MW00634385

DOWN BARNEGAT BAY

A Nor'easter Midnight Reader

The Sesquicentennial Edition

Robert Jahn

Plexus Publishing, Inc.
Medford, NJ

Published by:
Plexus Publishing Inc.
143 Old Marlton Pike
Medford, NJ 08055

Library of Congress Cataloging-in-Publication Data

Down Barnegat Bay : a nor'easter midnight reader / [edited by] Robert Jahn.—The Sesquicentennial ed.
p. cm.
Includes bibliographical references.
ISBN 0-937548-42-1
Barnegat Bay Region (N.J.)—History—Anecdotes. 2. Barnegat Bay Region (N.J.)—Social life and customs—Anecdotes. I. Jahn, Robert.

F142.O2 D68 2000
974.9'48—dc21

00-037318

Printed in Canada

For information about Plexus books, call 609-654-6500.

Down Barnegat Bay: A Nor'easter Midnight Reader

Table of Contents

Historical narrative, poems and photographs by the author, unless otherwise credited. The sources of reprinted material, where known, are credited in the body of the work.

Down Barnegat Bay Revisited 10
Preface to the Sesquicentennial Edition
- Down Barnegat Bay in Overview
- An Author in Full Immersion
- The First Voyage
- Perceptions of the First Voyage
- Celebrations of the Bay's Maritime History
- Travelling Through Time

"Down Barnegat Bay" 15

Foreword 16
- Grandfather Tales
- Folks Were Few and Far Between
- Salt Water Day

"Mantoloking" 20

The Ancient Seashore 23

Down Barnegat Bay to Cranberry Inlet . . . 24
- Early Explorers of the Coast
- A Very Good Land to Fall in With
- Natives of the Seashore
- The Grandfather of Nations
- New Netherlands and the English Invasion
- Whalers and Fishermen
- The Last of the Lenape
- The Settlement of the Seashore
- The Barnegat Spirit
- Seaports, Smugglers, and the Black Market
- Rebel Privateers and Redcoat Raiders
- The *Love and Unity* Wrecks on Squan Beach
- British Raids Along the Barnegat Coast
- The "Nest of Pirates" at Toms River
- The Storming of Toms River Block House
- The Massacre on Long Beach
- Privateering During the War of 1812
- "Old Ironsides' " Encounter with a British Squadron
- The Era of the Coastal Trade
- Cranberry Inlet Disappears in the Night
- The Founding of Ocean County
- The Clipper Ships

"The Maid of the Mist" 39

Fishing Off the Coast of New Jersey 41
- The Market Fishermen
- Never in a Hurry
- No Longer a Dreaded Coast

Squan Beach 45
A Secluded Watering Place
- Indian Will's Hole
- A Deadly Struggle in the Pines
- Seashore Longevity

The Ghostly Sphinx of Metedeconk . 48
- The Fisherman's Fright
- Source of the Mystery
- The Storm's Finale

Shipwrecks, Ghosts, and Tales of the Dunes 50
- A Beach Party at Uncle Jakey's Tavern
- Bill Chadwick's Establishment
- The Sportsman's Heart
- Evening at the House
- Tales of the Barnegat Pirates
- If You Had Seen What I Have
- A Mysterious Wreck
- Tales of the Dunes
- Ghosts in the Moonlight
- The Spirits of Mantoloking
- Uncle Jakey
- The Mare Saw It as Plain as I Did
- A Pleasant Week at the Beach

On The Bay At Chadwick's House 57
- A Shooting Match
- Birds of the Bay
- Blinds and Decoys
- By Stage Down the Beach
- The Baymen Are a Jolly Set
- Uncle Jimmy Loveland
- Uncle Charlie Stout
- Notes from the Chadwick House Register 1869 – 1899
- "Chadwick"

 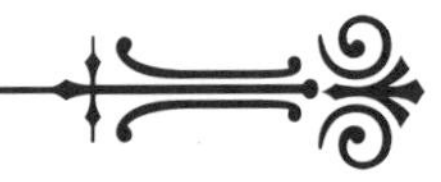

Table of Contents

An Historical Cabinet 63
Made from the Pieces of Twenty-Six Wrecked Vessels
The Locomotive's Whistle
A Famous Bayman
The Historical Cabinet
A Ghastly Record
Inside the Cabinet
A Well Versed Captain

A Moonlight Sail on Barnegat Bay 66
Rounding the Point
Fireflies in the Night
An Ocean Excursion
The One That Got Away
Out to the Fishing Banks

Captain Hen of Barnegat 70
The Old Salt Tells How the Yacht-Masters of the Bay Live
A Queer Old Fellow
Fishing the Bay
The Art of Duck Shooting
Inside the Yacht
Some Join the Life Saving Service
Setting Sail

Along Our Jersey Shore 75
Sunset on the Bay
Treasures from the Sea
A Sunday Cruise
Alone in the World
Barnegat Light
The End of the Journey

"The Wreck of *John Minturn*" 78

A Nor'easter Midnight Reader 81
Flotsam, Jetsam and Beachcombers
Shipwrecks and Wreckers
Tales of Barnegat Pirates
Inside the Pirate's Den
Captain Kidd and His Buried Treasure
Spanish Doubloons and Pieces of Eight
Indian Will's Discovery
Blackbeard and Richard Worley
The Sword with the Golden Hilt
Treasure on the Manasquan
Robert Louis Stevenson and Treasure Island
Charges of Piracy on the Barnegat Coast
Barnegat Light and the Great Storm of 1846
A First Rate Packet Ship
The Wreck of the *John Minturn*
The Deathwatch
Report of the Special Commission
The Life Saving Service
201 Saved on the *Ayrshire*
340 Lost on the *Powhattan*
Old Barney
A Close Call on the *Costa Rica*
The *Maid of the Mist* Meets the Barnegat Pirates
The Tragic Tale of the *David H. Tolck*
Last Days of the Volunteer Crews
Old Barney Saved from the Waves
The Mystery Wreck at Mantoloking
Were There Really Barnegat Pirates?

The Pirates of Barnegat 101
A Ghostly Heaving Form
In League with the Demon of the Tempest
A Dark Tradition of Wild Winter Nights
The Service Has Put an End to Wrecking
Joining the Circle Around the Stove

A Night with the Life Saving Service 104
Patrolling the Shore
A Bark Close Inshore and in Extreme Peril
Throwing a Life Line
Launching the Life-Car
A Cheer in the Wind

Heroism Rewarded 109
The George Taulane Wreck

Following the Bay 111
Sloops, Schooners, and Bluefish
Sailboat Racing
The Barnegat Sneak-Box
A Center for Sneak-Box Building
The Coming of the Railroad
The Flowering of Summer Resorts
Artists of the Seashore
Gerard R. Hardenbergh
The Photographic Record
Ducks, Geese, and Shore Birds
Gunning on the Bay
The Market Hunters
Barnegat Bay Decoys

"Salt Water Day" 122

The Barnegat Hotel 124
A Tavern by the Sea

On Board Captain Dorsett's Schooner . . . 127
Provisions for the Trip
The Boat and the Crew
The Fish of the Bay
The Favorite Old Schooner Yacht
Crabs, Oysters, and Clams
The Bones of Lost Ships
Bathing in the Ocean
The Wind Whistling in the Sails
Questions from the Quarter-Deck

"Her Eightieth Birthday" 134
—poem by Captain John Lott Dorsett.

Table of Contents

Surf Fishing 138

From the Manasquan River to Barnegat Inlet 139

A Man Who Has Cheated the Sea of Many Lives 152

Down the Beach 153

The View from the Life Saving Station Tower 162

Life at the Sea Shore 168

Sneakbox Racing 170

On the Bay 171

One Time the Beach Was Beautiful 187

- Beachcombing
- Warm Summer Days
- Squalls and Gale Force Winds
- On My Grandparents Farm
- No Ice-Boxes in Those Days
- Home Remedies
- Exploring the Attic
- Cranberries and Blueberries
- The Urge to Tramp
- Nothing Was Easy

One of the Heroes of the Jersey Coast . . . 190

Barnegat Ways 204

Uncle Charlie Broad

- Gathering at the General Store
- Shelter from the Nor'east Storm
- Uncle Charlie Broad: Born of Barnegat
- From the Head of the Bay to the Inlet

Tides of Barnegat 208

"A Song of Its Own" 211

Swapping Tales Around a Red-Hot Stove . . 213

Barnegat Baymen and Fresh-Water Salts

- Deep Sea Thrillers at the General Store
- Spitting on the Red-Hot Stove
- Dreams of Sailing Around the Horn
- Howard Rogers' Observation
- A Wonderful Vessel: The Emma C. Berry

Here One Forgets the Outside World 217

The Boardwalk 221

"Weather Eye" 222

Afterword 225

Last Summer

- The Sea and the Bay
- Omens on the Horizon
- A Homegrown Renaissance?
- The Spirit of Old Barnegat Bay

Acknowledgments 228

Travelling Through Time 233

Postscript to the Sesquicentennial Edition

- A Time Traveller
- Unexpected Moments
- Living History
- Honoring the Past
- Historic Sites
- Our Coastal Heritage
- The Past Remains
- Save Barnegat Bay
- A Part of Nature
- Storm of the Century
- A Nor'easter Classification System
- An Atlantis of the Future?
- These Days
- Welcome to the Jersey Shore!
- A Natural Identity

"Down Barnegat Bay" (Part II) 244

First Edition Crew 246

Sesquicentennial Edition Crew 247

Principal Maps

Barnegat Bay Region, 1878 9

Barnegat Inlet, 1889 14

Topographical Map of Barnegat Bay, 1872 17

Detail of Barnegat Coast, 1778 22

Map of New Netherlands, 1656 25

British Colony of New Jersey, 1758 35

Barnegat Bay Region, 1849 43

U.S. Life Saving Stations, 1889 103

Topographical Map of Barnegat Bay, 1889 120-121

National Park Service/N.J. Coastal Heritage Trail, 1999 231

For Gail — Happy Birthday!

For My Parents — Mr. and Mrs. Harold Jahn

And For My Grandparents — Mr. and Mrs. George Brower

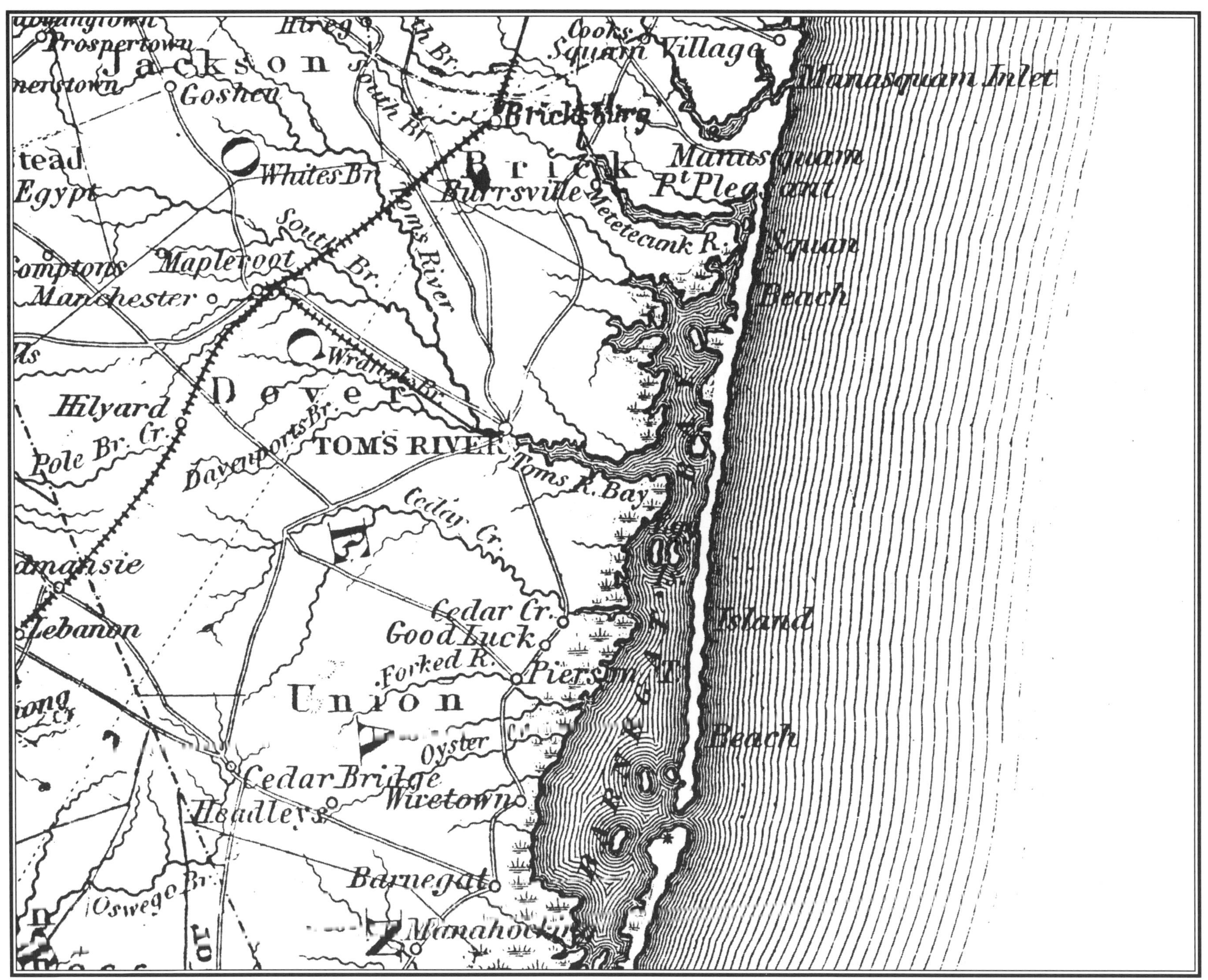

Barnegat Bay Region, 1878

Down Barnegat Bay Revisited

Preface to the Sesquicentennial Edition

On a squally November afternoon some five years ago, I first met Robert Jahn. Head bent down over maps and documents, he sat at a table drinking coffee in a darkened pub in the fast-fading light of the season. Imagination and time may have intervened, but I seem to remember the creaking of old timbers overhead. I was on a mission to obtain historical background for potential conservation areas on Barnegat Bay. My impressions on first meeting Robert were confirmed by a later reading of *Down Barnegat Bay*. On rare occasion, in my travels and conservation rounds, I have found someone who lives for a particular region so intensely that he or she can be said to personify that region.

A true chronicler of the bygone scene, Robert Jahn is fully absorbed in the folkways and historic past of Barnegat Bay. He brings to his analysis and presentation both insight and love. Moreover, as underscored by this Sesquicentennial edition of his book, Robert is fully concerned with the bay's present and future.

Due to its location within the highly developed metropolitan corridor of the Northeast, the bay region has faced and will continue to face great challenges in the form of loss and alteration of its open spaces. Regional history, as embodied by the present volume, has the potential to provide a yardstick for change, whether induced by nature or by man, and may serve as a reference point for land conservation and restoration efforts. Moreover, a rediscovery of the regional past can energize and educate all who come in contact with Barnegat Bay's landscapes — shores, waterways, marshes, forested uplands, and farmsteads — thereby reconnecting both natives and visitors with the land.

Down Barnegat Bay in Overview

Researched and written by Robert Jahn, *Down Barnegat Bay: A Nor'easter Midnight Reader* chronicles the maritime history of the seashore and the enduring cultural legacy of the baymen. With more than 177 illustrations, including seventy-five new images and nine maps, Jahn's updated narrative history is accompanied by rare historical accounts that feature recurring characters and events. Old timers such as Captain John Lott Dorsett, Uncle Jakey Herbert, and Captain William P. Chadwick are vividly depicted against the historic background of shipwrecks, lifesaving, and "following the bay." New additions to Jahn's original text include a review of significant cultural and environmental developments in the region. This expanded 248-page Sesquicentennial fourth edition, thoroughly revised and with a detailed table of contents, is published for the first time in hardcover with book jacket by Plexus Publishing, Inc., and also celebrates the twentieth anniversary of *Down Barnegat Bay*.

An Author in Full Immersion

Robert Jahn is a Jersey Shore native who has had a lifelong fascination with and, indeed, immersion in the region's maritime history. The span of the sea's horizon and the roll of the surf evidently captured his thoughts at an early age. Jahn grew up on the barrier beach in Mantoloking, where he still resides. In his youth, he worked at local boat yards and yacht clubs, as well as on the boardwalk and at Island Beach State Park. He holds a degree in journalism from Suffolk University in Boston, Massachusetts. As his latest edition appears, Jahn is already at work on a new book. During the moments when he is not researching, writing, and serving as a staunch advocate of the bay, Jahn can often be found photographing shore wildlife or on the water with friends.

The First Voyage

Down Barnegat Bay was first published in the summer of 1980 by Beachcomber Press of Mantoloking, in association with the author's late friend, Donald DuMont Jr., who died later that year as a result of an automobile accident. Three softcover editions of the original 208-page book have been sold out. Out of print now for several years, a New Jersey antiquarian book dealer recently was asking $125 for a first-edition copy autographed by the author!

A lifetime exposure to Barnegat Bay and a long family history in the region set the stage for Jahn's endeavor. His roots on the Atlantic shore can be traced back to the founding of New Amsterdam (now New York City) in the mid-1600s. In the nineteenth century, ancestors of both sides of his family volunteered for the U.S. Life Saving Service. Grandfather tales, according to Jahn, provided the original inspiration for his book. "In many ways," Jahn writes, "*Down Barnegat Bay* is an elegy to a vanished era, a time when it was still possible to live off the land and water. This new edition incorporates twenty years of new research and major developments in the region."

Having drawn upon both oral and written traditions in preparing the book, Jahn found that *Down Barnegat Bay* has had a wide resonance with readers who responded, in turn, with their own personal perspectives on the region's past. According to Jahn, "Many readers are very aware of their family history and deeply connected to their roots at the Jersey Shore. Most 'clamdiggers' express a great sense of longing for the way things used to be during the 'Good Old Days' before the local population explosion and widespread development that threaten to destroy our natural resources. Many other recent settlers in the area share a fascination with coastal history as well as a spiritual bond with the bay and the sea."

A shared resonance with the past may have verbal, written, and physical manifestations. Jahn continues, "The book struck a chord with readers of all ages. It seems more people are from New Jersey than live in New Jersey. We received book orders from all over the country and from as far away as England and Australia. It's always a pleasure meeting and hearing from people who have their own stories to tell. I've also heard from many people who are related to or descended from the old timers who are recurring figures in this history."

Captain John Lott Dorsett's 1880 "Historical Cabinet Made from Pieces of 26 Shipwrecks," the description of which is excerpted in this book, has resurfaced, courtesy of Dorsett's great-grandson, Coleman Brice, who has kindly allowed it to be exhibited at several of Jahn's programs at Ocean County Library. Descendants of Captain William P. Chadwick have shared their heirlooms and even invited the author to Chadwick family reunions!

Author Robert Jahn sailing down Barnegat Bay.
(Photograph, 1998, by Tom Barry)

Announcing

A Barnegat Bay Festival:
Year of the Coast Celebration

Ocean County College
Saturday, November 29, 1980

Featuring a Jersey Shore Symposium including:

Norman Brouwer, Ship Historian, South Street Seaport Museum, NYC, speaking on "The Last 100 Years of Sailing Ships," with slides.
Robert Jahn, *Down Barnegat Bay: A Nor'easter Midnight Reader*, speaking on his book and exhibiting maps, prints and photos.
James McCloy and Ray Miller, co-authors of *The Jersey Devil*, speaking on New Jersey folklore and legends.
Rick Geffken, Maritime Historian and Scuba Diver, speaking on "Shipwrecks Off The Jersey Coast," with slides.
William C. Schoettle, author of *Bay Head 1879-1911*, narrating his "Old Time Bay Head Slide Show."
Wayne L. Hartman, educator and literary authority, speaking on "Walt Whitman's Poetry of the Jersey Shore."

In the Gallery:

Exhibits by Regional Historical Societies and Private Collectors.
Historic and Contemporary Duck Decoys and Shorebirds.
Turn-of-the-Century Watercolors by Gerard R. Hardenbergh.
Rare and Authentic Models of Ships, Schooners and Sloops.
Contemporary Jersey Shore Art and Photography.

A tribute to the Jersey Shore's folk and maritime traditions with speakers, slide shows, regional art and music, historical, ecological, and cultural exhibits. All at the Fine Arts Center, Ocean County College, Toms River, N.J., from 11 A.M. to 5:30 P.M. General Admission: Adults, $3.00; Children, $1.00. Rain or Shine. For further information call the Dept. of Community Education at (201) 255-4000, ext. 356. Barnegat Light print from *Appleton's Journal*, 1871.

sponsored by

Ocean County College and Beachcomber Press
in association with
The Ocean County Cultural and Heritage Commission

Perceptions of the First Voyage

While it was advertised only by word of mouth, the first edition of Jahn's work received wide and favorable book reviews. S. J. Horner of *The New York Times* wrote, "*Down Barnegat Bay* evokes the area's romance and mystery." James S. Brown of *The Asbury Park Press* noted that the book was "a major contribution to Ocean County history." Deborah Coombe, in *The Newark Star Ledger*, commented that it was "written to be read on a cold winter night in front of a fire with a howling wind for accompaniment." John Haas wrote in *The Ocean Country Observer* that it was "a work of art on the way to becoming a classic!" And *New Jersey Monthly Magazine* said, "The history of the Jersey Shore is rich and fascinating, full of shipwrecks and ghostly folk tales. Jahn, a Mantoloking historian, is dedicated to keeping that lore alive in our consciousness."

Down Barnegat Bay was also singled out in 1983 as recommended reading in *History and People of New Jersey's Shore: A Teacher's Guide*, published by the New Jersey Museum and the New Jersey Historical Commission. In the same year, the book was also recommended by the Rutgers University Center for Coastal and Environmental Studies in its *New Jersey Barrier Islands: An Ever-Changing Public Resource*. Author David Oxenford also praised Jahn's work in his 1992 history *The People of Ocean County*.

One of the most unexpected moments in the book's history occurred in 1990 when the New Jersey State Department of Education included an excerpt ("There are times when the sea goes mad during northeast storms. . .") as a reading comprehension and vocabulary skill question in the annual High School Proficiency Test administered to all students. "I never dreamed of such a possibility," Jahn related, "and I might never have heard about it if not for the teenage daughter of old friends who managed to get me a copy from her teacher."

Celebrations of the Bay's Maritime History

As a writer and photographer, Jahn is a frequent contributor to area newspapers, historical publications, and television programs. He has also given slide-show talks for groups around the state, including the New Jersey Historical Society, Save Barnegat Bay, Surfrider Foundation, the New Jersey Archeological Society, the Barnegat Bay Decoy and Gunning Show, and the Ocean County Environmental Conference.

He organized and hosted the first Barnegat Bay Festival in 1980 at Ocean County College, which was billed as "a tribute to the Jersey Shore's folk and maritime traditions, with twelve speakers, slide shows, regional art and music, and historical, ecological, and cultural exhibits." Native American Chief Whip-poor-will opened the event with a traditional Lenape blessing; Captain Dorsett's grand-nephew, Herman Bennett, rang the ships' bell from the schooner *Rosamond*, and read the captain's poetry; and the Pinehawkers performed "The Clamdigger Song." The festival, which was co-sponsored by Jahn's first publisher, Beachcomber Press, and the Ocean County Cultural and Heritage Commission, drew over 500 people on Thanksgiving weekend.

The author expanded the multimedia approach with his continuing "Down Barnegat Bay Symposium" series, which in the summer of 1991 was the subject of a two-hour cable television documentary that has been broadcast many times over the years. The symposium explores the past, present, and future of the bay by bringing together experts from various fields who, along with Jahn, attempt to integrate cultural and scientific research. William de Camp Jr., Save Barnegat Bay president; Theresa Fowler, N.J. Department of Environmental Protection project manger; William C. Vibbert, Island Beach State Park superintendent; Cynthia Coritz, Barnegat Lighthouse State Park superintendent; Shaun O'Rourke, Cattus Island County Park naturalist; Terry O'Leary, Baymen's Museum historian; and this writer, have been occasional participants, along with many other speakers.

Travelling Through Time

For the past decade, Jahn has produced and hosted the popular "Travelling Through Time" cultural series at Point Pleasant Branch of Ocean County Library, where he presents slides, video, lectures, and special displays based on variations of themes in this book.

One notable program was "Jersey Shore Shipwrecks," commemorating the 150th anniversary of the *John Minturn* and the development of the U.S. Life Saving Service. Participants included representatives from the U.S. Coast Guard, F. Alan Vogel's screening of underwater video of offshore wrecks, and nautical artifacts from the collections of Dick Updike and several members of the N.J. Historical Wreck Divers Association.

"The Great Nor'easter of '92" program dealt with what many experts considered to be "the storm of the century." Participants included Susan D. Halsey, Division of Coastal Resources; Steve Kempf, Federal Emergency Management Agency; historian and meteorologist Jerry Woolley; and a major display of storm photographs by David May of *The Asbury Park Press*.

"A Very Good Land: New Amsterdam and the Early Settlement of the Shore" included N.J. Native American Association president Robert "Graywolf" Hamilton; historians Arthur J. Birdsall, Gene Donatiello, Sean Fleming, Wayne L. Hartman, and George Williams; descendants of original Dutch settlers who have formed the Jersey Shore Chapter of the Holland Society; and a genealogy panel discussion on researching family history with Lois Brown of Ocean County Library, and members of the Ocean County Historical Society including Carolyn Campbell, Betty Grant, Corinne Lill, and Richard Strickler.

Melissa Depp, reporting in *The Ocean County Observer*, wrote at the time that the series ". . . draws on people who are active in cultural, historical, and environmental groups, as well as individual writers, researchers, artists, and musicians, along with sailors, fishermen, and outdoorsmen. The common bond that unites them is a love of the shore."

The "Travelling Through Time" cultural series, inspired by *Down Barnegat Bay*, has become an experimental living history of the region. "The Jersey Shore has a natural identity that we are trying to preserve," notes the author. "As we honor Ocean County's Sesquicentennial and enter the twenty-first century, knowledge of the past is necessary to understand the present. We're just passing through. We have to think about the legacy that we are leaving for future generations."

Videos of many of the programs in the "Time" series are available at Ocean County Library. "I'd especially like to thank Barbara Kaden and the staff for their enthusiastic support. Some programs have featured as many as fourteen speakers and run for over four hours, with closed circuit television for standing-room-only audiences," Jahn says.

The winds are fair and promising for the fourth voyage of this book. Barnegat Bay, a magnificent natural, cultural, and historic resource, will be the beneficiary of Robert Jahn's love and perseverance.

"It's time to raise the sail again and celebrate Ocean County's Sesquicentennial. I hope readers enjoy the twentieth anniversary voyage down Barnegat Bay," says the author.

Peter P. Blanchard III
Principal Author, The Century Plan
Naturalist for the Trust for Public Land, Mid-Atlantic Region
New York, N.Y.
September 24, 1999

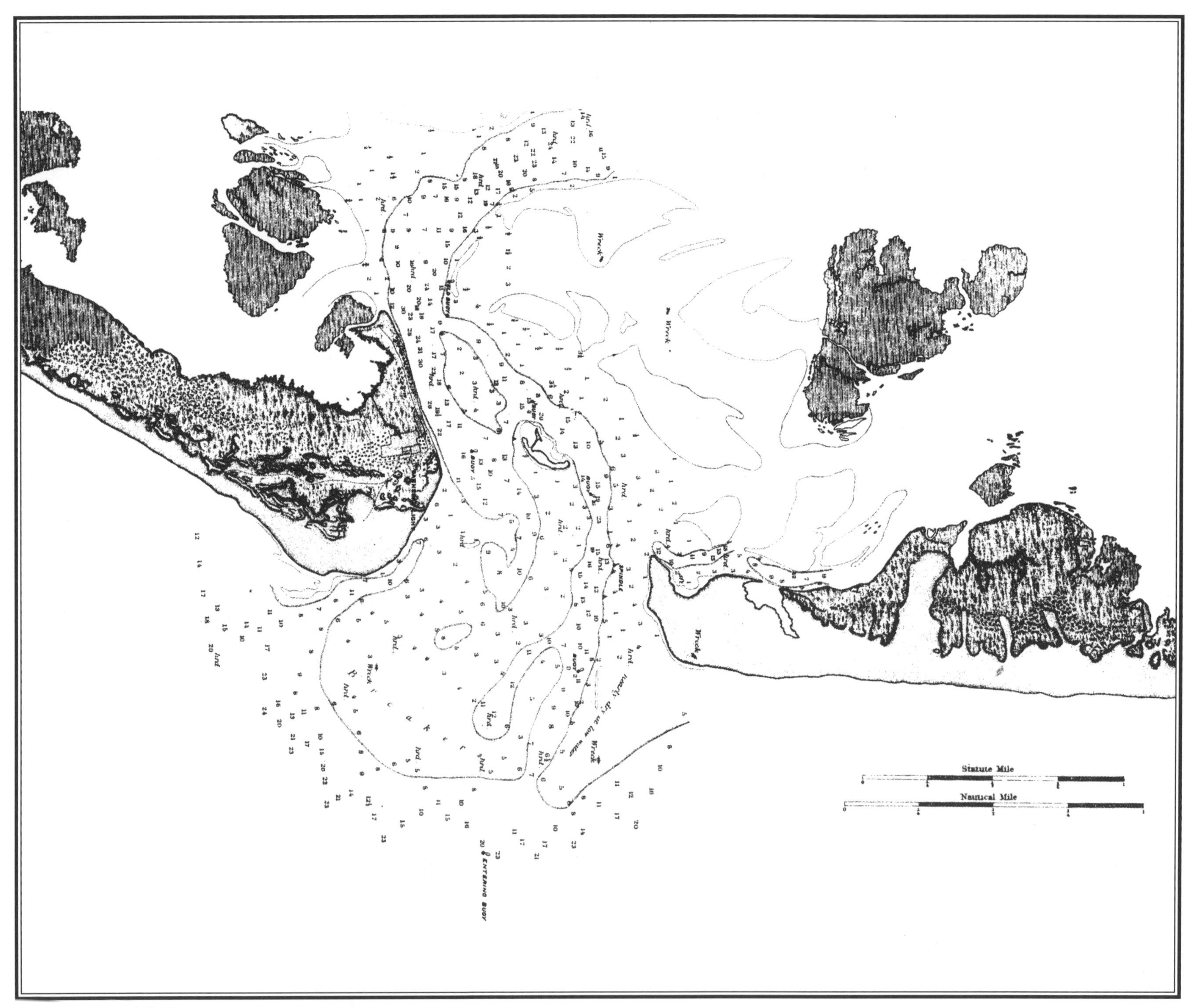

Barnegat Inlet, 1867. *(Map courtesy of Dick Updike)*

Down Barnegat Bay

A bright crimson eye
cast its light through the sky,
as we set out in the morning
and let the sails fly . . .

Down Barnegat Bay
on the wings of a dream,
to a time long forgotten,
downstream to the sea . . .

Sailing close to the wind
past the beaches and dunes,
a new day is dawning,
hear the laughing gulls cry:

Red sky at morning,
sailor take warning,
watch the waves as they dance
on the swelling high tide.

Watch out for those shoals,
when the wind's on the water;
watch the waves as they dance
to the bright sandy shore.

Down Barnegat Bay
on the wings of a dream,
to the time of the clippers,
downstream to the sea . . .

Foreword

Down Barnegat Bay is an illustrated folk history of the bay area and its maritime lore, from the Lenape to the days of the Life Saving Service and the coastal trade along the Jersey Shore. Images of the past bear witness to true tales from before the turn of the century, during the age of sail, when the bay was the highway connecting the scattered villages that lay between the Manasquan River and Barnegat Inlet.

This book is the record of a voyage through time, documented with contemporary accounts drawn from ships' logs, private journals, local histories, and early newspapers and magazines, as well as reminiscences of the old-timers — together with little-known selections of Barnegat Bay poetry and fiction.

More than 177 illustrations from museums, family albums, libraries, and private collections complement the text, many previously unpublished. Included are rare maps, prints, paintings, and historic photographs, which create an authentic portrait of the bay area as it once was, depicting the natural beauty of the seashore and the salty character of its pioneers.

Grandfather Tales

Down Barnegat Bay grew out of grandfather tales I heard long ago on summer nights on the side porch of a white clapboard farmhouse down the road from the bay. While my grandmother made tea in the kitchen, we'd sit outside in old rockers and watch the long shadows of twilight turn into nighttime.

The sea breeze always stirred the pines as darkness fell, and a whippoorwill would call from a willow by the pond. Rocking slowly in the creaking chair, my grandfather would light his pipe and sink back in deep thought, while crickets chattered in the summer heat. Then the stories came and went, between puffs of pipe smoke and long moments of silence — stories of growing up along the bay, tales of fishing and sailing and gunning.

Folks Were Few and Far Between

When he was a child in the 1870s folks were few and far between, and most people lived on the mainland, around Metedeconk, Burrsville, Cedarbridge, Silverton, Toms River, Barnegat, and Waretown. Family names like Havens, Miller, Johnson, Truax, Applegate, Hulse, Ware, Rogers, Clayton, Irons, Osborn, Herbert, Wardell, Gant, Pearce, Curtis, Brower, and Van Note were wide spread. Nearly everyone knew each other, and many were related by marriage.

Point Pleasant was an old farming and fishing village; Loveland-town had a few old bay houses, which had stood for seven decades, and Captain Elijah Chadwick had most of what he called "Bayhead" to himself. The beachfront south was nearly deserted, except for isolated Life Saving Stations and a couple of fishpounds with their surfboats, nets, and ice houses. Before this time only a few squatters had shanties here and there among the dunes. One of the earliest was David Mapes, a black Quaker who tended sheep and cattle in an area on the bayside of the peninsula, which old maps refer to as Nigger House Cove.

The only lodging available down the beach was at the old sportsmen's inns that had been built early in the century. They still stood, weatherbeaten by countless storms and known by the names of their keepers: Jacob Herbert's Tavern in Mantoloking, Bill Chadwick's House in Chadwick Beach, Michael Ortley's House in Ortley Beach, and John Reed's Hotel, which prospered for many years in Island Beach until a great hurricane blew it down in the late 1870s.

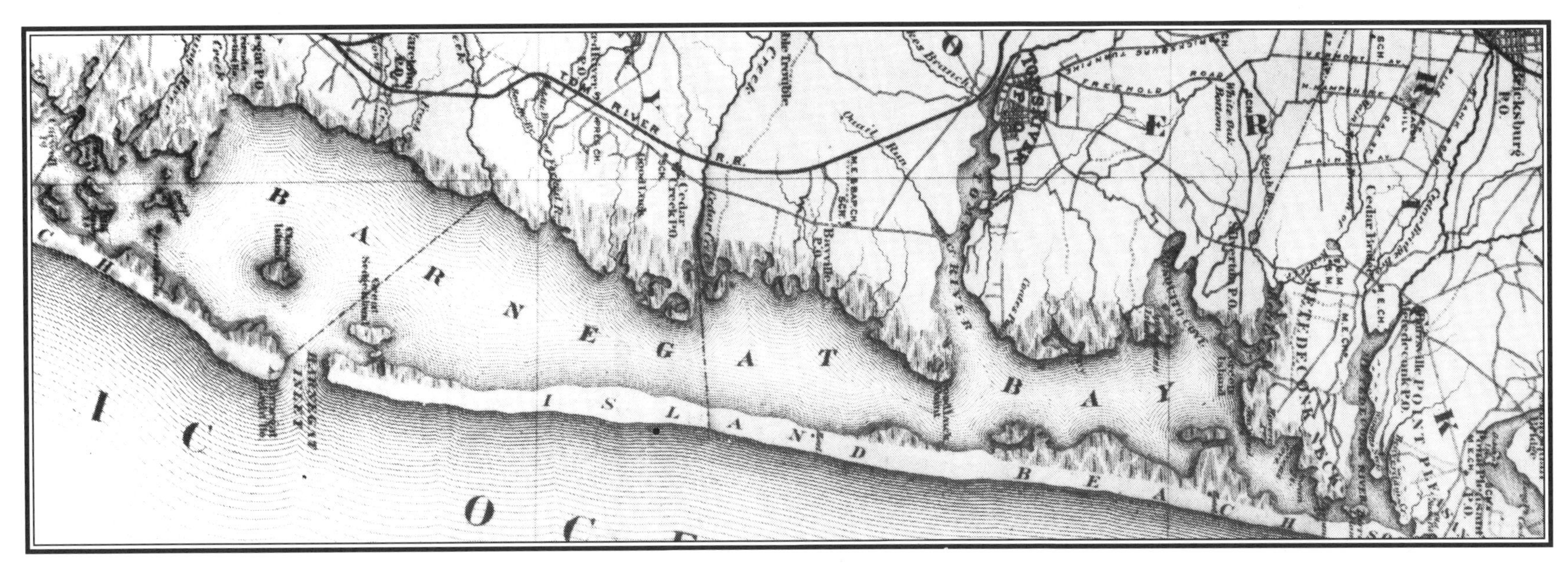

A 1872 topographic map of the Barnegat Bay region. ***(Map courtesy Ocean County College Library)***

Life was slow in those days and most people travelled by sailboat or wagon, or on foot. Not much happened out of the ordinary besides wild "nor'easters," which brought eighty-mile-per-hour winds and heavy flooding, as well as frequent shipwrecks on the shore. But times were changing fast. New towns were being founded on the coast: Point Pleasant Beach, in 1869; Mantoloking, in 1878; Bay Head, in 1879; Lavallette, in 1887; and Seaside Park, in 1876. The land rush was spurred by the coming of the Pennsylvania Railroad, which had crossed the bay from Toms River in 1881. During the next few years tracks were laid up the peninsula to meet with the New York Railroad, which ended at Manasquan.

Workmen were busy everywhere, levelling the dunes and clearing the thickets of briars and bayberry. Large summer "cottages" were built on the beach front and bay, and the railroad brought more people from the cities to the seashore every season.

Salt Water Day

The natives watched in wonder at the change. Once a year, in late summer, they gathered for a clambake on the beach at Uncle Jakey's Tavern. They called the celebration Salt Water Day. Captain John Lott Dorsett sailed down from Beaver Dam in his schooner *Rosamond.* "Uncle Tommy" Cook drove down the beach from his Point Pleasant farm with a wagon full of friends. And Bill Chadwick brought everyone up from his place in an overloaded carriage.

They came in droves from the farms and villages on the mainland, from Adamston, Osbornville, and Bricksburg. Families came from all over, jamming the sandy roads with traffic and filling the bay with wooden boats with sun-bleached sails. They came to laugh and splash in the surf, to feast on clams and crabs and corn, liberally washed down with beer and rum. At night they gathered driftwood for a big beach bonfire, and often danced around it beneath the starry sky.

Old Uncle Jakey, whose hawkish features and gold earrings made him look like the last of the Barnegat Pirates, welcomed them all.

What follows came out of those stories my grandfather told me and several years of research: tales of the bay and the sea — of sailboats, storms and shipwrecks — actual accounts of the usual and the unusual, from the Pirates of Barnegat to ghosts of the dunes, as they once happened, a long time ago, down Barnegat Bay.

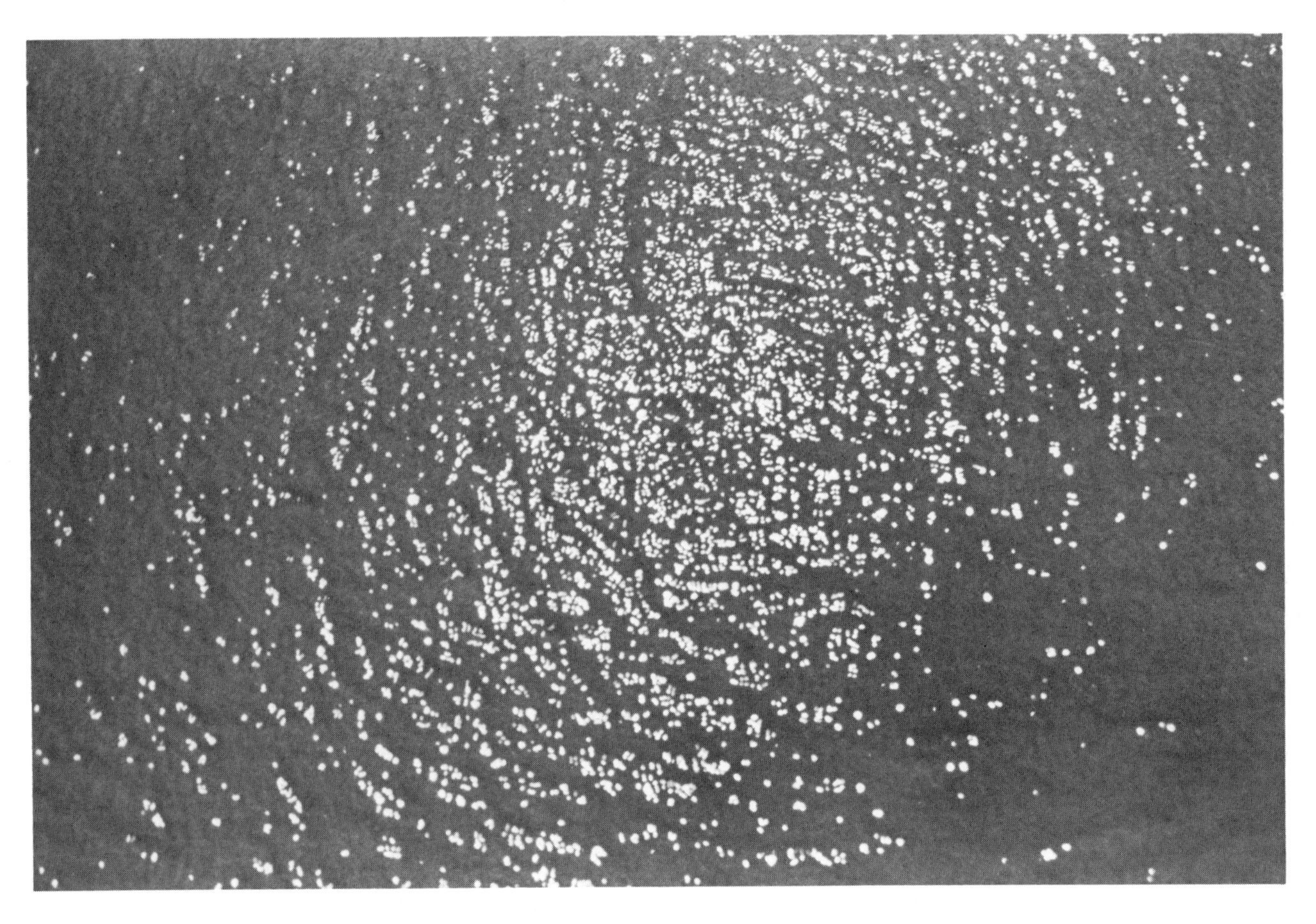

"I slept and dreamed beside the river,
River bearing Indian name,
Metedeconk, the Lenni Lenape
Called the stream ere white men came . . ."

Mantoloking

Captain John Lott Dorsett of Beaver Dam, Brick Township, is one of the quaint characters of the coast, unspoiled by the income of the summer visitor. Mariner, shipbuilder, wrecker, he has taken an active part in life for many long years, and is known from one end of the county to the other. Of late years he has knocked about the bay in his schooner *Rosamond*. The following is from his pen:

At the close of an early autumn day, I wandered alone on the banks of the Metedeconk and indulged in fantastic reverie. I thought of the time when the tall pines stood on the banks in majestic grandeur, when the beaver built his dams and the otter reveled in the stream, and the wild fowl, undisturbed by the sportsman's gun and the red deer, came and drank without fear. No sound disturbed the silence of nature save the ceaseless roar of the ocean and the breeze through the tree tops. Now, before me lay the towns of Bay Head and Mantoloking, a train of cars dashing along the beach railroad, numerous pleasure yachts, filled with merry people, skimming over the river, I mused on the wonderful change, and my brain filled with a wild phantasm and I slept and dreamed.

***"I am Chieftain Mantoloking,
All the tribes are ruled by me,
Hunted here and held possession,
of the lands along the sea..."***

I slept and dreamed beside the river,
River bearing Indian name,
Metedeconk, the Lenni Lenape,
Called the stream 'ere white men came.

And methought I saw approaching
Something in the form of boat,
Antique, odd and old appearing,
Shattered so she'd scarcely float.

He who rowed was grim and ghastly,
with long sweeps he plied the oars.
And I knew it was old Charon,
And the boat from Stygian shores.

Standing in the stern majestic,
Was an Indian chieftain tall,
Clad in furs with bow and quiver,
Eagle feathers crowning all.

Near they came and loud he hailed me,
And I seemed to understand
His language was the pure Algonquin,
That was spoken in the land.

What he said, was this in substance,
For I wrote it as I heard,
Careful not to miss a sentence,
Or to change a single word.

I am Chieftain Mantoloking,
All the tribes are ruled by me,
Hunted here and held possession,
Of the lands along the sea.

Here we came to spear the otter,
And to watch the beaver dams.
Caught our fish from out the water,
Many oysters, too, and clams.

And the wild fowl in their season
Swarmed along the marshy bank,
Oft we shot them with our arrows,
While we hid where reeds were rank.

In the woods we chased the red deer,
Shot him as he ran along;
Where my warriors laid in ambush,
With their bows made stout and strong.

Our canoes upon these waters,
All about would swiftly glide.
And we built our summer wigwams,
Close along the river side.

My people were content and happy,
We were free from all constraint,
And held high carnival for pastime,
Decked with feathers, furs and paint.

Where are the forests, tall and stately,
Where oft I've watched the nimble fawn,
Where are the beavers and the otters,
Alas! where are my warriors gone?

All, all are gone, he howled and gestured,
Charon plied his clumsy oars,
Off they started going westward,
Up along the river's shore.

Then I heard an awful wailing,
Sounding on the still, night air,
Like to some infernal Demon,
Roused from Hades dismal lair.

Then I awoke and looked around me,
Twilight gathering o'er the scene,
My wandering thoughts retracing slowly,
The wild phantasm of my dream.

—*from* The New Jersey Courier, *1908.*

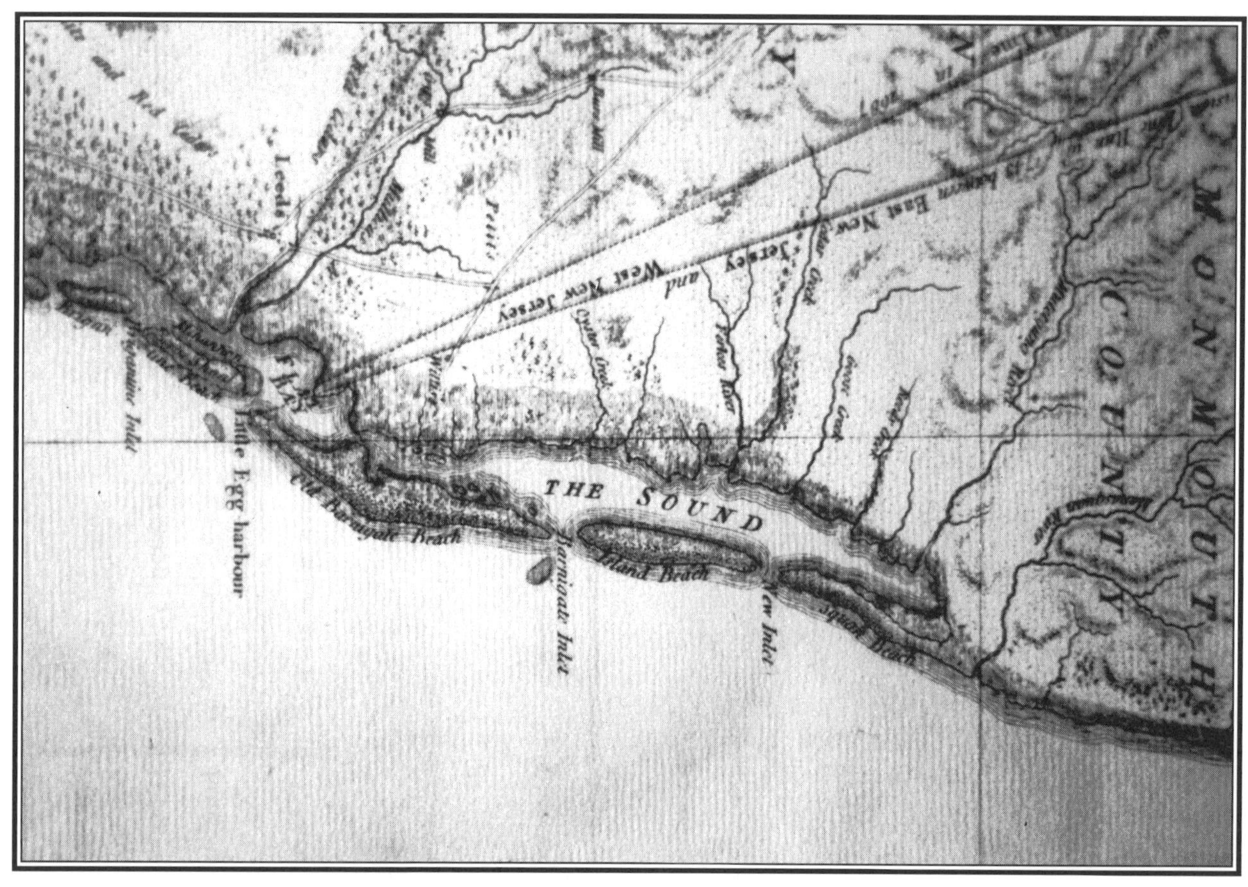

The Barnegat Coast in 1778, a detail from William Fadden's Province of New Jersey. "New Inlet" marks the location of Cranberry Inlet, opposite "Goose Creek" or Toms River. ***(Map courtesy Ocean County College Library.)***

The Ancient Seashore

In prehistoric times, before the age when mountains of ice moved south and covered much of the land by the edge of the sea, woolly mastodons and great dinosaurs roamed the primeval cedar swamps of Barnegat Bay. Lurking in shallow tidewaters that teemed with fish, crabs, and eels, were giant snapping turtles nearly six feet long, and crocodiles four times as large, which slithered up on the green sedge banks when the warming sun rose over a vast and rumbling sea.

Strange creatures with leathery wings — pterodactyls — soared through the air above the wild sand dunes, ancient ancestors of the seagull, but ten times their size. Their fossilized bones have been found, along with those of great sharks and whales that once swam in the deep. Least changed of all are the petrified clamshells, relics of that distant time when the ocean first cast life upon the beach.

In those days the prehistoric seashore is believed to have extended one hundred miles out from the present coastline where, over a range of a dozen miles, the ocean floor gradually descends from one hundred fathoms to more than a mile deep. Over the course of millions of years, the devouring sea slowly moves westward, its restless waves sweeping grains of white quartz sand, forming shoals and offshore islands. The beach advances upon the salt marsh, and the salt marsh advances upon the mainland.

The forces of erosion are continually at work, claiming two-and-a-half feet per year from the coastline. With the alongshore current flowing south, the surging sea gives as well as takes, building sand dunes and destroying them, closing old inlets and breaking new ones down the narrow finger of barrier beach that shelters Barnegat Bay from the blue North Atlantic.

Down Barnegat Bay to Cranberry Inlet

In the early 1700s, when whalers, smugglers, and pirates sailed the waters off these shores, Barnegat was the common name for the sparsely settled beach and mainland north of Barnegat Inlet up to the Metedeconk River. The bay — seventy-two square miles of shallow brackish water — was known as the Sound on early maps but, by 1750, local settlers referred to her as Barnegat Bay.

Before Dover Township was formed in 1767, this section was part of Shrewsbury Township, which was then the lower half of old Monmouth County. On the oceanfront and peninsula south of the Manasquan River, first surveyed by John Lawrence in 1740, lies Squan Beach — a nearly deserted stretch of meadows, cedar groves, and sand dunes running ten miles down to Cranberry Inlet.

A wild winter storm cut through the barrier beach around 1740, forming the 1,550-foot-wide inlet opposite Toms River. Named for the tart red berries that flourished in the bogs around its mouth, Cranberry Inlet was a vital channel, fifteen feet deep, for the sloops and schooners of the coastal trade. Many years before, Herring Inlet had opened and closed at the head of the bay near the Metedeconk River. The tallest sand dune on the Jersey Coast once stood here, known to mariners as High Hill Point.

By the early 1800s, Herring Inlet was fading from local memory, and a few farms and taverns had been built, widely separated along the seacoast. Small bands of fishermen lived among the dunes and served as volunteer lifesavers when passing ships struck offshore sandbars in foul weather. The beaches were strewn with the wrecks of lost vessels, timbers half buried in the shifting sands.

Below Cranberry Inlet lay Island Beach, once known as Lord Stirling's Isle, twelve miles of rolling dunes and marshes extending down to Barnegat Inlet, which has changed little in the past four hundred years. The foaming breakers of its shoals inspired Dutch Captain Cornelius Mey to name it Barendegat, or "breakers inlet," in 1614. Within a century, this original name became altered through common usage to Barnegat. The area from the inlet's southern bank down eighteen miles to Little Egg Harbor was once called Old Barnegat Beach, but came to be known as Long Beach Island by the time of the Revolutionary War.

Early Explorers of the Coast

It is possible that the first white men to see this coast were ancient Vikings who, more than a thousand years ago, made five voyages to the North American shore by way of Greenland and Iceland. They sailed so far south on one of these journeys that they saw green grass along the coast all winter long: Leif Ericson is believed to have passed this way around A.D. 985. According to historian Edwin Mitchell, the Vikings once had over ten thousand ships with more than one million sailors to man them. One of the largest ships was 475 feet long and had fourteen benches of oars.

The first European to set foot on New Jersey soil might have been John Cabot on an English exploratory expedition in 1498, six years after Christopher Columbus landed at San Salvador in the Bahamas. Giovanni Verrazano, an Italian navigator sailing for France, may have stopped for water somewhere along the Jersey Shore during his voyage up the North American coast in 1524.

A Very Good Land to Fall in With

But the best-documented account of the first sighting of Barnegat Bay was made by Captain Henry Hudson, who sailed west from Holland in 1609 aboard the *Half Moon*, with a crew of twenty. An Englishman in the employ of the Dutch East India Company, Hudson never accomplished his mission of finding a northwest passage to India. But he did navigate the northeastern coast of the great wilderness of North America from Cape Cod to Virginia.

It was on his return trip north that the *Half Moon,* an eighty-foot two-masted vessel, sailed close offshore the chain of barrier beaches and is believed to have dropped anchor for the night off Barnegat Inlet. The next morning, on September 2, 1609, first mate Robert Juet recorded the occasion in the ship's log:

When the sun arose we steered north again and saw land from the west by north to the northwest, all alike, broken islands. The course along the land we found to the noreast by north. From the land, which we first had sight of, until we came to a great lake of water, as we could judge it to be, being drowned land, which made it rise like islands, which was in length ten leagues. The mouth of the lake has many shoals, and the sea breaks upon them as it is cast out of the mouth of it. And from the lake or bay the land lies north by east, and we had a great stream out of the bay . . . This was a very good land to fall in with, and a pleasant land to see.

The view from the deck of the *Half Moon* must have been beautiful on that late summer morning. Long waves moved across the blue water, cresting and breaking on the shining white beaches. Sandpipers darted through the seaweed and clamshells in the foaming high tide. Rolling dunes lay behind the beach and all along the shore, covered with windswept salt grass and green tangled thickets of red cedar and bayberry. Swarms of seagulls filled the air, soaring in the morning sky. From the deck of the *Half Moon,* a new world lie waiting.

Natives of the Seashore

But beyond the dunes and across the bay lived an ancient race who called this land their own. The Lenape, natives of the woods, lived along nearly all the cedar creeks and rivers that flowed into the bay, following a seasonal ritual hundreds of years old. They called themselves Scheyechbi, or "original people." They believed that the great spirit Manitou lived in this land of sunrise, and took the form of the terrapin to reveal himself in

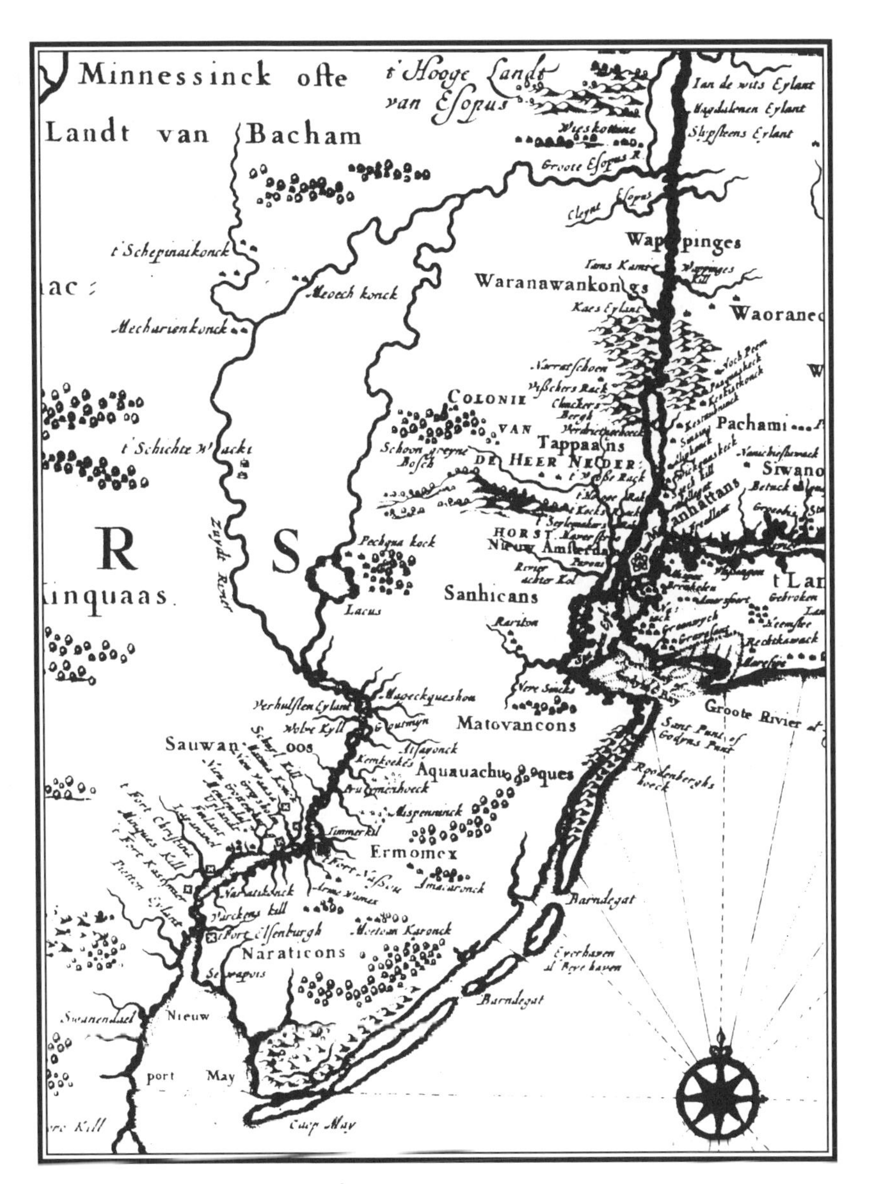

Nicolas Visscher's 1656 map of New Netherlands

The Lenape, natives of the woods, lived along nearly all the cedar creeks and streams that flowed into the bay.
(Print courtesy of Ruth and Dr. James Reese)

dreams. News of the coming of the white men on board the *Half Moon* spread through Lenape camps like a fire in the pines.

Dutch navigator Adrian Vanderdonck spoke with several Indians who had experienced that moment, and recorded their account in his *Journal of 1656*:

Indians or natives of the land, many of whom are still living, and with whom I have conversed, declare freely that they are old enough to remember distinctly that before the arrival of our Netherland ship the Half Moon, *in the year 1609, they did not know there were any other people in the world than those who were like themselves, much less any people who differed from them so much in race and fashion. Their men were bare on their breast and about the mouth, and their women, like ours, very hairy. They were unclothed and almost naked, especially in summer, while we were all the time clad and covered. When some of them saw our ship approaching afar off they did not know what to think but stood in deep and solemn amazement, wondering whether it was a spook or apparition, and whether it came from heaven or hell. Others of them supposed it might be a strange fish or sea monster. They supposed those on board to be rather devils than human beings, thus they differed among each other. A strange report soon spread throughout their country about our visit, and created great talk and comment among all the Indians.*

They belonged to the Unami tribe of Lenape. The first white settlers called them Delaware Indians, because so many lived near that river. They were a branch of the great northwestern family of Algonquin, who wandered across the continent thousands of years before. The remarkable story of that epic journey is recorded in painted pictures on a sacred bark scroll called the *Walum Olum,* which was discovered by anthropologists in 1833.

Small groups of Lenape lived along the coast all year long, but in the spring several thousand more would travel to the seashore from their inland winter grounds. The Manasquan, Metedeconk, and Toms River areas were major campgrounds for them. Here they cut saplings and stripped bark for their lodges, which they built near the mouths of waterways running into the bay. Some carried portable tepees with them and moved from place to place. During the warm summer months the men fished, clammed, and gathered oysters from their dugout canoes. They fashioned crude bird decoys out of straw and mud, and hunted with spears and bows and arrows.

The squaws stayed close to the campsites, raising children and caring for the elderly. They planted corn and beans, and picked wild herbs and berries. Narrow and sandy Indian trails snaked through the pine-needle-covered forest floor from the woods of Metedeconk and West Mantoloking down past West Creek. For many years Indians from all over gathered at the head of the

Lenape Indians encounter the Half Moon, 1609: "When some of them saw our ship approaching afar off, they did not know what to think but stood in deep and solemn amazement, wondering whether it was a spook or apparition, and whether it came from heaven or hell." ***(Print credit: Bank of Bergen, N.J.)***

Metedeconk River for an annual summer powwow to celebrate and smoke the peace pipe. When the red and yellow leaves of fall appeared, most of them followed the setting sun west to their winter homes in the forest.

The Grandfather of Nations

The Lenape were eulogized in *The Leatherstocking Tales* by James Fenimore Cooper, which was one of the first major works of American literature. Natty Bumppo's Indian friend Chingachgook tells the story of his people in the following excerpt:

My tribe is the grandfather of nations, but I am an un-mixed man. The blood of chiefs is in my veins, where it must stay forever . . . The salt lake gave us its fish, the woods its deer and the air its birds. We took wives who bore us children; we worshipped the Great Spirit . . . The first paleface who came among us spoke no English. They came in a large canoe, when my fathers had buried the tomahawk with the red-men around them. We were one people and we were happy. The Dutch landed, and gave my people the firewater; they drank until the heavens and earth seemed to meet, and they foolishly thought they had found the Great Spirit. Then they parted with their land. Foot by foot, they were driven back from the shores.

New Netherlands and the English Invasion

A few years after Hudson's voyage of discovery, the Dutch East India Company established a trading post at New Amsterdam, on the island of Manhattan. Company sea captains brought in the first settlers who bartered with local Indians for furs and food. Although the Swedes had laid claim to the territory later known as New Jersey, which they dubbed New Sweden, the Dutch invaded in 1654. They called the land New Belgium, a part of their great New Netherlands empire. Bergen was the site of their first outpost in North Jersey. Within a few years, villages were founded in Middletown and Freehold. Two of the earliest-settled areas along the shore were at Manasquan, in 1664, and at Barnegat, four years later.

Dutch rule came to an end in 1664 when the English took possession of New Netherlands. They renamed the area New York and New Jersey. Sir George Carteret was granted title to the land along the shore. The rule of the English Crown lasted for more than one hundred years. New Jersey became a province in 1673, and a Royal colony thirty years later.

Whalers and Fishermen

The first white settlers that the local Indians encountered were probably fishermen and whalers who sailed south from Cape Cod and Long Island. They built outposts on the beaches above and below Barnegat Inlet in the mid-1600s. There was an abundance of whales offshore, and two or three whales per season was considered a lucrative catch. At these temporary settlements, they watched the seas from high towers and pursued passing whales in six-man whaleboats. They dragged the huge carcasses onto the beach and sold the meat, bone, and oil. Harvey Cedars was the site of one of the first permanent whaling quarters. After more than a century of wholesale slaughter, the whales nearly vanished from offshore waters and their bones bleached in the sun on the white sand.

As late as 1758 a few Indians held title to large tracts of land along the bay between Metedeconk and Toms River, and these were among the last to be given up to white settlers. Although the Lenape were once a flourishing culture believed to number more than ten thousand before the coming of the Europeans, by 1775 less than two hundred Indians remained in South Jersey. Most Lenape left the state in 1802 to reunite with other tribes in New York. Despite this, there were some Indian families who stayed at the seashore, adjusted to their new neighbors, and made their living by fishing, hunting, and weaving baskets.

The Last of the Lenape

Relations with the white settlers were generally peaceful, and colonial authorities often relied on the Lenape to act as mediators in disputes with other tribes. Although local Indians legally signed away the rights to their lands, most of them did not fully understand the meaning of private property, and sometimes conflicts arose with the settlers when Indians persisted in returning to their old fishing and hunting grounds. According to Alfred Hulse, an Osbornville old-timer, six of the last Lenape around Metedeconk were lynched in the 1850s by an angry white mob because the Indians refused to stay away. Their bodies were buried in a common grave near the old Wardell farm and in later years the site became known as the Old Indian Burial Ground.

Dark spots on the high ground in the meadows and woods surrounding the bay mark the locations of their vanished bark lodges. Arrowheads, pottery, and worn grinding stones are sometimes still found. Large mounds of oyster and clamshells still stand on the sedgelands at the foot of the bay, accumulated by countless generations of Indians. The bones of ancient chiefs have been discovered beneath some of them, and a few of these skeletons measured six feet, eight inches tall. One of the biggest mounds, near Tuckerton, was one twelve feet high, one hundred feet long, and fifty feet wide. The Lenape language survives in local place names like Mantoloking (mantuah-leuku-ink or "tribal sand place"), Manasquan (manatah-squaw-han, or "stream of island for squaws"), Metedeconk (metu-saconk, or "medicine man outlet of stream") and Manahawkin (min-na-ac-un, or "a place where there is good land").

The Settlement of the Seashore

From the beginning of the European settlement, New Amsterdam was a maritime center, only thirty-five miles away, by water, from the head of the bay. The first vessel built in North America, the sloop *Restless*, was launched in New Amsterdam in 1614, and she explored Barnegat Bay on her maiden voyage down the Jersey Coast.

Early navigators recognized the possibilities for future settlement of the Barnegat region, and this foresight is well documented in Vanderdonck's *Journal of 1656*:

The coast has double forelands with many islands which in some places lie two or three deep. These forelands, as well as the islands, are well situated for seaboard towns, and all kinds of fisheries, and also for the cultivation of grain, vinyards, and gardenings, and the keeping of stock, for which purposes the land is tolerably good. Those lands are now mostly overgrown with different

Whalers established outposts on the beaches around Barnegat Bay in the late 1600s.
Whaling continued for more than a century, until the great mammals nearly vanished from coastal waters.
(Print from the collection of the author)

kinds of trees and grapevines; having many palms, hazelnuts, and strawberries, and much grass. The waters abound with oysters, having many convenient banks where they may be taken. Besides the many islands which lie between the aforesaid bays, many of which are high land, there are also several fine bays and inland waters which form good sea harbors for those who are acquainted with the inlets . . . but as New Netherlands is not yet well peopled, and as there are but few Christians settled at those places, the harbors are seldom used unless winds and weather render it necessary for safety.

By 1684 the following description of the Barnegat Coast appeared in Samuel Smith's *History of the Colony of Nova-Caesana*:

Barnegat or Burning-Hole, is said to be a very good place for fishing; and there is some desiring to take up land there, who inform that it is good land, and abundance of meadow lying to it. There are no fishermen that follow only that trade, save some that go a whaling upon the coasts; and for other fish there is abundance to be had every where through the country, in all the rivers; and the people commonly fish with long sives or long nets, and will catch with a sive, one, sometimes two barrels of good fish, which they salt up mostly for their own use, and to sell to others . . . There are several places of the country fit for mills; and several, both corn and saw mills already set up . . . There are but few Indian natives in this country, their strength is inconsiderable, they live in the woods, and have small towns in some places far up in the country . . . They have kings among themselves to govern them; for religion they have none at all; they do not refuse to sell lands at occasion.

Within a century, a few hundred settlers lived around the bay area. Early whalers — including the Applegates, Harveys, Irons, and Lawrences — worked along the beaches in the late 1680s, and their families were among the first permanent settlers in the area. Thomas Luker, an English immigrant, moved from Connecticut to New Jersey around 1700. He lived with his Indian bride in a wigwam on the banks of Goose Creek, later known as "Tom's" River. Princess Ann, his wife, was the daughter of a local Lenape chief who bestowed upon Luker the Indian name Pumha, or "white friend."

Three saw mills were established around Kettle Creek in the mid-1700s by Ebenezer Applegate, Job Cook, and Benjamin Wooley, and others soon followed on the Toms River, the Metedeconk, and the Manasquan. Most of the early settlers were farmers, fishermen, and tradesmen whose great-grandparents had colonized New England. These settlers usually lived on the mainland away from the beachfront hazards of storm and vagabond pirates.

The Barnegat Spirit

The traditional Barnegat spirit of stubborn self-sufficiency was nurtured by living off the land in sandy pine woods that abounded with deer, bears, wolves, wild cats, foxes, and beavers. Pine wood was used for everything from making tar, turpentine, and charcoal, to constructing small cabins. They also used durable white cedar, which was specially valued for boat building, as well as for making clam rakes, baskets, and cranberry scoops. Spruce, walnut, cherry, and mahogany were also commonly employed.

Many of the early coastal pioneers were Quakers, but they welcomed wandering ministers of different persuasions. One of these was Rev. Thomas Thompson, preaching for the Church of England, who settled in Monmouth County in 1745. Fresh from the old country, he was not too pleased by the attitudes he encountered when he journeyed around the bay area. In his *Journal of 1751*, Rev. Thompson wrote:

From Manasquan, for twenty miles further on in the country, is all one pine forest. I travelled through this desert four times to a place called Barnegat, and thence to Manahawkin, almost sixty miles from home, and preached at places where no foot of minister had ever come. In this section I had my views of heathenism just as thoroughly as I have ever since beheld it. The inhabitants are thinly scattered in regions of solid wood. Some are decent people who had lived in better places, but those who were born and bred here have neither religion nor manners, and do not know so much as a letter in a book. . . . These poor people call themselves Quakers, but they have no meetings, and many of them make no distinction of days, neither observing Lord's Day nor the Sabbath. In my journeyings through this part of the country I had many conferences and disputes with the people. Some of them were willing to see their errors, and others were as obstinent in defending theirs. . . .

Free churches were soon established in Manahawkin and Barnegat. Thomas Potter built one in the village of Good Luck in 1760, but its first regular minister did not arrive until ten years later, when the brig *Hand in Hand* stranded off Cranberry Inlet. One of her seamen was John Murray, a former Universalist preacher from England. Potter, who had long waited patiently for his minister to arrive, had a premonition about the shipwreck. He was not at all surprised when Murray arrived one morning at his house, asking for food, and Potter came right to the point:

My friends have often asked me, "Where is the preacher of whom you spoke?" and my constant reply was, "He will by-and-by make his appearance." The moment, sir, I saw your vessel on shore, it seemed as though a voice had audibly sounded in my ears: "There, Potter, in that vessel, cast away on that shore, is that preacher you have so long been expecting."

Amazed by the fateful encounter, Murray accepted the honor and became the first Universalist preacher in America. He also named the village "Good Luck" in tribute to the providential nature of his arrival.

Around the same time the Rev. John Brainerd travelled throughout the area, spreading the Presbyterian gospel to whites and Indians alike. His *Journal of January 1761 – October 1762* tells of how he lived with the Lenape in the village of Shamong, north of Atsion, after the death of his wife and two children. Here he preached to the Indians — in their own language — and taught them how to sow crops and fence their lands. He also warned them of the hazards of firewater and the "cupidity of white men," and sometimes acted as a mediator in settling disputes. He journeyed from Great Egg Harbor to Manahawkin, Toms River and Cedar Bridge, at the head of the Metedeconk, and preached to both Indians and white men. One of the entries in his *Journal* reads:

Lord's Day, Sept. 5. — Preach'd in the Forenoon at the Shore near Tom's River, in the south part of the Township of Shrewsbury, to a large congregation. And after Divine Services, promoted a subscription for the building of a Meeting House, which I think there is considerable prospect for.

Seaports, Smugglers, and the Black Market

During the late 1700s, small, busy seaports sprang up around the bay from Toms River to Barnegat and on down to Tuckerton. The Continental Congress designated Tuckerton as the third port of entry in the United States, after New York and Philadelphia. Up around the headwaters of the Manasquan, Crabtown grew from a small farming village to an active trading and boat-building center, later known as Squan Bridge. Smugglers sailed their sloops and schooners by night through the inlets and around the hidden coves of the bay. The black market flourished at local seaports where "free traders" were warmly welcomed.

Rebel Privateers and Redcoat Raiders

When the American colonies rebelled against the King in 1775, many bay area smugglers, whalers, and fishermen aided the cause of independence by attacking British shipping all along the coast. These privateers were commissioned by both the Continental Congress and the State of New Jersey. During the course of the war they engaged in seventy-seven naval battles off the Jersey Shore. Although considered common pirates by the enemy, the privateers

Captain Kidd, Blackbeard, and Richard Worley were among the pirates who sailed offshore during the late 1600s and early 1700s. Tales of piracy and buried treasure survived long after the buccaneers disappeared from the Jersey Coast. *(Illustration by Howard Pyle from* Harper's New Monthly Magazine, *courtesy of Kim and Bert Mauro)*

Attack by the British on the rebel Block House at Toms River, 1782.
(1891 engraving from the collection of the author)

played a crucial role in winning the war by cutting the British line of supplies and capturing their ships and cargoes.

Daring and high-spirited by nature, Barnegat seamen welcomed the opportunity to strike back at the Royal Navy, which had long made a practice of seizing American vessels and sailors on the high seas, and forcing them into service. Since the French, Spanish, and Danes were also guilty of this habit, American privateers frequently drew blood wherever they could find it.

Toms River, Tuckerton, and Little Egg Harbor were major centers of privateering on the Jersey Coast. Rebel sloops and schooners made frequent strikes on British shipping. They took captured vessels and cargo into port to be sold at public auction. It was hazardous duty, however, and the British did not give up their ships easily. They often retaliated by retaking their vessels, only to lose them again to the Rebels.

The *Love and Unity* Wrecks on Squan Beach

One of the largest prizes captured by local privateers was the three-masted British ship *Love and Unity,* which stranded on Squan Beach in August 1778. She was seized with her cargo, and an advertisement of her auction appeared in the August 15th issue of the *New Jersey Gazette*:

To be sold at publick Vendue, On Monday, the 31st. of August, The Ship LOVE AND UNITY, lying at Toms River, New Jersey, together with her tackle, apparel, furniture, and cargo, consisting of Bristol beer in bottles, Porter, Red and white Port wine, Bristol cyder, Salt, flour, cheese, Queen's and delft ware, And a small quantity of double flint ware, wine glasses, and tumblers.

Purchased by three Rebel merchants, the ship was renamed the *Washington* and armed as a privateer. British authorities in New York were enraged. A few weeks later, on September 18th, two Royal men-of-war and two brigs sailed down to Cranberry Inlet. At sunrise, armed troops in seven whaleboats rowed into the bay and recaptured the *Washington* and two other sloops. They also took several prisoners.

Revolutionary sympathizers organized a militia — composed of men from all over the region — and built a blockhouse at Toms River on a knoll overlooking the town bridge. When the Battle of Monmouth was fought in late June 1778, and made Molly Pitcher a legend, the sound of cannon fire

Pirates and privateers haunted the coves and inlets of Barnegat Bay in the 1700s, sailing in sloops, schooners, barks, and brigs.

rumbled down the coast. A large body of local militia assembled and marched through the pines to Freehold but arrived too late to join the battle.

British Raids Along the Barnegat Coast

British troops made several raids along the coast during the same year, stealing cattle, taking American vessels, and destroying salt works. Salt was a crucial commodity during the war, used for making gunpowder and preserving food. It sold for $35 a bushel. The Union Saltworks, on the south bank of the Manasquan River, about a mile inland, was one of the largest. In early April, 135 Redcoats landed and destroyed the saltworks and more than one hundred houses in the river area, as well as copper kettles used for boiling salt. There was no opposition to the raiders.

The Pennsylvania Saltworks lay near the mouth of Toms River, on the marshlands of its northern bank. A tall windmill stood facing Cranberry Inlet. It was used for pumping salt water into a large stove inside the main building, which was 169 feet long and twenty-nine feet wide. Several small houses stood nearby, including a blacksmith shop, a small kitchen, and two storehouses. A platoon of militiamen protected these works, with the aid of two howitzers and an armed sloop, the *Delaware*, which patrolled the bay and neighboring coast, on the lookout for British raiders.

Although the British did not succeed in striking the Pennsylvania Saltworks in 1778, they burned it two or three times a few years later, and also destroyed the smaller saltworks located at Forked River, Waretown, and Barnegat.

In the course of war, the Toms River militia engaged in twenty-three skirmishes with British and Tory soldiers. Privateering went on as usual, with the capture of many British vessels, including the *Hazard*, the *Dove*, the *Experiment,* the *Fanny*, the *Hope*, and the *Lively*. One privateer ship, the *Dart*, sailing under Captain William Gray with a crew of seven, was seized while chasing a British brig outside Cranberry Inlet.

The "Nest of Pirates" at Toms River

Rebel spirit was so strong around the bay that William Franklin, the exiled Royal Governor of New Jersey, decided to destroy the "nest of pirates" at Toms River. Franklin, who was an illegitimate offspring of Benjamin Franklin, raised a British expedition that sailed out of New York bound for the Jersey Shore. On the chilly gray night of March 23rd, 1782, the British brig *Arrogant* and three armed whaleboats anchored off the Southern end of Squan Beach.

Under cover of darkness, eighty Redcoats and forty Refugee Tories boarded the boats and rowed through Cranberry Inlet and across the choppy waters of Barnegat Bay. Landing on the marsh near Coats Point, north of Toms River, they were joined by local turncoats, who served as guides on the midnight march upriver to the seaport. Along the way they raided farms and took several hostages.

The sleeping village lay waiting, a dozen small houses, with a boatworks, saw mill, and grist mill. Captain Joshua Huddy, the commander of the militia, received word of the coming attack. With twenty-five men, he prepared to defend the log blockhouse near the bank of the river. Protected by a seven-foot stockade and brass swivel guns, the blockhouse was the only fortified position in the area.

The Storming of Toms River Block House

Shortly after dawn that Sabbath morning, about 125 British Redcoats and Refugee soldiers launched their attack. They swarmed down Squan Road and through the narrow lanes of Toms River, brandishing swords and flintlocks with fixed bayonets. The village lay deserted, and a crying rooster broke the eerie calm. Crouched behind the log stockade, the Rebels watched as the Redcoats and Tories surrounded the small blockhouse. Their commander ordered the militiamen to give up their fort. Captain Huddy replied, "Come and take it!"

The roar of yelling men and musket fire shook the morning air as the Redcoats marched forward with ladders and stormed over the stockade. Faced with overwhelming odds, the Rebels fought desperately until their ammunition ran out. Then they fought with swords, pikes, and their bare hands against the oncoming British bayonets. Confusion reigned in the smoky haze of battle. Seven militiamen escaped. Nine were killed and twelve taken prisoner, including Captain Huddy, who was captured in Randolph's mill. The British force suffered three dead and nine casualties. Their mission accomplished, the Redcoats spiked the village cannon and dumped it in the river. Then they put the town to the torch and marched back to the bay as a cold rain washed in from the sea.

A brief account of the battle was published soon after in the *Royal Gazette of New York*:

Lieutenant Blanchard summoned them to surrender, which they not only refused, but bid the party defiance; on which he immediately ordered the placed to be stormed, which was accordingly done, and though defended with obstinancy, was soon carried.

A few weeks later, the British hanged Captain Huddy at Atlantic Highlands, despite his prisoner-of-war status. The incident drew a formal protest from Commander in Chief George Washington, and created an international furor. The bay area Rebels suffered a stunning blow with the loss of many brave men and the destruction of their major seaport, which they rapidly rebuilt. Disaster struck again on October 25th, six months after the attack on Toms River.

The Massacre on Long Beach

Sailing up the coast in the privateer galley *Alligator*, Captain Andrew Steelman and his nine-man crew discovered an abandoned British cutter stranded off Long Beach, one mile south of Barnegat Inlet. Seizing the wreck, Captain Steelman sent for help in removing the valuable cargo of tea and transporting it to the mainland. Seventeen men from Waretown and Barnegat answered his call. Laboring feverishly until nightfall, the crew of the *Alligator* and the volunteers set up camp and slept soundly on the beach, hoping to complete the task of unloading the next day before the British had time to send a rescue salvage ship.

Word of the Rebels at work on the wreck quickly reached Captain John Bacon and his notorious band of Refugee Tories and runaway slaves, who were using Island Beach as a base for piracy and raiding parties on the mainland. Late that night, Bacon and his men sailed across Barnegat Inlet in a small sloop called the *Heroes Revenge.* They landed on Long Beach, a short distance from the Rebel camp. Sneaking through the shadowy dunes on a damp fall morning, they encircled the sleeping men and massacred them. Twenty-one Rebels were killed in cold blood. Five managed to flee in the night.

Bacon's band went into hiding in the forest south of Toms River. Outraged Rebels organized search parties and proclaimed a bounty of 50 pounds for Bacon's head. In April 1783, Bacon was trapped inside a tavern near West Creek and shot down as he attempted to flee into the pines.

Privateering During the War of 1812

Thirty years later, during the War of 1812, privateers again took to the waters to harass British shipping. Since the enemy held no American

A detail of New Jersey from Thomas Jeffreys' 1758 *General Map of the Middle British Colonies in America* (Map courtesy of O.C.C.L.)

A British fleet pursuing the *U.S.S. Constitution* up the New Jersey coast during the War of 1812. Trapped on a windless sea, "Old Ironsides" set out longboats to haul her out of harms way. Cannon fire thundered across the coast during the desperate three-day engagement. ***(Print courtesy of Wayne L. Hartman)***

port, the privateers served mainly as blockade runners and frequently skirmished with British vessels. Commodore Hardy's seventy-four-gun, three-deck Royal man-of-war *Ramilles* patrolled the Jersey Shore, enforcing the blockade of New York.

Redcoats again landed on the coast to raid local farms and destroy American vessels and boatworks. In July 1813, two Barnegat Bay sloops, returning from New York, were sighted by a British brig, which pursued them to Manasquan Inlet. Captain James Warren, in the *Maria,* and Captain Thomas Mills, in the *Friendship,* raced for the safe shallow waters of the river but stranded on the bar outside the entrance. The American crews jumped ship and swam to shore as barges set out from the warship to plunder the sloops. Musket fire from the men on the beach drove the raiders off. In retaliation, the brig swung around and fired more than two hundred cannonballs at the stranded vessels, breaking their masts and battering their hulls.

John S. Forman was an eyewitness and gave the following report:

After they were out of the way and the tide had risen, we got the sloops over the bar and up the inlet where they could be repaired and used later . . . We expected the British would land that night and there were 180 of us under arms and on the lookout. We would have given a good deal to induce them to do so, but they were all very timid about venturing on shore and preferred to drop a shot now and then upon us from their men-of-war, or to land only long enough to steal cattle and make off again.

Four months earlier, on March 31, the *Ramilles* stood off Barnegat Inlet and sent armed barges into the bay to burn two privateer schooners that lay at anchor. As local residents watched from rooftops in Forked River and Waretown, Redcoat raiders also landed on Long Beach Island, according to a contemporary account:

While the barges were at the inlet, a party landed on the beach and killed fifteen head of cattle. The British left word that if the owners presented a bill to

Commodore Hardy, he would settle it. But the owners were too patriotic to attempt anything that seemed like furnishing supplies to the enemy.

During the same year the British privateer ship *Thistle* sunk off Manasquan Inlet, where she still lies under twenty feet of water.

"Old Ironsides' " Encounter with a British Squadron

One of the strangest sea chases in naval history took place a month after the war began when the *U.S.S. Constitution*, later known as "Old Ironsides," encountered five British warships off the Jersey Shore. The 54-gun frigate *Constitution*, under Captain Isaac Hull, was sailing up the coast from Chesapeake to rendezvous with an American squadron outside New York harbor. Around sundown on July 17th, Captain Hull sighted dead ahead what he believed to be the sails of the American force, and he decided to drop anchor for the night off the southern end of Long Beach Island.

When the sun rose and the morning fog cleared, Captain Hull discovered his ship was moored on a calm, windless sea in the midst of a formidable British squadron. Astern the *Constitution* lay the sixty-four-gun man-of-war *Africa* and two thirty-eight-gun frigates, *Belvidera* and *Shannon*. On her leeward lie the thirty-two-gun frigate *Aeolus* and the thirty-eight-gun frigate *Guerriere*.

Faced with a dead wind and outgunned four-to-one, Captain Hull ordered his crew to quietly lower the ships' boats and sent men ahead to tow the *Constitution* out of harm's way. When the British realized what was happening, the American frigate opened fire with her stern guns. The five Royal warships responded with thundering broadsides. One of the American gunners, Moses Smith, described the tense moment in his pamphlet, *Naval Scenes in the Last War*:

Captain Hull came aft, coolly surveyed the scene, took a match in his hand, and ordered the quarter-master to hoist the American flag. I stood within a few feet of Hull at the time. He clapped the fire to my gun, No.1, and such a barking as sounded over the sea! It was worth hearing. No sooner had our iron dog opened his mouth in this manner, than the whole enemy opened the whole of theirs. Every one of the ships fired directly toward us. Those nearest kept up their firing for some time; but of course not a shot reached us then, at the distance we were. Captain Hull gave up the match to the captain of the gun, and we kept blazing away with our stern chasers. The shots we fired helped send us ahead; but we resolved to save ourselves from capture, or sink in the conflict. We soon found, however, that we made but slow work in getting ahead.

Recognizing how dire their situation was, the American boat crews began kedging: setting sea anchors out ahead while seamen on board the *Constitution* pulled the lines in to haul the ship forward. They worked throughout the night to stay ahead of the pursuing British vessels, which adopted similar tactics.

During the next three days, the thunder of sporadic cannon fire rolled across the waves as the desperate chase continued up the coast past Barnegat Inlet and Island Beach. When the angry gray clouds of a summer squall began gathering, Captain Hull quickly took in his sails. Seeing the coming storm, the British also struck their sails, as the *Constitution* vanished in the downpour. Seizing the opportunity, Captain Hull re-rigged his frigate for full sail, and the *Constitution* escaped the British squadron on the gusting winds of the storm.

A month later, the *Constitution* engaged one of these pursuers on the high seas when she encountered and sank the *Guerriere* in a furious battle, which brought her the nickname "Old Ironsides."

The Era of the Coastal Trade

The 1800 edition of the *American Coast Pilot* offered the following warning to coastal mariners:

The shoal of Barnegat does not extend beyond three miles from the beach and is very steep too; you may turn this shoal in six fathoms of water within pistol shot of the outward breakers . . . By passing Barnegat in the daytime it may easily be known, should you be so far off as not to see the breakers; you will see a long grove of wood back in the country, apparently three or four miles long, known to the coasters by the name of Little Swamp, *and lies directly in the rear of the inlet of Barnegat.*

After the war ended in 1815, the maritime commerce of the Northeast boomed, as American shipping began to compete with European powers for foreign trade. New York rapidly grew as an international port during the next half-century, and a colorful parade of ships of all flags regularly passed off the Jersey Shore. Standing on a sand dune on Squan Beach, one could see the billowing sails of French barks, Dutch galleys, English merchantmen, coastal packet ships, and Yankee Clippers. On an average summer day in 1850, 313 ships, 524 brigs, and 247 steamships plowed through the offshore seas. They sailed through the night, their glowing lanterns bobbing on the water in the dark like floating stars.

Barnegat Bay sloops and schooners fished the local waters and traded up and down the coast, from New England to Southern ports. These vessels sailed in and out of the bay, carrying lumber, charcoal, tobacco, tea, vegetables, and many other goods. The bay was the highway between the scattered villages that lay on her shores. Enclosed by a surrounding pine forest, the bay area was a world in itself, facing out on the broad North Atlantic. The coastal trade expanded the sense of possibility for local youths who dreamed of seafaring. Many "coast-wise" Barnegat sailors went on to other ships and seas.

Cranberry Inlet Disappears in the Night

Cranberry Inlet began shoaling up early in the nineteenth century. One morning in 1812, after a great northeast storm, David Mapes, the shepherd of Squan Beach, woke up to find the inlet had closed entirely during the midnight gale. Squan Beach and Island Beach were joined to become a twenty-two-mile-long peninsula. Captains from the head of the bay and Toms River were forced to sail twelve miles south of old Cranberry to Barnegat Inlet.

Around 1818, Michael Ortley purchased land north of the old inlet and, with the help of local fishermen, began the backbreaking work of digging a new channel. He had hopes of reaping a fortune by charging tolls for passage. Finally in 1821, Ortley celebrated the completion of his dream with a keg party on the beach as the last ground was broken, and the sea once again washed into the bay. Disappointment dawned the morning after when Ortley discovered the longshore tide had worked during the night to shoal the channel closed. Only after repeated failure did Ortley give up his dream.

Twenty-six years later, Anthony Ivins recruited a few hundred local volunteers and made another effort at reopening an inlet a short distance south of where Ortley had failed. The running tide again refused to cooperate. Shoals built up in the northern half of the bay, where the depth averaged fifteen feet in her channels but less than five feet close to shore. South of Barnegat Inlet, around Lovelady Island, the bay was nearly twenty feet deep. As a result of the shoaling, passage on the bay became limited to shallow draught vessels. Nearly sixty sloops and schooners worked out of Toms River by 1850, carrying charcoal, lumber, and cordwood.

The Founding of Ocean County

In the same year, Ocean County was formed, with the longest coastline in the state, running forty miles from Manasquan Inlet to Little Egg Harbor. Barnegat Bay was the largest body of water in New Jersey, stretching thirty-five miles from Bay Head to Gunning Ditch, and ranging in breadth from one to five miles wide. Ocean County had a population of 10,032 at this time, and Toms River was selected as the county seat.

Stagecoaches carried passengers and goods between the shore towns, and followed sandy trails through the desolate pines to the inland cities. A one-way ticket from Point Pleasant to New York overland by stage cost 87 cents. In the summer, many people sailed or steamed down from the northern cities on small passenger vessels to vacation at the fashionable watering places that were flowering along the seashore.

The Clipper Ships

The great era of the clipper ship peaked around this time, when 120 of these magnificent vessels were launched in this country in 1853. American ship builders applied all their skill in developing faster ships with finer lines that could hold more canvas. Their efforts resulted in the clipper ship, which builder David McKay called "the thoroughbred of the seas."

The Baltimore clipper evolved out of schooners built during the early 1800s in Maryland. With raking masts, their schooner rigged sails were adapted to the winds and currents of the Eastern shore. They were fast vessels with long, narrow hulls, and rarely weighed more than two hundred tons. As a result, they could not carry much cargo and were used by the Navy during the War of 1812 and later as pilot boats. Pirates and slavers also found them to be very seaworthy vessels. One of the largest was the *Ann McKim*, which was launched in 1832 and weighed 493 tons.

The Baltimore clippers bore little resemblance to the classic clipper ships built by Donald McKay in Boston during the 1850s, such as the famous *Sovereign of the Seas*, which weighed 2,421 tons. She was one of the fastest clippers, capable of sailing at twenty-two knots. Another McKay ship, the *Flying Cloud*, once sailed 374 miles in one day during a remarkable voyage from New York to San Francisco, arriving eighty-nine days and twenty hours after departure. His greatest feat, however, was the giant *Great Republic*, which, at 4,357 tons, was the largest wooden vessel ever built.

Although construction began to decline as early as 1855, when only forty-two of them were launched, for many years later these magnificent clipper ships were a common sight sailing off the Jersey Shore. Beachcombers and clam diggers watched them from the beaches, heading out for the California gold fields and coming home from the China Run, racing on the wind.

The Maid of the Mist

The Maid of the Mist

When a scrimshaw moon glows
with an ivory light,
the Maid of the Mist
walks the shore in the night,
and moans the sad song
of her lost lover's plight,
as she wanders beside
the foggy low tide . . .

"Oh, where have you gone,
oh, where can you be,
when will the sea
return you to me?
You left without warning,
no word of farewell,
your sloop slipped its mooring,
lost to Heaven or Hell . . ."

And the wind seems to answer
through the deep ocean roar,
with the power of love
while the waves wash ashore.
His song for his lover
who walks in moonlight,
tolls like a bell
in the fog of the night . . .

"My sloop, she weighed anchor
and left Barnegat Bay,
set sail for the sunrise,
a squall struck underway —
but I sent you my love
as the circling gulls cried,
corked in a bottle
to ride the high tide."

Still the Maid of the Mist
walks the shore in the night,
with a willow-like grace
and wet seashell eyes.
If you spy her, don't linger,
let the poor widow by,
she's been walking this shore
for a century or more.

"Oh, where have you gone,
oh, where can you be,
when will the sea
return you to me?
You left without warning,
no word of farewell,
and I walk these beaches
still under your spell. . . ."

Barnegat Lighthouse, July 14, 1865, from a pencil sketch by George Tenils.
(Picture courtesy of Rutgers University Library)

Fishing Off the Coast of New Jersey

Sunrise at Mantoloking. The shipwreck in the foreground at the water's edge might be the *Creole* or the *John Minturn*. *(Watercolor by G. M. McCord, 1878, courtesy of L.E.C.)*

The rough line of sea front extending from the entrance of the harbor of New York to the Capes of the Delaware, a distance of one hundred and twenty miles, affords within its comparatively limited space one of the choicest fishing grounds in the world. For many generations the inhabitants occupying this somewhat desolate and isolated region of the Atlantic coast have made "fishing" a business; the ancestors of the present active generation found the sterile soil little adapted to agriculture, but the unprecedented abundance of Old Ocean was ever at the command of "easy industry," and thus the people always thrived, and in latter days have made a great and most profitable business in supplying the surrounding population with fish.

By some law that governs the migration of ocean-life, fish, which are more especially esteemed valuable for food in early spring, seem to head toward the Jersey coast, and here they remain through the entire summer and late in the fall; in fact, it is not until the fresh airs of coming winter chill the shallow water that they seek the more genial regions of the South, or sink into the depths of the sea, below the influence of borean blasts. Thus, it is in the finest weather the great self-produced crop of fish is gathered.

The Market Fishermen

The appliances of the market fishermen are, as a rule, simple and inexpensive. The little skiff, the more pretentious but still small sailboat, make up the list of water-craft, to which must be added the strong nets, many of the simplest contrivance, such as Peter and his companions, over eighteen hundred years ago, used in the Sea of Galilee.

But modern American mechanical ingenuity, illustrated by the fishermen of the Jersey coast, has added the "pound." Its principle of action is very similar to the gin used by "pot-hunters" to secure the bright-eyed quail. In a favorable position, and at a right angle from the shore, a "net-fence" is erected, from nine hundred to a thousand feet in length. At the extreme end of this obstruction is placed the pound, another strong net, arranged so that its walls represent a room about twenty feet square. Everything properly disposed of, the waters far above and below the trap are rudely disturbed, and the fish, all unconscious of danger, leisurely pursue their way until they strike the fence, then, alarmed, they rush toward deep water and are guided into the pound, where their captors leave them until ready to ship them to market. The

Two Barnegat Bay catboats off to the fishing grounds. ***(Lithograph from water-color by G. R. Hardenbergh, 1909, courtesy of Mr. and Mrs. C.J.H.)***

"catches" on many occasions are thousands and thousands of every variety of fish known to the coast.

Never in a Hurry

The fishermen have their professional peculiarities. Like all disciples of the "rod and line," they are hospitably disposed, and steady-going and quiet in their demeanor they are, as a class, never in a hurry, and give little heed to the cares and excitements of the outer world. Their game is noiseless and timid, their homes are isolated, and they (the fishermen) insensibly conform their thoughts and manners to their surroundings.

Nor is the theory that, as fish contain an unusual amount of phosphorus, therefore the eating of them especially strengthens the brain, rendering the consumers of flounders and horse-mackeral poets and statesmen, sustained by intercourse with the semi-marine population of Squan Beach or Tuckahoe Inlet; on the contrary, they are very practical people, sharp at a bargain, and greatly given to thrift and to putting their surplus dollars in farms and savings-banks.

All along, from Sandy Hook to the Capes, hidden away in the broken and cosy nooks of this apparently arid soil, are the single cottages and little villages of the professional fishermen. Their lives are not spent in hardship, nor are their rewards for labor meagre. The consequence is that you will find them living cosily, and often blessed with much of the world's goods.

In addition to fishing the bays, the men employed in their small sail-boats go some distance from the mainland, where, in deep water, they secure the finer specimens, which are so attractive to old gentlemen with large purses, large girth, large appetites, and large families, and to ambitious keepers of popular hotels. Trolling for fish is one of the most exciting sports, and, as success is not the result of experience, it is sometimes a matter of grave speculation to decide whether the tyro in the boat, or the blue-fish at the end of the line, is most astonished.

No Longer a Dreaded Coast

Fifty years ago, our pleasant fishing-coast of New Jersey, now the seat of happiness and prosperity, was one of the horrors of the hardy children of the sea. The stern, repulsive headlands from Sandy Hook southward to Cape May, were associated with marine disaster. Human hearts, however brave, and human hands, however strong, too often failed in the hour of peril off this dreaded coast. But when the untiring arm of the steam came, as an obedient assistant to the over-wrought sailor, and the dreaded shoals and precipices had their towers by day and their warning lights by night, the Jersey coast became less traditionary of danger.

— by T.B. Thorpe, writing in **Appleton's Journal*****, June 24, 1871***

An 1849 view of the Barnegat Bay area from Thomas Gordon's map of New Jersey.
(Engraved by Edward Yeager, of Philadelphia, courtesy of David Harrison and the Ocean County Historical Society)

Tales of Barnegat Pirates haunting the beaches on stormy nights and luring ships ashore for wreck and plunder, made the Jersey Shore notorious during the nineteenth century. The seacoast was strewn with the hulks of lost vessels, and many people believed they were caused by more than the chance combination of foul weather, sandbars, and fate. *(Print from the collection of the author)*

Squan Beach
A Secluded Watering Place

Something less than 20 miles to the south of Long Branch lies the straggling village of Point Pleasant, whose beach has been a favorite resort for a full hundred years. During the first century, the sturdy farmers of New Jersey and Pennsylvania drove hither in their wagons, and engaged in hunting and clamming, while they lodged in the old house now kept by "Uncle Tommy" Cook, then under the care of his grandfather. He died at a ripe old age and it then passed into the hands of his son, who lived his 80th year, and in such feeble health that the place has been closed to all except very few visitors.

During the past decade, other boarding houses have been erected, and at the present writing hundreds are quartered here, and many more have been turned away, unable to find accommodations. The soil is sandy, but a plentiful distribution of the great Jersey fertilizer known as marl give abundant crops, and enables those farmers who devote their summer months to the comfort of their visitors, to make an exceedingly good thing of it.

A place as old as this cannot fail to have many reminiscences connected with it. Upon the remarkable little register at "Uncle Tommy's" can be seen the names of more than one governor, cabinet officer, and men ranking high in the army and navy of the country.

And there are others who have come here regularly for more than 30 years without the intermission of a single summer. The bride and groom who spent their honeymoon here many years ago are now old and bent, but their delight and pleasure in making their annual visit is scarcely less today than it was on that bright summer evening in the dim sweet past, when the lumbering old coach drew up in front of the old farmhouse, after its 40 miles and more of wear dragging through the hot sand and permitting them to rest under the shade of giant willows where the cool breeze of the Atlantic could fan their faces. The salt air carried life and health and vigor to all.

Times have changed since then. Twenty years ago the railroad was completed to Freehold, and the enervating stage ride through the heat and sand and pines was greatly lessened. Then it was cut down to a dozen miles by the extension of the line to Farmingdale, and during the present season it has been halved again by the spur that runs from the latter place to Squan Village.

Indian Will's Hole

Along the shore of the Squan River, but a few hundred yards from the spot, a small inlet was pointed out to me, which is known as "Indian Will's Hole." Some three-quarters of a century ago an old Indian chief made his home in the woods attached to the Cook farm. He was a brawny, muscular savage, peaceably inclined toward the whites and suffered no molestation from them. Many of his people lived around him, but he preferred to occupy his cabin along with his wife, while he spent most of his time in hunting and fishing.

But one day Indian Will brought home a muskrat which he ordered his wife to prepare for dinner. She obeyed, but when it was placed on the table she refused to partake of it. "Very well," grunted the noble red man, "If you are too good to eat muskrat, you are too good to live with me." And there upon he took her down to the little bay spoken of and caused her to sink so effectively that she has not yet come to the surface.

Indian Will had three brothers-in-law, two of whom were residing on Long Island, and when in the course of time word reached them of the manner in which Indian Will put away their sister, they went down to New Jersey to avenge her death. When they reached his cabin he sat inside eating clam soup. Knowing their errand, he invited them in to dinner, telling them he would fight it out with them as soon as the meal was concluded. "Barkis was willing," and they gathered around the aboriginal board, complementing the steaming soup which was placed before them, and scooped it into their spacious jaws in the very felicity of sensuous enjoyment.

Before the dinner was over, Indian Will pretended that he heard someone approaching, and springing up hurried out of his cabin to meet him. But the instant he was out of their sight he scooped up their guns, which they had left leaning against the door in full trust of his honor, and through the open door

Along the Metedeconk. *(From lithograph by G. R. Hardenbergh, 1909, courtesy of Mr. and Mrs. Curles J. Hulse)*

he shot them both, the last redskin falling dead as he was rushing out to close with his treacherous host.

A Deadly Struggle in the Pines

In those days it was the custom of the Indians to hold a yearly meeting or council at a place now known as Burrsville (Laurelton), something like a dozen miles from this point. It was here that Indian Will encountered the third brother-in-law, and they started homeward together, having no weapons with them, but carrying a jug of whiskey. Deep in the gloomy recesses of the pine woods, when his blood was enflamed with fire water, this Indian told the chief that he must die, as the death of his relatives must be avenged.

They halted and both closed in the deadly struggle. Both were active and powerful men, and it was a fight to the death. But late that evening Indian Will appeared at his cabin with no companion but his whiskey jug. The next day he received several visitors of his race that had been at the council and who had seen the two depart together. Inquiring as to what had happened to his comrade, he told them to search and they would probably find out.

They took the back trail of the chief and after an hour's tramping they found the dead body. The crushed skull and the bloody pine knot lying nearby told the tale. Henceforth, Indian Will was left alone, and quietly died in his cabin many years later. I find that in the deed of the Cook farm, this "Indian Will's Hole" is recognized and its margin is given as one of the landmarks.

Seashore Longevity

Just 25 years ago a character died here who was known as "Uncle Billy" Chamberlain. His wife preceeded him a few months, and was considerably over 90, while he was in his own 105th year at the time of his decease. Dr. Laird, who is still a hale old physician, actively practicing in this place, attended him in his last illness, if such it may be termed, and he tells me that for 40 years of his life he drank an average of a quart of whiskey a day. This was not during the later part of his career, however. He held up towards the last, and died without a particle of pain.

Another of the physician's patients, "Aunty Philips," was in her 108th year at her death. She was temperate in every respect, thereby refuting any theory that might be built upon the career of the other centenarian.

— by E.M.E., from the **New York Press,** *1878*

On the beach between Bay Head and Mantoloking — two fish pound boats in left foreground and a passing two-masted coastal schooner on the horizon.
(Watercolor by G. R. Hardenbergh, 1895, courtesy of Mr. and Mrs. Joseph Forsyth)

The Ghostly Sphinx of Metedeconk

About a mile south of here, on the low brown bluff that overlooks the ocean, there is an old house to which the inhabitants of the place have attached a portentous gruesome legend. It is here that the white lady, a moaning, mourning thing of the mist, walks to and fro, haunting the beach at the edge of the surf in midnight searches for the body of her lover. The legend was born, it is said, in 1815, and since that time Metedeconk has devoted much breath to the discussion of it, orating in the village stores, haranguing in the post office, until the story has become a religion, a sacred tale, and he who scorns it receives the opprobrium of all Metedeconk.

It is claimed that when this phantom meets a human being face to face, she asks a question — a terrible, direct interrogation. She will ask concerning the body of her lover, who was drowned in 1815, and if the chattering mortal cannot at once give her an intelligent answer, containing terse information relating to the corpse, he is forthwith doomed, and his friends will find him the next day lying pallid upon the shore. So, for fear of being nonplussed by this sphinx, the man of Metedeconk, when he sees white at night, runs like a hare.

There have been those who come here and openly derided the legend, but they have always departed wiser. Once a young man, who believed in the materialism of everything, came to town and perambulated up and down the beach during three midnights. He had requested the inhabitants to bring forth their phantom. She did not appear. During some following days the young man poked all of the leading citizens in the ribs and laughed loudly, but he was whipped within an inch of his life by an old retired sea captain named Josiah Simpson. Since then the legend has obtained a much wider credit, and for miles around Metedeconk the people evince a great faith in it.

The Fisherman's Fright

The last man to assert definitely that he has encountered the specter is a bronzed and blase young fisherman, who assured the world that the matter of its believing his story is of no consequence to him. He relates that one night, when swift scudding clouds flew before the face of the moon, which was like a huge silver platter in the sky, he had occasion to pass this old house, with its battered sides, caving roof, and yard overgrown with brambles. The passing of the clouds before the moon made each somber shadow of the earth waver suggestively and the wind tossed the branches of the trees in strange and uncouth gestures. Within the house the old timbers creaked and moaned in a weird and low chant. By a desperate effort the fisherman dragged himself past the dark residence of the specter. Each wail of the old timbers was a voice that went to his soul, and each contortion of the shadows made by the wind-waved trees seemed to him to be the movement of a black and sinister figure creeping upon him.

But it was when he was obliged to turn his back upon the old house that he suffered the most agony of mind. There was a little patch of flesh between his shoulder-blades that continually created the impression that a deathlike hand was about to be laid upon him. His trembling nerves told him that he was being approached by a mystic thing. He gave an involuntary cry and turned to look behind him.

There stood the ghostly form of the white lady. Her hair fell in disheveled masses over her shoulders, her hands were clasped appealingly, and her large eyes gleamed with the one eternal and dread interrogation. Her lips parted and she was on the verge of propounding the awful question, when the fisherman howled and started wildly for Metedeconk. There rang through the night the specter's cry of anger and despair, and the fisherman, although he was burdened with heavy boots, ran so fast that he fell from sheer exhaustion upon the threshold of his home. From that time forward it became habitual with him to wind up his lines when the sun was high over the pines on the western shores of Barnegat, and to reach his home before the chickens had gone to bed.

Source of the Mystery

It seems that long ago a young lady lived in this house which then was gorgeous with green blinds and enormous red chimneys. The paths in the grounds had rows of boxwood shrubbery laid down their sides with exquisite accuracy, and each geometrical flower bed upon the lawn looked like a problem in polygons. The maiden had a lover who was captain of a ship that was given to long voyages. They loved each other dearly, and, in consequence of these long voyages, they were obliged to part with protestations of undying affection about three times a year. But once when the handsome sailor luffed his ship into the wind and had himself rowed ashore to bid goodbye to his love, she chose that time to pout. He spent a good deal of time in oration and argument, he proved to her in sixty ways that she was foolish to act thus at the moment of his departure, but she remained perverse, and during his most solemn abjurations she lightly and blithely caroled a little ditty of the day. Finally, in despair, he placed his hand upon his lacerated heart and left for Buenos Ayres.

But his ship had not passed Absecon Inlet before the maiden was torn with regret and repentance, and by the time the craft was a white glimmer upon the edge of the horizon she began to mourn and mourn in the way that has since become famous. As the days passed, her sorrow grew, and the fishermen used often to see her walking slowly back and forth, gazing eagerly into the southeast for the sail that would bear her lover to her. During great storms she never seemed able to remain quietly in the house, but always went out to watch the white turmoil of the sea.

The round, tanned cheeks grew thin and pale. She became frail, and would have appeared listless if it were not for the feverish gleam of those large eyes, which eternally searched the sea for a belated sail.

The Storm's Finale

One winter's day a storm came from the wild wastes of the unknown and broke upon the coast with extraordinary fury. The tremendous breakers thundered upon the beach until it seemed that the earth shook from the blows. Clouds of sand whirled along the beach. The wind blew so that it was nearly impossible to make headway, but still the young girl came out to stare at the impenetrable curtains of clouds in the southeast.

That evening as she made her difficult way along the beach, a rocket went up out at sea, leaving for a moment a train of red sparks across the black sky. Then she knew that sailor lads were in peril. After a time a green light flashed over the water, and finally she could perceive a large ship on the bar. Above the roar of the waves she imagined she could hear the cries of the men.

The fishermen, notified by the rocket, came to the shore by twos and threes. No boat could live in such a sea, and the sailors of the ship were doomed. The fishermen bustled to and fro, impatiently shouting and gesturing, but in those days their greatest efforts could consist in no more than providing fires, drink, and warm blankets for any who by some astounding chance should escape through the terrible surf. From time to time seamen tried to swim to the shore, and for an instant a head would shine like a black bead on this wild fabric of white foam. Bodies began to wash up, and the fishermen, congregating about huge fires devoted their attention to trying to recall life in these limp, pale things that the sea cast up one by one.

The maiden paced the beach praying for the souls of the sailors who, upon this black night, were to be swallowed in a chaos of waters for the unknown reasons of the sea.

Once she espied something floating on the surf. Because of the small gruesome wake, typical of a floating corpse, she knew what it was, and she awaited it. A monstrous wave hurled the thing to her feet and she saw that her lover had come back from Buenos Ayres.

This is the specter that haunts the beach at the edge of the surf and who lies in wait to pour questions into the ears of the agitated citizens of Metedeconk.

– by Stephen Crane, from the **New York Press,** ***1895***

Shipwrecks, Ghosts, and Tales of the Dunes

The bay between the mainland and the sand bar, known everywhere as "The Beach," was narrow, winding slowly as we advanced, until at the end of our seven miles' journey, it was nearly three miles across. There was little vegetation besides salt grass and bay-berry bushes; but of the animal kingdom the only representatives — the mosquitoes — were thicker than the mind of man can conceive; they rose in crowds, pursuing us fiercely, covering the horses in an unbroken mass, settling upon ourselves, flying into our eyes, crawling upon our necks, stinging through our clothes, and filling the air. Although small, they were hungry beyond belief, and, following their prey relentlessly, compelled us to fight them off with bushes of bay-berry for our lives.

A Beach Party at Uncle Jakey's Tavern

One good effect they had, however, was to compel the driver to urge on his weary team, and leave him no time to gossip at Jakey's Tavern, over the beach party that was to be held there the next day. A beach party is another delightful institution of the Jerseyites, and consists of a congregation of the youths of both sexes, especially the female, collected from the main shore, and meeting on the beach for a frolic, a dance, and a bath. As it rarely breaks up till daylight, the pleasantest intimacies are sometimes formed, and soft words uttered that could not be wrung from blushing beauty in broad day.

Bill Chadwick's Establishment

The establishment of the "old man" — the sporting "old man," not the political one — since he has been gathered to his forefathers, is kept up by his son-in-law, usually known by the abbreviation Bill. It is not an elegant place; sportsmen do not demand elegance, and willingly sleep, if not in the same room, in chambers that lead into one another; but it is as situated within a hundred yards of the best shooting ground, and is as well kept as any other tavern on the beach. Sportsmen do not mind waiting their turn to use the solitary wash basin, drawing water from the hogshead, or wiping on the same towel, but are thankful for good food, and the luxury of a well filled ice-house.

The best days are those with a cloudy sky, and a south-westerly wind. On such occasions the birds often come in myriads, delighting the sportsman's heart, testing his nerves, and filling his bag to repletion. When the object is to kill the greatest number possible, they are permitted to alight among the stools and collect together before the gun is fired; then the first discharge is followed rapidly by the second, which tears among their thinned ranks as they rise; and,

Mantoloking seascape, with passing schooner and steamer on the horizon. *(Lithograph from watercolor by G.R. Hardenbergh, courtesy Mr. and Mrs. Curles Hulse)*

if there be a second gun, by the third and fourth barrel, till frequently all are killed. The scientific and sportsmanlike mode is to fire before they alight, selecting two or three together and firing at the foremost.

The Sportsman's Heart

It is a glorious thing to see a flock of marlin or willet, or perhaps the chief of all, the sickle-bills, swerve from their course away up in the heavens, and after a moment's uncertainty reply to the sportsman's deceitful call and turn towards his false copies of themselves.

As they approach the rich sienna brown of the marlin and curlew seems to color the sky and reflect a ruddy hue upon surrounding objects; or the black and white of the barred wings of the willet makes them resemble birds hewn from veined marble. The sportsman's heart leaps to his throat, as crouching down with straining eye and nerve, grasping his faithful gun, he awaits with eager anxiety the proper moment; then, rising ere they are aware of the danger, he selects the spot where their crowding bodies and jostling wings shut out the clouds beyond, and pours in his first most deadly barrel; and quickly bringing to bear the other as best lie may among the now frightened creatures as they dart about, he delivers it before he has noticed how many fell to the first. Dropping back to his position of concealment, he recommences whistling, and the poor things, forgetting their fright and anxious to know why their friends alighted amid a roar like thunder, return to the fatal spot, and again give the fortunate sportsman a chance for his reloaded gun.

Evening at the House

Towards evening the flight diminished, and when the horn announced that supper was ready, the different parties met once more at the house to compare notes and relate adventures. All had met with excellent success, but our stand carried off the palm.

"Bill," commenced some unhappy person, after we had left the close, hot dining-room, "Why do you not enlarge your house?"

"Bill is waiting for another wreck," was the volunteer response. "The whole coast is fed, clothed and sheltered by the wrecks. The house is built from the remnants of unfortunate ships, as you perceive by the name-boards of the Arion, Pilgrim Samuel Willets, J. Harthorn, and Johanna, that form so conspicuous a part of the front under the porch. When a vessel is driven ashore, and the crew and passengers who are not quite dead are disposed of by the aid of a stone in the corner of a hankerchief, which makes an unsuspicious bruise, the prize is fought over by the natives, and not only the cargo, but the very ribs and planks of the vessel appropriated."

"Now that's not fair," replied Bill, aroused. "No man, except my father-in-law, has done more to save drowning men than I have. I tell you it's an awful sight to see the poor creatures clinging to the rigging and bowsprit, to see them washed off before your eyes, sometimes close to you, without your being able to help them, and their dead bodies thrown up by the waves on the sand. You don't feel like stealing or murder at such times; and besides, I never knew a dead man come ashore that had anything in his pockets."

A peal of laughter greet this naive remark, together with the ready response: "Bill, you were too late; some Barnegat pirate had been before you."

Tales of the Barnegat Pirates

"No, the Barnegat pirates are kinder than the Government. We do our best to save the poor fellows, but the Government puts men in charge of their station-houses that know nothing about their business. My father-in-law was the first man that threw a line with the cannon over a ship, and he was presented with a medal by the Humane Society. He never was paid a dollar for taking charge of the station, the life-boat, and the cannon. Since he died I kept it for five years, and was paid two years; now men are selected for their politics. One lives on the main land two miles from his station-house, another never fired a gun, and a third never rowed a boat."

"But, Bill, tell us about the Barnegat pirates leading a lame horse with a lantern tied to his neck over the sand hills in imitation of a ship's light, and thus inveigling vessels ashore."

"I can only say I have never heard of it. As quick as a vessel comes ashore, the insurance agent is telegraphed for, and he takes charge of everything. Why, we even buy the wrecks and pay well for them too. Now and then something is washed up like that coal in front of the house, but it is not often."

"Now, Bill, stop your talk about the public wrongs, and tell us something more interesting. Have you ever heard one of Bill's ghost stories?" This inquiry was addressed to the public.

Bill's face lengthened; he sat silently nursing his leg and smoking his briarwood pipe, while a shadow seemed to settle on his countenance. "Come, Bill," we responded, "let's have the story."

Bill answered not, and the shadow deepened, and the smoke was puffed in heavier masses from his lips.

"Bill is afraid; he doesn't like ghosts, and don't dare to talk of them."

Crossing Barnegat Bay, from *Harper's Monthly Magazine*, 1878. *(Courtesy of William C. Schoettle)*

If You Had Seen What I Have

"I am not easily skeered," he answered at last; "but if you had seen what I have on this shore, you would not talk so easy about it. 'Lige, do you remember the time we saw that ship? There had been a heavy storm, and when we got up next day early, there lay a vessel on the beach; she must have been most everlastingly a harpin' it."

"What is that?" was asked wonderly, on the utterance of this peculiar expression.

"Why, she had come clear in over the bar, and must have been going some to do that; for there she lay, bow on, with her bowsprit sticking way up ashore, just below the station yonder. Her masts were standing, and we clapped on our clothes and started for the beach. The wind was blowin' hard, and the sand and drizzle driving in our faces as we walked over, and we kept our heads down most of the time. When we got to the sand hills we looked up, and the ship was gone. I thought that likely enough, for she must have broken up and gone to pieces soon in that surf, so we hurried along as fast as we could; and sure enough, when we rounded the point, the little cove in which she lay was full of truck. 'Lige was there, and he saw it as plain as I did. The water was full of drift-boxes, barrels, planks, and all sorts of things, pitching and rolling about; and some of them had been carried up onto the sand and were strewed about in all directions."

A Mysterious Wreck

"It was early, and the day was misty, but we could see plain enough, and we saw all that stuff knocking about as plain as I see you now. There was a big timber in my way — a stick — well, thirty feet long and two feet or two and a half square, so that I had to raise my foot high to clear it; I stepped one leg over, and drew the other along to feel it, but it didn't touch anything; then I stopped and looked down — there was no timber there; I looked back towards the sea — the drift had disappeared, the barrels and boxes and truck of one sort or another was gone. There was nothing on shore or in the water. Now you may laugh, but 'Lige knows whether what I've told you is true."

"Bill, that is a pretty good story, but it is not the one I meant," persisted the individual who had commenced the attack.

Tales of the Dunes

"Well, another time, Zeph and I were at work getting the copper bolts out of an old wreck, when we happened to look up and saw two carriages coming along, up the beach. I spoke to Zeph about it, but as they came along slowly, we went on with our work, and when we looked up again there was only one. That came one closer and closer till I could tell the horses; they were two bays of Squire Jones' down at the inlet; they drove right on towards us till they were so near that I did not like to stare the people in the face, and looked down again to my work. There were two men, and I saw them so plain that I should know 'em anywhere. Well, I raised my head a second after, and they were gone; and there never had been any wagon, for Zeph and I hunted all over the beach to find the tracks in the sand."

"I guess that was another misty day, and you hadn't had your eye-opener," was the appreciative response.

"No, it was three o'clock in the day, and bright sunshine; but at that time, as near as can be, Tommy Smith was drowned at the inlet, and the very next day at the very same hour, the 'Squire's wagon did come up the beach, with the same two men driving, and the body in a box in the back part."

Ghosts in the Moonlight

Bill fell silent, again looking off into the distance as though he saw something that others could not see. He pulled away nervously on his pipe, which had gone out, but answered not.

Snipe-Shooting at "Chadwick's." From *Scribner's Monthly*, 1876.

"Bill's afraid," was the tantalizing suggestion.

"There's Sam," said Bill suddenly. "He's not afeard of man or devil; ask him what he saw."

The person referred to was a large, broad-shouldered, pleasant-faced man, with a clear blue eye that looked as though it would not quail easily, and he responded at once:

"I never saw anything; but one night when I was coming by the cove where the *Johanna* was cast away, and where three hundred bodies were picked up and buried, I heard a loud scream. It sounded like a woman's voice, and was repeated three or four times; but I couldn't find anything, although I spent an hour hunting among the sand-hills, and it was bright moonlight. It may have been some sort of animal, but I don't know exactly what."

"Bill's adventure happened in the same neighborhood, so let's have it," continued the persistent man.

The Spirits of Mantoloking

"As Sam says," commenced Bill, at last, "the *Johanna* went ashore one awful north-easter in winter about six miles above here, near Old Jakey's tavern; she broke up before we could do anything for her, and three hundred men, women, and children — for she was an emigrant ship — were washed ashore during the following week; most of them had been drifted by the set of the tide into the cove, and they were buried there; so you see it ain't a nice place of a dark night.

"I was driving down the beach about a year after she was lost, with my old jagger wagon, and a heavy load on of groceries and stores of one kind or other. It was about one o'clock at night, mighty cold, but bright moonlight; and I was coming along by the corner of the fence, you know, just above Jakey's, when the mare stopped short.

"Now she was the best beast to drive you ever saw. I could drive her into the bay or right over into the ocean, and she was never skeered at anything. But this time she come right back in the shafts and began to tremble all over; I gave her a touch of the whip, and she was just as full of spirit as a horse can be, but she only reared up and snorted and trembled worse than ever. So I knew something must be wrong, and looked ahead pretty sharp; and there, sure enough, right across the road, lay a man."

Uncle Jakey

"Jakey was a little too fond of rum at that time, and I made up my mind he had got drunk and tumbled down on his way home; it was cold, and I didn't want to get out of the wagon where I was nicely tucked in, and thought I would drive round out of the road and wake him up with my whip as I passed.

"I tried to pull the mare off to one side to go by, but she only reared and snorted and trembled, so that I was afraid she would fall. She had a tender mouth, but although I pulled my best I could not budge her; at last, getting mad, I laid the gad over her just as hard as I could draw it. Instead of obeying the rein, however, she plunged straight on, made a tremendous leap over the body, and dragged the wagon after her.

"I pulled her in all I knew how, and no mistake; but it was no use, and I felt the front wheels strike, lift, and go over him, and then the hind wheels, but I couldn't stop her. That was a heavy load, and enough to crush anyone, and as soon as I could fetch the mare down — for she had started to run — I jumped out quick enough then, you may bet your life. I tied her up to the fence, although she was still so uneasy I daresen't hardly leave her, and hurried back to see if I could do anything for Jakie."

The Mare Saw It as Plain as I Did

"Would you believe it, there was nothing there! I tell you I felt the wagon go over him, and what's more, I looked down as I passed and saw his clothes and his hair straggling out over the snow, for he had no hat on; though I noticed at the time that I didn't see any flesh, but supposed his face was turned from me. There was no rise to the ground and not a cloud in the sky; the moon was nearly full, and there wasn't any man, and never had been any man there; but whatever there was, the mare saw it as plain as I did."

"Now let's turn in," said a sleepy individual, who had first been nodding over Bill's statement of public wrongs, and had taken several short naps in the course of his ghost story; "and as there was something said yesterday about a smoke driving away mosquitoes, for heaven's sakes let's make a big one; the infernal pests kept me awake all last night."

A Pleasant Week at the Beach

Never did mortals pass a pleasanter week than that week at the beach, and it is impossible to chronicle all the good shots, to repeat all the amusing stories or merry jokes, or to record all the valuable instruction; and to obtain an inkling even, the reader had better make a firm resolve that next August will not pass over his head without devoting at least one week to bay-snipe shooting.

When at last the time came to part, and the baggage was packed, and the guns reluctantly bestowed in their cases, we bade our farewell with sincere regret, praying that often thereafter might we find such sport, and meet such companionship.

Bill harnessed his ponies — for, wonderful to say, a few horses and cattle manage to live on the beach and sustain existence in spite of the mosquitoes — and we stowed ourselves and our luggage in his well worn wagon. The road lay over the barren beach, deep and heavy with sand, and hardly distinguishable after a heavy rain; the one-story shanty, that had been our resting place, soon faded from view, and we had nothing in prospect but the dreary journey home.

— By Robert Barnwell Roosevelt,

from* Game Water Birds of the Atlantic Coast, *1884

The Return.
From *Appleton's Journal*, 1871
(Print courtesy of Ocean County Cultural Commission)

On the bay at Chadwick's House, one of the earliest lodges on the beachfront, built in 1830. View is looking to the northeast on Chadwick Beach.
(Watercolor by G. R. Hardenbergh, 1895, courtesy of L.E.C.)

On The Bay At Chadwick's House

Bill Chadwick's gunning house, in the upper part of the bay, is perhaps the best known sporting hostelry in the vicinity of New York; thirty years ago it was known as John Maxon's, and many a gentleman of the old school, who long since has laid aside his gun for a staff, has pleasant recollection of the little fishing-hut on Squan Beach.

"That tavern old and quaint,
and all devoid of paint, —
A long, low building stretched a
hundred feet or more,
With many a curious name
Set round with guilded frame,
Nailed and fashioned over and up
against the door."

Chadwick, like Maxon, his father-in-law, is to the manor born, and has inherited all genial and sporting qualities. He is a typical character of the beach, and king-bee among the fraternity. A daring surfman, he has assisted in saving the lives of over two hundred and fifty shipwrecked people; as a gunner and fisherman he has no superior, and as a practical joker he is simply incorrigible. If one betrays any marked peculiarity, it is sure to serve as a peg whereon he may hang innumerable tricks.

A Shooting Match

Once a gentleman who was enthusiastic over a new and very expensive breech-loader of his, which was purposely pooh-poohed by Bill, offered to shoot it against Chadwick's celebrated "Old Tom" (a muzzle loader) for a basket of champagne. Two targets were procured, in order that the penetration and shooting qualities of each gun might be separately and fairly tested, and six shots were to be allowed to each gun. The cartridges of the breech-loader were duly charged with the prescribed quantity of ammunition and placed on a table ready for use, when the owner of the gun (by preconcerted arrangement) was called up to the balcony to see a passing vessel; during his absence Bill cooly substituted six cartridges loaded with less than half the prescribed charge.

At last the match begun. The shooting was led off by Bill, who made a splendid target. The owner of the breech-loader then fired six shots, but failed to put a single pellet into his target. His astonishment and dismay may well be imagined — his expression of countenance was too ludicrous to be looked at with a straight face. Having loaded his own cartridges he was satisfied that there could be no trick, and with this conviction he spent the rest of the day in cursing his gun-maker, and promising to "make it lively" for him on his return to town.

With such jokes the weary hours of a stormy day, or a long winter evening, are whiled away.

Birds of the Bay

The shooting here commences on the 20th of October, the earlier birds having reached here on their way south about that time. The blue and green-winged teal are then killed in large quantities. In fact the shooting is generally very good about this time, as the birds, not having been shot at, are not so wary. But if you ask one of the old gunners when to come, he will say "'bout 'lection time" and "just at the end of a heavy storm," for in fine mild weather the fowl congregate during the day-time in the middle of the bay, and it requires a hard storm to break them up into small bunches, when they naturally take shelter under the lee of the meadows and close in shore, giving the gunner a chance after the storm is over.

The bay opposite Chadwick's is about three miles wide, and jutting out into it from the beach are meadows which are intersected by water-lanes, or thoroughfares the fowl feed at night on the rich grasses of which they are so fond, and in some localities upon the wild celery, and then establish there what is technically called a "trade;" and if they are not disturbed at night they fly in and about these places all day long, from one point to another, affording capital shooting.

Every point of the meadow has its proper designation, which is as familiar to the gunner as is the location of his own house. These points are occupied, or not, according to the state of the tide and wind. Some command the fowl "trading" up and down the thoroughfares, while others command the middle of the bay, the decoys attracting the large flocks passing up and down, as well as the new-comers constantly arriving. Thus, "the north-west and south-west points of the great and little sedge," "big and little cormorant," and a host of others are daily selected by gunners for the scene of their operations; sometimes they go all the way across the bay and shoot from the sand-pits on the main at red-head and canvas-back, as they are trading in and out of the creeks and the coves.

A Snipe Blind. From *Scribner's Monthly*, 1876. *(Print courtesy of Toms River Seaport)*

Blinds and Decoys

The shooting being from "points," a little circular fortification, two-feet high, of seaweed and grass is erected on their extreme edge, and inside of it and sheltered by it from the wind the gunners spread their blankets and, lying down, peer through its crevices for coming game. The decoys of wood are anchored in the water at about twenty yards distance.

Sometimes the flight is enormous, the whole air being thick with ducks and geese, but the bay being so extensive, not one flock in ten will come near the points, or one in twenty within shot. Usually, in the height of the season, ten of Bill's points will be occupied, and the average is not over seven ducks killed to a point, although, on good days, "north-west" will kill twenty-five.

In this vicinity, the wild celery and duckgrasses flourish, attracting the better varieties of duck; and in both autumn and spring, vast numbers of canvas-backs, red-heads, widgeon, teal, dippers, and sprig-tale are killed. The canvas-backs and red-heads have as fine a flavor as those shot in the Chesapeake, while in the lower part of the bay, about the inlet, the water is salt and the marine plants do not thrive; consequently, the fowl of that vicinity are obliged to live upon the abundant smaller crustacia, and their flavor is apt to be fishy, excepting the brant (the most delicious of fowl), which feeds upon a kind of sand-worm.

By Stage Down the Beach

Chadwick's can be reached by land by the Central railroad of New Jersey to Squan, and thence by Charley Maxon's stage down the beach seven miles; but those seven miles are through deep sand, and, as the winter winds have a clear sweep across the spit, it is an exceedingly uncomfortable drive. It can be done in the way above described in four hours and a half, at an expense of about six dollars; the pleasanter way, however, is to take the New Jersey Southern Railroad by steam-boat to Sandy Hook, thence by rail to Tom's River, and thence by Captain Gulick's boat the "Zouave," across to Bill's (a pleasant sail of seven miles).

There is a capital hotel, Cowdrick & Cook's, at Toms River. The cost will be the same as by way of Squam. The expense of shooting at Chadwick's — and the same may be said of all the gunning houses on the beach — is about $5 per day; $2 for board, and $3 for the gunner, who furnishes boat and decoys; but the gunner must be provided with ammunition, or with a money equivalent.

Some twenty miles below Chadwick's, the beach is penetrated by an inlet, on the southern point of which is situated the well-known Barnegat Light.

The Baymen Are a Jolly Set

In the upper part of the bay the men are a jolly set, and their facility of adaptation to almost any circumstances in which they may be placed is remarkable. Take "Zeph" Chadwick, for instance (it is a mooted point whether he was christened Zephyr or Zephaniah), — who, with his brother "John," was born on the beach. Both are natural sailors and surfmen. When a regatta is sailed, they usually are found at the helm of the winning boat; and when the birds are flying, they shoot; if a ship comes ashore, they lend a hand to save the people and "wrack" the vessel; when nothing else offers, "Zeph" works as a ship or house carpenter, it don't appear to make much odds to him which.

Uncle Jimmy Loveland

One of the oldest of the gunners of this region is Uncle Jimmy Loveland, who, in spite of his age, is a crack shot, and can even now knock over a duck going sixty miles an hour, or drop an English snipe with the best of them. He has an eye like a hawk, and can see a bunch of ducks and describe their species, when, to an inexperienced eye they are mere specks on the horizon.

The unerring certainty with which old gunners can distinguish different fowl at immense distances is most remarkable, and is, of course, the result of years of observation, — the different kinds of fowl having certain peculiarities of flight, with which, by degrees, the gunner becomes familiar.

Before going down we telegraph Jimmy at his residence at Point Pleasant, to meet us at Chadwick's on a certain day. When we meet him the first question is, "Many ducks in the bay, Uncle Jimmy?" to which he replies in this strain, "Yes, sir-r-h; I see a power of canvas-backs and red-head a-settin' off n'ar West P'int, as I cum down in my box from the head of the bay — there must 'a 'bin six thousand of 'em a-feedin' on the flat. I sailed as nigh to 'em as I could git, and then they got up with a noise as ef a thunder-cloud had busted."

Uncle Charlie Stout

The wag of the beach is Charlie Stout, a herculean gunner. During the war he was drafted, and, after having been wounded in the thigh before Fredericksburg, saved his life by rolling behind a fence, where his blanket, which he had rolled in a ball to represent his head, was absolutely riddled by bullets.

He owns a small thirty-ton sloop, ycleped "Old Hickory," the age whereof no man of the present generation can pretend to guess; he calls her his yacht, and employs her "oysterin' and clammin' when there ain't no gunnin'." The writer once went on a gunning excursion in her, when she got hard and fast aground. There was little on board to eat, and that little not nice. Stout's paternal injunction to his son, who acted as chef de cuisine: "Simon Solomon, cook us a mess!" having been productive of a pot-pourri which none but a strong stomach could digest. After lying aground all night and part of the next day, Charlie became disgusted, and not-withstanding it was midwinter, he jumped overboard, and putting his shoulder under the counter, actually boosted her off into deeper water.

Once, when Charlie was returning from gunning on a sand-spit, just inside the inlet, where he had been induced to stay longer than was prudent, at the earnest solicitation of his "gentleman," who was having elegant sport, the wind began blowing a heavy gale from the westward, and Charlie, seeing that his companion's boat was drifting seaward, took him in tow. Both men began to pull for dear life, for, if driven out on the bar, they must inevitably perish. The gentleman, who was a cool hand too, shouted:

"I say, Charlie, if we can't make the point at the light, it will be all up, won't it?"

"It will be all up with you, Mr. L.," replied Charlie, "for I shall cut the tow-line if we drift much further, and go ashore and tell the folks that the last I seed of you, you was a-headin' for Europe! I don't want to go there myself!"

— from "Bay Shooting,"* Scribner's Monthly, *1876

The Snipe

Notes from the Chadwick House Register
1869 – 1899

Dec. 19, 1869 — Steamer Cacassian came ashore this Evening abreast this House — Wm. Ellis, the Captain's wife and passengers were brot ashore by Wm. Chadwick in a life car in one hour from the time she stranded.

Aug. 9, 1869 — Mr. Roosevelt, Peter Balm, Chas. Newman, (from) Albany by (way of) Freehold.

Oct. 20, 1872 — Horace Greeley, Nyack, with a full stumach and He got it at Chadwicks — and don't you forget it!

Gathering Bait. From *Appleton's Journal*, 1871.

July 13, 1877 — A large "Sea Serpent" was seen by Captain James Loveland off North West Point, in the deep waters today. Captain Bozier of the yacht Annie gave chase and succeeded in capturing it, Captain Loveland being completely paralyzed with fright.

July 25, 1878 — US Grant, GB McClellan, Paul Tilden — all drunk as owls.

Aug. 19, 1881 — First P.R.R. Passenger Train came into Seaside Park.

May 1, 1885 — Wind NE blowing a gale, raining in torrents — Cold as Greenland & no birds. Capt. Chadwick deserted to Toms River.

Oct. 20, 1887 — Steamer Chas. F. Mayer, Capt. Seth Hand, a collier bound from Boston to Baltimore, came ashore about a half mile below the Life Saving Station at 9:40PM, wind blowing a gale from ENE. A line was shot over her by the mortar and the Captain & crew, 17 in all, were brought ashore by means of the breeches buoy. She lies high on the beach.

William R. Kelsey Assumed Proprietorship of the Chadwick House April 1, 1892, and extends to former patrons, his friends and other driftwood a hearty & sincere WELCOME.

Aug. 1, 1896 — Capt. William Chadwick ate 49 clams, drank 6 bottles of beer & gave three cheers for the Hon. William McKinley, the next President. Captain Bill, although just under 100 years old, executed a complicated double shuffle lasting two hours, to juba time, in a manner that could not be duplicated by any body half his age.

Sept. 8, 1896 — On this day Gerard R. Hardenbergh, Morgan Davis and George Endicott, killed 63 yellow-legs & 2 gelpers. The first good shooting of the season. Yesterday we shot 43 yellow-legs.

1899 —

CHADWICK

by Capt. Bunk

There is a land of pure delight
where bums supremely reign,
there poker takes up half the night,
and liquor banish pains.

All is sands and flowing tides,
meadows and salt hay,
a narrow strip of land divides
the ocean from the bay.

It is a gunman's favorite site
with snipe and ducks galore,
in the bay the weakfish bite
and blue fish swim near shore.

And there are many captains bold,
much whiskey they can swig,
the biggest stories ever told
are not for them too big.

From the Woolman and Rose *Atlas of the New Jersey Coast*, 1878. *(Print courtesy of William Gregor)*

Beaver Dam Creek, Point Pleasant. *(Watercolor by G. R. Hardenbergh, 1896, courtesy of Mr. and Mrs. Alfred Johnson)*

An Historical Cabinet

Made From The Pieces of Twenty-Six Wrecked Vessels

Nestled snugly among the pines in Ocean County, and standing back about five hundred yards from Beaver Dam Creek, is one of those old fashioned houses whose corner stone was laid sometime during the Revolutionary period. Its quaint look and utter loneliness causes the traveller to pause. There is something about the place that makes him forget the present and wander back into the past. He peoples the house with the quaint Hollander and imagination runs riot as he places his characters, taken from early history, about the premises.

As his eyes wander from the house to the stream, taking in the wild beauty of the scene, the dream is broken. Riding gracefully at anchor, on its placid bosom, is a handsome yacht, a thing of beauty, whose lines and curves denote swiftness; and craft that is not in keeping with the surroundings, and such a one as the wildest dreams of the simple Hollander had never pictured.

The Locomotive's Whistle

Further east, above the line of the horizon, the picturesque cottages of Mantoloking can be discerned, while the faint-sound of the locomotive's whistle in the distance tell him that ere long the peaceful spot will assume a different aspect, and the relic of bygone days give way to one of those airy structures in which the wealthy denizens of the great cities delight to spend the hot summer days.

A Famous Bayman

Indeed, the place is not unknown to them now. Many of the most wealthy citizens of New York and Philadelphia have partaken of the hospitalities of the master of the house, who is no more or less a personage than Capt. John L. Dorsett, whose fame as a bayman, boat builder and life saver has gone abroad. The Captain, straight as an arrow, old fashioned, yet keenly alive to the doings of the outer world, is in full harmony with his surroundings. A lover of antiquities; a hoarder of relics of by gone days.

The interior of the house has a comfortable appearance. Its low raftered ceilings have been nicely painted; the walls are covered with a neat design of paper, while furniture of modern make goes far toward subduing the grim roughness of the ancient cerpentary.

In the neat sitting room on the west of the house, the visitor's searching gaze is arrested by a cabinet containing many rare and curious articles. The cabinet itself attracts attention from the many different woods of which it is composed. But there is nothing, except small figures in gilt, to indicate that each piece of wood has a history; that each piece represents the loss of thousands of dollars, and that many of the pieces have witnessed the death struggle of many brave men. But such is the fact.

The Historical Cabinet

The cabinet is made of wood taken from twenty-six different vessels wrecked on the Jersey shore, during a period of sixty years, and in which eight hundred and sixty-nine lives have been lost. It is a ghastly record thus perpetuated, but interesting withal, and at our reporter's request the captain gave the names of the vessels whose timbers furnished material for the cabinet.

A Ghastly Record

No. 1, is a piece of walnut taken from the ship *Donaldson*, wrecked on Squan Beach in 1808. No. 2, is a piece of cherry taken from the schooner Alabama wrecked on Squan Beach, February 15, 1846; the entire crew, consisting of seven men, being lost. No. 3, is a piece of mahogany taken from the bark *Argyle* wrecked on Squan Beach in February 1854, in which eleven lives were lost.

Captain Dorsett has in his possession the "figure head" of the *Argyle* in his possession, which represents the Duke of Argyle in full Highland costume. It is in a good state of preservation, with the exception of one foot which has rotted off.

No. 4, is a piece of mahogany somewhat darker than that taken from the *Argyle*, which was taken from the bark *John Farnum*, wrecked on Squan Beach, February 7, 1855. No. 5, is a piece of walnut taken from the ship *Clara*

"A Sea Serpent Sighted Off the Jersey Shore," from the *New York World*, 1880. Such creatures were frequently seen along the East Coast in the nineteenth century — with many reports in 1806, 1818, 1826, and the mid 1840s. The captain of the schooner *Eliza Ann Steele* spotted one off Long Beach in the spring of 1856. He testified he had never seen anything like it before: The creature was forty feet long, three feet wide, with shiny black skin, a large rough head, and a flat tail like an eel.

Brookman, wrecked on Squan Beach, August 28th., 1857. No. 6, is a piece of baywood taken from the brig *Axel* wrecked during the terrible winter of 1847. No. 7, comprises the stiles of the cabinet and is part of the stair rail of the ship *Sovereign*, which was wrecked in the spring of 1836, on Squan Beach, one life being lost.

No. 8, is a piece of oak taken from the steamship *Mediator*, wrecked at Barnegat February 1st., 1875. No. 9, is a piece of maple taken from the steam tug *Titan* which was wrecked September 8th., 1855, on Squan Beach.

Captain Dorsett waded into the surf and rescued the captain of the tug who was completely exhausted, and who, no doubt, would have perished had it not been for the timely arrival of Dorsett. The captain stated that the tug was on its way to a stranded vessel further down the coast, and that the night before being clear, they had indulged freely in liquor and had neglected to set a watch. During the night a storm came up and the men were in no condition to do battle with it, and the gray September morning broke over the ruins of the rescuer whose merciful mission was thwarted and brought to an untimely end by the demon rum.

No. 10, is a piece of white pine taken from the memorable wreck *John Minturn* which came ashore at Squan Beach on February 15, 1846, the same day that the *Alabama* came ashore, and which added fifty more to the death roll. Captain Dorsett has possession of the name board of the vessel. It is about five feet long with carved letters, gilded.

No. 11, is white pine from the wrecked ship *Minerva* which came ashore at Cranberry Inlet in March 1857. No. 12, a piece of walnut from the *Ayershire*, wrecked on Squan Beach January 12th., 1850. The *Ayershire* had three hundred passengers aboard and was the first wreck where the life-saving car was used. Only one person was drowned.

No. 13, a piece of walnut taken from the steamship *Creole*, wrecked on Squan Beach on March 17, 1868. No. 14, is a piece of mahogany from the ship *Powhatten* wrecked at Long Beach in 1854. All her passengers and crew, numbering three hundred and eleven, were lost. The wood is very dark and considerably wormeaten. No. 15, is a piece of beech from the bark *William Enges*, wrecked in the spring of 1848. No. 16 is also beech from the French bark *Fauvette*, which came ashore on Squan Beach in 1847.

No. 17, is spruce taken from the bark *Arion* wrecked at Cranberry Inlet in 1852. No. 18, is oak from the ship *Samuel Willets* wrecked July 7th., 1857. No.19, is maple from the schooner *Cora A. Lindsay* wrecked on Squan Beach in February 1854. No. 20, is mahogany from the ship *New Era* wrecked at Great Pond, November 13th., 1854. This ship contributed four hundred and eighty four to the death roll, over one half of the entire number.

No. 21, is a piece of walnut taken from the cabin of the schooner *Tremlet* which was wrecked in April 1852 on Squan Beach, and which added four lives to the fatal list. No. 22, is rosewood from the brig *Governor Bull*, wrecked on Squan Beach May 4th., 1861. No. 23, is mahogany from the ship *New York*, wrecked on Island Beach, December 19th., 1856. No. 24, is ash from the schooner *Brazil* wrecked in 1860. No. 25, is also ash from the brig *Fortunato*, wrecked at Lavallette City, August 21st., 1860. This vessel was loaded with marble, and the cargo still lies buried in the sand although two attempts have been made to recover it.

No. 26, is a piece of the mizzenmast of the steamship Black Warrior, which completes the list, was wrecked on the Long Island shore in 1855.

Inside the Cabinet

Within the cabinet are articles whose past history contains nothing of the ghastliness of the wood which encloses and protects them. The center piece is a dish brought from Holland and made sometime during the 15th century. It is curiously decorated and is made of some very light material.

On a shelf above the dish is an old Dutch Bible bound with boards, with heavy brass clasps, bearing the date of 1741. It was at one time the property of John Lot, a grandfather of Captain Dorsett, an old Revolutionary soldier who was with Washington at Trenton, and who was detailed by him to keep the camp fires burning in order to deceive the British while the main body of the army fell back to Princeton.

Besides this rests two other copies of the Word bearing the dates 1746 and 1748 respectively. Below these hang an old wooden spoon rack, such as was used in the last century when the good housewives loved to display their highly polished pewter. Along side of this rests a piece of the British Man of War Augusta, blowed up at Fort Miflin while coming up the Delaware ladened with British gold to pay off the King's troops.

Keeping it company is a piece of the old frigate *Constitution*, which was presented to Captain Dorsett by the late Admiral Marston. Just beneath is a pair of snow white stockings worn by Captain Dorsett's grandfather at his wedding in 1782, and which the worthy Captain did himself the honor of wearing at his own wedding. In a little cluster to the right of the stockings, is a stock-buckle, knee-buckle, brooch and buttons from the wedding suit of James Dorsett, a minute man in the Revolutionary war and who did duty at Middletown, N.J.

Seventy-one dollars in continental currency with a six shilling and thirty shilling note rest on a little shelf, and behind it are deeds executed in 1752 and in the twenty-fifth year of the reign of King George II, conveying certain lands bordering Beaver Dam Creek to one Joseph Pearce. Next there is a piece of the old Treasury building which was built in St. Augustine, Florida, in 1513.

The above mentioned are the most prominent in the collection of relics within the cabinet. Captain Dorsett has also a number of rare and curious prints. Among them being a reprint of "the travels and observations of Captain John Smith in Europe, Asia, Afrike and America. Beginning about the year 1593 and continued to the present 1629."

A Well Versed Captain

Captain Dorsett is well versed in the happenings along the shore during the past sixty years, and has during his lifetime assisted work on sixty three wrecked vessels, helping and succoring many persons who have been cast ashore on the bleak Jersey coast.

The captain sails a handsome yacht on Barnegat Bay during the summer and in the winter pursues the boat building trade. He is now engaged in building a very pretty yacht for Mr. Edgar Herbert, who intends placing her on the Manasquan River.

— from **The Manasquan Sea Side,** ***1888***

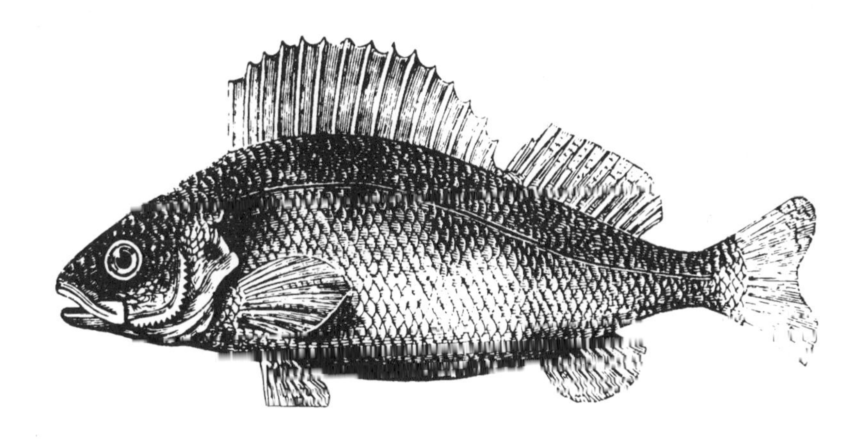

A Moonlight Sail on Barnegat Bay

Tom's River. From *Harpers*, 1878.

At the invitation of Mr. G. A. Bennett, of the Resort House, at Point Pleasant, my friend Hall and myself packed our satchels and took the morning train on Wednesday for a moonlight sail on Barnegat Bay that evening. We arrived at Resort House near noon, and after an enjoyable dinner of soft shell clams and clam fritters, we made a tour of observation of the improvements that have been made at this favorite summer hostelry, and an inspection of the new cottages that have been erected, we drifted down to the beach, along which we wandered as far down as the Ocean House, where we saw the fishing boats come in from sea laden with fish, principally sea bass.

These fishermen follow this business for a livelihood, going out from five to ten miles on what they call the banks, which are rocky bottoms, around which the fish come for feeding purposes on mussels, & c., which adhere to the rocks. The depth of the water is from 60 to 75 or 100 feet. The boats are only about 20 feet long, 4 feet wide and about two feet deep, with two pairs of oars and fitted with a sail which they can put up or take down in a few seconds.

There are two men to each boat. The bait is sea clams or soft shell crabs. The fish not disposed of to the summer hotels and residents are packed in ice and shipped to the large cities.

After tea we took the Resort House coach, some nine of us, and rode over through the pines to the head of Barnegat Bay, about a mile and a half, where lay the handsome and commodious yacht, *Bertie Jardin*, for a moonlight sail with Captain Dorsett. This pretty yacht is of ten tons measurement, with a neat cabin, and sleeping accommodations for eight persons besides the captain and one man, with galley, & c., and mealing arrangements for that number of people as long as they wish to stay out.

Last summer we spent a couple of days fishing and sailing on her with a party of twelve. While anchored fishing late in the afternoon of the first day, a storm came up, and we ran to Waretown for supplies, but before we reached there the water came down in bucketsful. We had arranged for most of the party to sleep on deck that night, but the rain confined us all to the cabin where the heat, with the number and the windows and doors closed to keep out the water, made the atmosphere most oppressive.

As soon as the captain returned from shore in the skiff with bread and butter, & c., we made sail in the rain and started for the floating hotel, which was anchored in the bay, half way between Barnegat light and the shore. Here we had a midnight lunch and a jolly time until morning, when we returned to the yacht, anchored but a few feet away, and made sail for the fishing ground, which we reached in a short time and had lively sport, taking in weak fish and barb as fast as the captain and his man could take them off the hooks and put on the bait.

Rounding the Point

In less than two hours we had taken two hundred, which with the fifty we had caught the day previous, was all we could take care of with the ice we had on board — and keep our lager cool. But I am digressing from our moonlight sail. As soon as we were aboard the sheet rope was hauled in, the main sail being already up, the jib hoisted and we were off. We rounded the point and sailed up the broad Metedeconk river as far as the residence of Superintendent Havens, of the Life Saving Service, when the yacht went about and we headed for the bay, when the wind died down and we scarcely moved.

Captain Dorsett being apprehensive that we would not have wind enough to get back in season if we went far, we "bouted" on a drift homeward, there being scarcely wind enough to feel any motion on the water. With the stillness on the water we knew that the atmosphere must be very oppressive at home, so we congratulated ourselves that "we were where we were."

Fireflies in the Night

The millions of fireflies on the land gave it the appearance of a large panoramic city at night, and with the rising moon abaft served to give us the appearance of the "painted ship upon the painted ocean." Afterward, however, a breeze sufficient to waft us homeward sprang up and we dropped anchor and went ashore, where we found our stage, which soon rattled us through the pine forest to the "Resort" a little after midnight.

The *Bertie Jarden* is kept for the accommodation of fishing and sailing parties through the Summer, and gunning parties in the Fall; she is a splendid boat, perfectly safe for parties of either ladies or children, numbers of whom

Seaside Park. From *Harpers*, 1878.

enjoy a sail on her in the Bay during the season, and when the weather permits, out on the broad Atlantic through Barnegat inlet.

Captain Dorsett is a Christian gentleman, and when a party is on board he is at their service to give them a good time and make everything pleasant.

An Ocean Excursion

On Thursday morning Hall and myself were up early for a fishing excursion "outside." I had always wanted a little experience of this kind, but the occasion had never before offered. When we arrived at the landing near the Ocean House we found that all the other boats had been gone since daylight, and Captain James Fleming, an old sea dog, who had been a follower of the water for over forty years, with his son Joseph, one of the crew of the Life Saving Station No. 9, during the Winter, were waiting for us with the bow of their boat towards the water and ready for the launch.

Further up the coast men and boys were hauling in large blue fish from the shore as rapidly as they could throw out and haul in their squid lines. This was the first run of the blue fish for the season and the water seemed to be alive with them. Over two hundred, weighing from three to six pounds apiece, were taken in this way, and as many more could have been hauled in had there been more fishermen. We wanted to take a few but time was pressing, and we should have been on our way to the fishing banks two hours before. The sea was as smooth as the water of the Delaware river when we pushed off and passed over the bar in our own fishing boat about 18 feet in length, 4 feet beam and two feet deep. After a long pull with the oars a breeze sprang up and the sail was hoisted, the captain steering with an oar on the side of the boat.

On our way out we had a view of the half dozen comfortable story-and-a-half cozy cottages with plenty of piazzas, erected on the bluff of the ocean, at the head of the bay, and occupied by families from Princeton. It is called Bayhead and is a charming location for a summer residence, being but a few steps from either the Bay or Ocean, near the life saving station, and on an elevation sufficiently high to get every wave of air that may be wafted from the ocean.

The boiler from the steamer *Creole*, which was wrecked on the bar within a short distance from the shore, is exposed at low water. The water is not deep enough to permit the wrecking craft to come in with her machinery and raise it, and the breakers would make the work difficult from the shore side.

Salt Meadows on Long Beach. From *Harpers*, 1878.

Out to the Fishing Banks

After a delightful sail we reached the fishing banks, between three and five miles from shore, and cast our anchor in sixty feet of water. Soon we had about a dozen sea bass and black fish in the boat, but afterwards we only had nibbles, and the fishermen anchored around us said that the blue fish had driven all the other fish away, and they pulled up anchors and started sailing for blue fish. We wanted bass and kept on fishing on the banks while we could see them sailing back and forth, hauling in blue fish at a tremendous rate, until we caught the fever, and our anchor was raised and sail made.

Over twenty yards of line with the bright block tin squib and large hook on the end, were cast astern, while the sail of our little boat bent itself to the breeze with her head towards the green isle source 3,500 miles away.

The One That Got Away

Above five miles in that direction was as far as we cared to go just then, and we tacked on another course. All at once Hall jumped up in the boat, and with his eyes dancing, began to haul in. He had hooked a tremendous blue fish, and as he hauled away the fish thought he would prefer to go towards Cape May, and made a dash in that direction. But he kept the line taut and brought him up alongside the boat. He lifted the fish up to grab him but at that moment he gave a flirt, tore himself lose from the hook and fell back into the "big drink."

A sickly smile circulated around the quartet in the boat, which ended in a good laugh, and hopes of better luck next time. We sailed on and in a few minutes both of us had hooked fish. I drew mine but a few yards when I lost him, but Hall got his, a five pounder, into the boat. I had another shortly and had him half way into the boat, when he bit the squid clean from the line and left.

Hall landed another, a four pounder, but after hooking two or three and losing them we squared away for a sail with a good breeze and a chop sea, which gave the boat a delightful roll. The captain and his son seemed surprised that the motion did not make us two "landlubbers" feed the fishes, and complimented us on the behavior of our stomachs on our first expedition on the ocean in a fishing boat.

We "just landed" about two o'clock coming through the surf without shipping a gill of water or wetting the soles of our feet. Captain James Fleming has fished off the coast for over forty years, and had five sons now in the same business, but if you want to go on a fishing and sailing excursion with a couple of accommodating and careful seamen, just get him and his son Joseph to take you out, and you will return pleased with your experience.

—from **The Daily Emporium,** ***1880***

Harvey Cedars, Long Beach, below Barnegat Light. From *Harper's*, 1878.

Captain Hen of Barnegat

The Old Salt Tells How the Yacht-Masters of the Bay Live

The captains of the yachts of Barnegat are indeed queer characters. Their lives are fully as romantic as the lives of the hunters or the trappers in the far west. They see many hardships that very few people believe exist, and perform far greater deeds of bravery than any Western trapper. It takes a great deal of courage for a number of men to put off to sea in a small boat in the midst of a raging storm in the middle of winter in order to help some shipwrecked crew.

This many of the Barnegat captains do as members of the life saving service that guard the seacoast. Anybody who has seen a storm on the ocean, especially in winter, can imagine what an undertaking it must be for these men to breast that seething, hissing, formidable line of roaring breakers in the darkness of night as they are sometimes compelled to do. The members of the New Jersey life-saving crews do, indeed, lead a life of hardship and danger. They have to keep a sharp lookout all the time, keep track of all the vessels that pass, and patrol the beach for miles in the middle of winter night, and day, in all kinds of weather.

A World representative yesterday visited Seaside Park, where many of these captains keep their yachts, and from which place they can put out for the fishing grounds.

A Queer Old Fellow

One of the captains met was a queer old fellow, with sharp, black eyes. His comrades call him "Hen," which is probably an abbreviation of Henry, though his laughter sounds exactly like the cackling of a hen after laying an egg. What his other name is could not be learned, and it is rather doubtful he has any other. He is an honest old chap, and has courage marked on every lineament of his countenance. Tanned by exposure to all sorts of weather, and with skin hardened by honest toil, he is not what a city belle would call beautiful, but he is as pure at heart as his exterior is plain, and he is the soul of bravery.

These Barnegat men are unread, uneducated and unrefined in their manners, but yet they have implicit faith in the Bible. They know no wit but their own, and often "crack" rude and pointless jokes among themselves and laugh heartily.

Old "Hen" at first regarded the reporter as a kind of a suspicious character, and finally, after surveying him from head to foot, said, in a drawling tone: "You're a fine sucker, ain't you?"

His mind was soon disabused of that idea.

"How do we live?" he said, "Why we live by what we honestly earn, of course."

"Yes, but how do you earn anything?"

"Oh, that's what you want to know, is it? Well, in the summer we take parties out fishing in our yachts, and it pays us pretty well, too. A great many people come here to go weakfishing in the summer, and that is when we reap our harvest. You see, Barnegat is the best fishing and gunning grounds anywhere along the coast of the United States, except Chesapeake Bay, and when people come here they have got to hire a boat and hire some one to take them to the fishing grounds. Without doing this you may bet they won't get any fish, for there are only certain places where fish can be caught, and it is only the men who were brought up on the bay who know how to keep track of them."

"The people that come here fishing come from nearly all the Jersey summer resorts, and many come from the large cities. Some come hundreds of miles just for two days fishing. In the latter part of July and nearly the whole of August we have our hands and pockets more than full. Besides the pay these people give us for taking them fishing, a great many give us the fish

Bluefishing. ***(Print courtesy of Mr. and Mrs. Joseph Forsyth)***

they catch, which is quite an item. We don't get any chance to fish ourselves, because we are kept baiting the people's hooks and unhooking the fish."

"Beg pardon, but did you ask where I live? Why I live over to the other side of the bay. I sail over home in my yacht every night when my work is done, and I generally take along a mess of fish, too, for the parties I take out nearly always give me some fish. We all have large families, and it takes quite a number of fish to keep the young ones' mouths busy. We eat all we can get."

Fishing the Bay

"Oh, they catch many different kinds. Nearly all the parties that I take out go for weakfish. Quite a few go bluefishing, and once in a while a party of gentlemen will want to catch pike. Very few people know that there is any pikefishing on Barnegat. I think the pike in Barnegat are larger than anywhere else in the state. The place for pike is over to the other side of the bay, up in the streams that run back into the country."

Gathering Moss-Bunkers. From *Appleton's Journal*, 1871.

"The fish that stay at the mouth of these streams are not so large, but if you go up to the head the pike can be found very big, both in numbers and size. Some of them will weigh four pounds, and it is a very rare thing to catch one weighing less than two. Many parties that I take catch well on to a hundred fish. Pike fishing is very exciting — probably more exciting than any other kind of fishing. At least the parties seem to enjoy it more and make more fuss when they pull in fish."

"I only take gentlemen after pike, for you see we have to scull about in a row boat after the fish. I scull the boat slowly along at the edge of the bull-rushes, the fishers trolling their lines in and around the dark recesses. Suddenly you will see a gray streak shoot through the water. Then a swirl will follow and you jerk on the pole and you've hooked your fish. And a pike can make a great fuss in the water, I can tell you. Beaver Dam Creek seems to be the best place. That is just beyond the wagon bridge towards Bay head. It is four or five miles long and is full of pike."

"What do you fishermen do in the winter?" he was asked.

"Why, we do different things," replied the old salt. "Some of us make a business of duck shooting, selling what we shoot in the New York markets. They command pretty good prices. We often take parties out gunning in our sneak-boats. A great many sports come to Barnegat in the winter on purpose to go duck shooting, and, of course, they always want an experienced man who knows the waters and the habits of the ducks, and their feeding grounds."

The Art of Duck Shooting

"There is quite an art in duck shooting. You get your man — the gentleman who hires you — and start out early in the morning, before the sun rises, for the feeding grounds. Then you lie concealed in the sneak-boat, which is covered with green branches. After awhile you will see a dark looking cloud in the sky, which will keep on gradually coming nearer, until you can see that it is a flock of ducks. An experienced gunner can always tell as far as he can see what kind of ducks are coming, and he can always utter the correct call for them.

"When lured on by the call the ducks will come very near and fly low, affording a good shot. You can nearly always get four or five ducks out of a flock. Did you ever see my 'Ole Sal'? She's a dandy, I can tell you. I've killed five ducks with her many a time. Well, would you like to see her? Yes? Come on board."

Inside the Yacht

The old captain led the way into the cabin of his yacht, and took down from the rack "Ole Sal." She was a "dandy," indeed. The barrel was about six feet long and fully an inch and a half at the muzzle. The gun weighed about twenty pounds, and it would take a giant to shoulder it. What a shock the shooter of the weapon must experience can well be imagined. The stock was made of oak, and the hammer, which looked like a letter S, was about four inches long. There was a very strong spring in the weapon, and it would severely tax an ordinary man's strength to cock it. "Old Sal" was indeed a beauty, and her owner took great pride in exhibiting her fine qualities. "You see," said Captain Hen, "I call her 'Ole Sal' because a gun is called a 'she.' "

He continued: "All the Barnegat men don't shoot ducks. Some go codfishing. This pays pretty well, but it is hard work, and is attended with many dangers. You have to put out to sea in a skiff. The cold tells on the codfishers. You have to get wet going through the breakers. It is not like going after bass in the summer, when the air and water are warm and the sea isn't so rough."

Some Join the Life Saving Service

"Then some of us are members of the Life Saving crews, which pays pretty well, though there is some pretty hard work to be done. We have to take turns keeping lookout and patrolling the beach. We have to patrol four miles from one station to another. The men have to practice in working the apparatus every once in a while. We run out a life-line and get the life-car and breeches-buoy in operation, shoot out lines and go off in the life-boat. Sometimes we are called up in the middle of the night to do this, just for practice. We have to learn our parts out of a book and recite to the captain. If a man don't say the lesson just right, then he gets it, I can tell you."

Going Out for Weak-Fish. From *Appleton's Journal*, 1871.

"Sometimes what we have learned and practiced actually comes into play. Only last winter a schooner came ashore in a blinding snow-storm. We had to go out to her, and we got everybody off alive, too. If you look over to the northeast you'll see her bones rising above that sand dune."

Setting Sail

"We have no easy life, and what we earn we earn by hard, honest toil, that is one thing sure." And the old captain, as he finished talking, lighted his pipe, set his sails and was soon speeding over the waters of the bay.

—from* The World, *1887

The Great Ocean Yacht Race, 1867, by Currier and Ives. ***(Print courtesy of Gail Reese)***

Along Our Jersey Shore

We had intended to hire the boat of Aaron Pharo for our cruise, but as he was away fishing, we accepted the offer of his brother to take us to him. Brother Bill is a celebrity from Cape May to Squan, and his character is so luminous that I think it would project itself in any community.

A little boastfulness; a good deal of a certain kind of knowledge; a clear perception of what is wrong, and a total inability to live up to the precepts which he reiterates oftenest; much good nature, and no means to substantially gratify it; a flood of profanity and irreligion, with a Gulf Stream of sentiment mellowing parts, and putting around his nature some of the pleasant mistiness through which we now see it — these are some of the boldest headlands in his moral coastline, and they are, after all, the salient features of many others; but what leaves him in one's memory as a gleaming point of humor is the very oddest face I ever saw, and a most wonderful pair of trousers.

The trousers he wore rose from the knees like a springtide to within a few inches of the shoulders, where a pair of determined looking suspenders caught them, and they were as voluminous behind as a Chinese novel. His face is long and red, two high cheek-bones pressing against two saucer-like, deep-set eyes, with a craggy forehead hanging over them, and a comical seriousness flashing in them. His conversation covered a wide variety of subjects; it was his opinion that what is now New Jersey was recently, geologically speaking, part of the bottom of the sea, and in proof thereof he adduced the fact that oyster shells have been found very much farther inland than the present coast-line.

We arrived on a Saturday evening. Fiddles were scraping and feet shuffling in the halls of the big hotels; the broad piazzas were crowded with loungers and promenaders, mostly fair maidens and stately matrons in refrigerant summer dress that reached their necks in diaphanous snowy muslins; the men were happy in a surfeit of tender attentions; and at the close of day, all the yachting parties having come home to supper, the wharf on the bay was left to us.

Sunset on the Bay

The sun was setting on the brilliant plain of sedge as we looked landward, and beheld the spires of West Creek and Tuckerton rising out of the distant woods, which changed from blue to purple, and from purple to a smoky crimson, until the great globe of fire sunk well behind them and left them a chilly black. But before this, the whole sky was transformed into a sea full of flaming shoals; a mass of cirro-cumuli had become detached, and the fragments floated against the pearly blue of the sky and burned with the reflected glow.

Green never before seemed so green, or so capable of many shades, as it did on the marshes, which, as the sun disappeared behind the woods, were momentarily tipped with gold, and then left to brooding green and blue. In the far north a storm was bursting of tumultuous clouds, which had also caught some of the rosy magnificence of the sunset, and were laced with the vivid thrusts of forked lightning.

The night came upon us, advancing from a tender pearl blue to a steel blue, and from a steel blue to an unsympathetic grey, which grew darker until the last light from the west had been extinguished, and the stars pierced the sky with incisive brilliancy. The myriad stars that shone in the opaline moonlight night were as nothing compared in numbers with the gnats and mosquitoes; but who would not have endured even greater torments for a sight so memorable? It was such a sunset as can be seen nowhere else than on those plaintive marshes and barren sands of the Jersey coast.

The sandy strip upon which the "practical sea-side resort" is situated is nearly twenty miles long, and is called Long Beach, its northern extremity being formed by the Barnegat Inlet, and its southern extremity by the Little Egg Harbor Inlet. Along this desolate coast so many vessels have been washed ashore, that it is known among fishermen as the Graveyard.

Treasures from the Sea

Treasures from many lands are gathered from wrecks, and a fisherman's family is often helped through a trying winter by the provisions which the sea casts up. When an orange schooner is wrecked, there is dessert after every meal at the cottages; or should the cargo be prunes, that fruit becomes a common article of diet. A visitor is sometimes surprised to see foreign brands of olives and canned stuffs on the shelves of the village stores; he learns that they have been secured from a wreck; and the host of one inn at which we spent the night had some excellent Maria Bonvennto claret, labelled, with grim suggestiveness, "Importation direct via Barnegat Shoals."

Much queerer things than these are occasionally picked up. A forlorn old parrot, feeble from its un-English complainings, drifted in on a spar, and at another time a pair of Manx cats were saved from a wreck by a noted old beach-man,

Caleb Parker, of Harvey Cedars, near the Barnegat light, who raised a family of eleven more, and meets a visitor at the door of his cottage with a purring retinue of his furry friends, one of them perched on his cap, two others playing on his shoulders, and the rest brushing his legs. "Dad" Parker is one of the heroes of the coast, and carries a silver medal presented to him for life-saving.

Fashionable summer resorts are new things to the outer beach. Formerly a small house was erected here and there for the accommodation of sportsmen and parties of fishermen, who came over from the mainland with their wives, daughters, and sweethearts for an evening dance. The gayety of one of these gatherings at Harvey Cedars was eclipsed by the startling announcement that a ship had gone ashore, and was making signals of distress; whereupon the whole company made for the beach, including the women in all their holiday finery, and not a ribbon or flounce was thought of until the last man had been landed from the wreck.

A Sunday Cruise

Bill's brother Aaron came to Beach Haven for us on Sunday morning, and we embarked in his yacht on a cruise up and down the coast.

A fair wind carried our little yacht seven or eight miles north in a hour, and at sunset we were gliding, with a faint ripple at the bow, through a narrow "thorough-fare" of the bay. The marshes were on each side of us; behind and ahead a motionless sea, varying from a most vivid emerald to a dusky cedar green.

The water was like a mirror, except where a school of small fish broke it into a thousand ripples, and our boat was inert, the sail hanging loosely from the mast. As the sun fell closer to the blue line of the main-land woods from a heaven of unspeakable color, the evening star and a crescent moon were growing more radiant in the pale gray-blue east, and cast a reflection on the water while it still held the imprint of the more passionate orb.

Alone in the World

We were alone in the world at that moment, and the world was motionless. There was a wan, pitiful look on the meadows, which, lying in a death-like lull, gave the scene its salience, and despite the rosy ardor of the western sky, Nature desponded and fell into a sad sleep. Sunsets at second-hand are not satisfactory, but those that we saw night after night along the Jersey coast were so individualized in their contrasted splendor and melancholy undertone that they really seemed to belong to its topography.

The wind fell altogether at dark, and as we drifted through the winding reaches of the thoroughfare, our ecstasies were overcome by a plague of mosquitoes and gnats, which attacked us so seriously that one member of our expedition was threatened with delirium. We had to propel the boat with poles. From time to time we grounded, and it was after midnight we reached Bonds — a summer hotel south of Beach Haven.

The next day was cloudy and gray, and a variable wind took us through the bay to Barnegat inlet, off the Barnegat Shoals. It was sunset when we reached our boat, and great flocks of birds flew out of the reeds, uttering wild and melancholy cries. A schooner lay at anchor near the inlet, and the wreck of the steamer *Mediator* was visible. One wreck is no sooner out of sight than another happens, and in such terrible evidences the few inhabitants of the settlement at the inlet are constantly reminded of how inhospitable a coast theirs is.

Barnegat Light

Barnegat Light is famous, and we stood under it as it was ignited. The shaft towers from a bed of sand, which has formed a ridge twenty or thirty feet high around the base, and out of which a few cedars grow. The great brilliancy of the lantern, which makes it visible to vessels some twenty miles away, is lost to people standing at the base, and the only indication of it is in the prismatic glass. The keeper's house is nearby, and the children sleep while the father watches and works in that radiant crown on the tower.

Farther northward. The wind was now in our favor, and we ran up to Toms River past Waretown, where an old grave-yard sadly overlooks the sea, and past Seaside Park, another of the fashionable places which have appeared within the last three or four years on the outer beach.

The End of the Journey

Toms River is charming, and the village is one of the prettiest in America. Then we took the railway again and went to Sea Bright, where we spent a happy day with the fishermen. There is no settlement more picturesque or interesting than this along the shore, although summer boarding-houses and hotels are crowding the old huts away. Small boats, white, green, and red, line the beach, their bronze sails flapping idly in the wind. Here an old fisherman sits mending his nets; there a boat with a load of shining mackerel has just been beached, and a lot of tawny men, bare-legged and bare-armed, are transferring her cargo to small hand-carts. The huts are built among the sand-hills, and the peculiar, conical roofs of the ice-houses give the village a foreign look.

When we reached Pier No. 8, North River, where we ended our journey, we landed with faces as brown and weather-beaten as Bill Pharo's.

— from **Harper's New Monthly Magazine,** *1878*

Fishing Off Barnegat Lighthouse. *(From* **Appleton's Journal,** *1871)*

The Wreck of John Minturn

In the foul winter of 'forty-six
came high tide at Squan Beach:
three days of storm across the reach,
the north-east wind did wail,
and took ten tall ships or more,
the demon tempest hailed . . .

But the worst on Jersey shore, we learn,
was the wreck of John Minturn,
a proud packet ship, dark bottle-green,
New York-bound from New Orleans,
three masts and oaken keel,
Captain Stark behind the wheel . . .

Though she cut salt-water like a sword,
of the tragic fifty-one on board,
few lived to tell the tale:
how she struck the bar
in dead of night,
and went down in the gale . . .

Now the clippers are long gone,
and their sailors sail no more,
on the sandy shore the old folk know
how those fierce nor'easters blow . . .

And some still hear that awful sound,
the Minturn *moaned, hard run aground;*
though they tried to get a life-line through,
there was nothing surfmen could do,
but watch and wait
while the cruel wind blew . . .

And the proud ship, with her sails all torn,
rocked wildly in the raging storm,
the pounding waves like cannon roared,
all on deck washed overboard . . .

She broke apart and left her bones,
and Captain Stark met Davy Jones,
on that cold sand bar
off Barnegat—
and there was nothing surfmen could do,
but watch and wait while the cruel wind blew . . .

In the foul winter of 'forty-six
came high tide at Squan Beach:
three days of storm across the reach,
the north-east wind did wail,
and took ten tall ships or more,
the demon tempest hailed . . .
but the worst on Jersey shore, we learn,
was the wreck of John Minturn.

The *John Minturn* tragedy shocked the American public and brought about a demand for the formation of a regular Life Saving Service.
(Print by Nathaniel Currier, courtesy of the Harry T. Peters Collection, Museum of the City of New York)

A Nor'easter Midnight Reader

There are times when the sea goes mad during northeast storms, when the crashing waves and dark, swirling clouds become a nightmare vision. Over the years, more than three thousand ships sailed into that nightmare and met their doom on the treacherous shoals off the New Jersey coast. According to local records, 125 of those vessels came ashore between the Manasquan River and Barnegat Inlet from 1838 to 1878. For eleven years after that, one ship a year struck sand bars off Bay Head, with four wrecks occurring at the same spot, one piling up on top of another.

Nautical relics from distant shores were commonly used in building and decorating the early shanties of the dunes. Ship wheels, timbers, masts, and figureheads became a part of the seascape. Their colorful quarter-boards were prominently displayed at the old beachfront inns like the Chadwick House. The wrecks they came from — the *Ayrshire*, the *Powhattan*, the *John Minturn* — entered local lore and legend.

Flotsam, Jetsam, and Beachcombers

Beachcombers walked the beaches in the early morning hours after a storm, and sometimes found unexpected treasures mingled among the seashells and driftwood. Everything from food and clothing to silver, china, and furniture washed ashore during the old days. Natives sometimes found gold rings and old bottles with scrawled messages inside. Beachcombers considered the flotsam and jetsam, thrown overboard from ships in distress, as a bounty from God by way of the sea. The waves were often very generous, and occasionally large kegs of uncut rum, 180 proof, rolled onto the beach and into the hands of some lucky bystander who happened to be in the right place at the right time. On other days the beaches might be barren, instilling a philosophical attitude among beachcombers: Sometimes the magic worked, and sometimes it didn't.

Shipwrecks and Wreckers

The first recorded notice of shipwreck off the Barnegat shore was printed in the May 1705 issue of the *Boston News Letter*:

> *New York, April 30 — Yesterday came hither the masters of the three sloops which were cast away near Barnegat by the late easterly storms, viz: Archibald Morris, who was bound from Pennsylvania for New York and Boston, and one Saunders, bound from Roanoke to Boston. Saunders*

The howling gale of a northeast storm at sea, under the influence of a full-moon flood tide, which sent ten ships ashore on the Jersey Coast during the Great Storm of 1846. ***(The painting on the facing page,*** **High Seas,** ***by Edward Moran 1902, courtesy of Ralph Autorino)***

THE WRECKERS:

OR, THE

SHIP-PLUNDERERS OF BARNEGAT.

A Startling Story of the Mysteries of the Sea-shore.

Rodolf Raven luring seamen and vessel to shipwreck and death —See p. 12.

BY CHARLES E. AVERILL,

F. GLEASON'S PUBLISHING HALL,
CORNER COURT AND TREMONT STREETS, BOSTON.
S. FRENCH, 293 Broadway, New York.—A. WINCH, 116 Chestnut Street, Philadelphia.—STRATTON & BARNARD, 121 Main Street, Cincinnati.—J. A. ROYS, 37 Woodward Avenue, Detroit.—E. K. WOODWARD, 91 Chestnut Street, and NAFIS, CORNISH & CO., 266 Main Street, St. Louis.—WM. TAYLOR, North Street, Baltimore. JOHN CARTER, JR., 11 Wall Street, Louisville, Ky.—JOHN SELLERS, Rue Champs Elysees, New Orleans.

The Wreckers: Melodramatic fictional accounts of piracy on the Jersey Shore were popular themes in romantic novels of the mid-nineteenth century. ***(Book title page courtesy of Rutgers University Library Special Collections Department)***

had one man drowned and saved nothing at all, and the others saved very little besides lives.

Authorized wreckmasters were appointed by the provincial governor as far back as 1696, and held responsible for salvaging foundered vessels that came within their jurisdiction. They returned the vessels, if possible, or sold them with their cargos, at public auction. By the 1850s, shipping and insurance companies had their own salvage crews. Wreckers were experienced seamen, usually locally hired, and wrecking was a hazardous business despite its lucrative fringe benefits.

Tales of Barnegat Pirates

Throughout the nineteenth century, the Barnegat coast was one of the most dreaded passages along the Atlantic seaboard. It was widely believed that the tragic toll of shipwrecks was the result of darker forces than the chance combination of foul weather, sandbars, and fate. Late-night tavern tales told of ruthless pirates haunting the beaches on stormy nights, luring passing ships ashore to loot and plunder. Some tales said they led a donkey down the beach with a lighted lantern tied to its neck, glowing in the windy darkness. There were reports they built large bonfires on the seaward edge of the dunes, in hope of attracting passing vessels closer to the submerged offshore shoals.

Although these tales were never proved — or disproved — the legends of the Barnegat Pirates provoked terror in mariners sailing by these shores. Charges of piracy along the Jersey Coast grew out of an era when real pirates roamed the offshore waters from New England to the Carribean. It was a dangerous age, when most seagoing vessels were well armed with cannons, muskets, and cutlasses, always on the lookout for rogue ships that struck without warning. With the rapid expansion of American maritime interests in the early 1800s, tales of pirates and piracy fired the popular imagination. But real cutthroats actually prowled the seas as late as 1834, when seven pirates were captured by the Navy and hanged on Boston Common.

Barnegat Pirates entered American literature in 1856, when Walt Whitman published *Leaves of Grass*, one of the great works of modern poetry. Among several poems dealing with the sea and nature, Whitman introduces the element of human evil in "Patrolling Barnegat," his vision of pirates waiting on shore for a ship to come their way:

Wild, wild the storm, and the sea high running,
Steady the roar of the gale, with incessant undertone muttering,
Shouts of demoniac laughter fitfully piercing and pealing,
Waves, air, midnight, their savagest trinity lashing,
Out in the shadows there milk-white combs careering,

On beachy slush and sand spirts of snow fierce slanting,
Where through the murk the easterly death-wind breasting,
Through the cutting swirl and spray watchful and firm advancing,
(That in the distance! is that a wreck? is the red signal flaring?)
Slush and sand of the beach tireless till daylight wending,
Steadily, slowly, through hoarse roar never remitting,
Along the midnight edge by those milk-white combs careering,
A group of dim, weird forms, struggling, the night confronting,
That savage trinity warily watching.

Melodramatic fictional accounts of piracy on the Jersey Shore were popular themes in Romantic novels of the nineteenth century. One of them was called *The Wreckers: or the Ship-Plunderers of Barnegat, A Startling Story of the Mysteries of the Sea-Shore.* Published in Boston in 1848, this novel was written by Charles B. Averill, and tells of "the lawless wreckers of the Jersey Coast, with whose striking report of horrors the land still rings."

The title page features an illustration of Captain Rudolf Raven, the head pirate of the bay, standing on a high dune looking out on the sea, raising a cutlass in one hand and waving a black banner with the other. The legend on the banner reads "Woe to the Mariner." Silhouetted against a stormy sky, Captain Raven wears seven-league boots, a windblown black long-coat, and an ancient helmet with flowing plumes. Behind him stands a tall mast with a hoisted false beacon. Beneath the picture the caption reads: "Rudolf Raven luring seamen and vessel to shipwreck and death."

Inside the Pirate's Den

Another novel, *Barnegat Pirates*, was written by Howard Van Sant, and published in New York in 1897. Van Sant based his tale on the notorious deeds of Captain John Bacon and his band of renegades during the Revolutionary War. In his story, Van Sant's hero, Tim Berryman, is cast ashore on Island Beach, the sole survivor of a harrowing shipwreck. Wandering across the desolate dunes, Berryman stumbles onto one of the pirates, a runaway slave. The pirate offers him food and drink — for a price — and takes him to the hidden pirate den concealed in a cave inside a dugout sand dune:

A dimly lighted lantern, which hung from a broad rafter above, revealed the interior of a long, gloomy cave, probably thirty feet in length and half as broad, and high enough for him to walk erect. A number of timbers braced against the ship's planking at the top prevented the sand from falling, while the sides were supported in a similar manner . . . In one corner a considerable amount of booty such as chains, windlasses, anchors, brasswork, ship's rigging, provisions, several chests and a varied assortment of odds and ends, were gathered. The only furniture was a half dozen ship's chairs, mostly broken, and several long boxes, used for tables and stands, while a few robes and blankets were strewn about the floor at one side of the fireplace and an extra heap of hay, the sleeping quarters of the place.

Bewildered by his surroundings, Berryman asks if this is the home port of the Barnegat Pirates. "Dat's what de settlers call us," replies the black man, "but Capt'n Bacon says he ain't no more pirate than anyone else around here. He's fighting for de king . . ." In fact, Bacon was an outlaw before the war, and treacherous by nature. While most Tories were decent men loyal to their king, the Revolution brought out the worst in some people. The hostilities between local Tory and Rebel neighbors rapidly escalated to a state of bitter civil war. There were marauding gangs of outlaws and runaway slaves, like Bacon's band and Davenport's Pine Robbers, who responded to the conflict for the same reason vultures circle a battlefield. Even old Indian Tom, who lived alone in his wigwam on the bluffs of the Toms River, was suspected by the Rebels of spying for the British.

In the preface to *Barnegat Pirates*, Van Sant explained the historical basis of his novel, and absolved coastal residents of any blame:

Most of the piratical practices and murders so much talked of along this section were confined to war times. That there was depradation of a greater or less degree several years before and for some years since the war of independence, is granted; but that a major portion of the shore population countenanced or in any way aided in piratical practices is denied, and is without real foundation. The whole country was little more than a forest, and the beach a barren, uninhabited waste, where it was easy for lawlessness to thrive and escape punishment.

Captain Kidd and His Buried Treasure

There were real pirates operating off the New Jersey shore in the old days. One of the most notorious was Captain William Kidd, who sailed by the Barnegat shores in 1699 aboard the pirate galley *San Antonio.* Captain Kidd was a respected British navigator and privateer before he raised the *Jolly Roger* in 1696. His crew was frequently seen around Middletown, in Monmouth County, where one of his men, Moses Butterworth, once went on trial for piracy. According to tradition, his armed shipmates burst into the courtroom and freed the defendant. Then they seized the judges, court lawyers, and even the Royal Governor, and held them hostage for four days.

Another legend holds that Captain Kidd romanced a Barnegat farm girl by the name of Amanda, and buried a treasure chest near Oyster Creek. A different old story claims Kidd sailed up from Barnegat Inlet and landed on an island near Toms River, long since known as Money Island. Around this time a few of his men jumped ship while Kidd's galley was moored near the mouth of the Mullica River. The turncoats fled to New York, where they informed the Royal Governor. With pirate's luck on his side, Kidd sighted the British warships approaching and, rigging the *San Antonio* for full sail, escaped to the south on the running tide.

Spanish Doubloons and Pieces of Eight

Tales of Kidd's treasure lingered around the shore area long after the Captain was finally captured by Royal authorities in 1701. Kidd was taken to London in chains, where he was tried and convicted of piracy. He went to the gallows on May 24th, and the news of his execution inspired a popular ballad of the time called "The Dying Words of Captain Kidd":

Come all ye young and old,
you're welcome to my gold,
for by it I've lost my soul,
and must die . . .

One hundred and thirty years later, Captain Kidd was the model for the central character of the Skimmer in James Fenimore Cooper's *Water Witch*, a novel of piracy and buried treasure on the Jersey Shore. Down through the years, wandering beachcombers have occasionally found Spanish doubloons and pieces-of-eight, washed up on the beach at low tide. Such incidents always revive the whispered rumors that larger treasures have been discovered but not reported, or that they still lie buried in the white sands, waiting to be found. These rumors also say that Captain Kidd landed during his last voyage and hid several chests filled with silver and gold near a pond behind a range of dunes by the shore, somewhere between Old Barnegat Beach and Sandy Hook.

Indian Will's Discovery

A legend from the late 1700s suggests that Indian Will may have found part of the treasure, according to Salter's *Old Times In Old Monmouth County*, published in 1887. Indian Will lived in a wigwam on a cove known as Will's Hole near the Manasquan Inlet, in what is now Point Pleasant Beach. He was a stocky, broad-shouldered fellow, who frequently wore gold earrings and a large nose ring. Some reports claim he was often seen wearing a tricornered cocked hat and a crimson long coat.

An Ocean County old-timer remembered him well: "Indian Will sometimes travelled down along the shore as far as Barnegat Inlet and always attended by a lot of big, lean, hungry-looking dogs, to help him fight off other Indians."

THE BARNEGAT PIRATES.—Information was received at the New York Police Office on Saturday of the arrest of the Barnegat Magistrate, Platt, alleged to have been the ringleader of the Barnegat gang of pirates. After a chase of three days through the dense woods of that neighbourhood, his pursuers overtook and secured him, though he at first flourished a formidable display of weapons, which he threatened to use on them, but prudently suffered his threats to evaporate in words. He was held to bail in the sum of $5000, which he procured.

The Barnegat Pirates made sensational headlines in the *Philadelphia Saturday Courier* on January 17, 1835. *(From the collection of the author)*

Apparently on one of these beachcombing journeys Indian Will stumbled onto an old pirate treasure. According to Salter:

Indian Will often visited the family of Derrick Longstreet at Manasquan, and one time showed them some silver money which excited their surprise; they wished to know where he got it, and wanted Will to let them have it. Will refused to part with it, but told them he had found it in a trunk along the beach, and there was plenty of yellow money beside; but as the yellow money was not as pretty as the white, he didn't want that, and Longstreet might have it. So Longstreet went with him, and found the money in a trunk covered over with a tarpaulin buried in the sand; Will kept the white money and Longstreet the yellow (gold), and this satisfactory division made the Longstreets quite wealthy.

Blackbeard and Richard Worley

John Teach and Richard Worley were two other freebooters who sailed this way in the early 1700s. Better known as Blackbeard the Pirate, Captain Teach was the scourge of the Carolinas who once fled north to the Jersey Shore to escape a pursuing fleet. There is a tradition that says he entered Barnegat Bay and anchored his eight-gun pirate schooner, *Queen Ann's Revenge*, among the reeds and cattails of the sedge islands. Blackbeard and his thrity-man crew were reportedly seen on the mainland, around Lower Bank, and raided farms around Middletown. Shortly after, in 1718, he was trapped and killed on Ocracoke Island, on North Carolina's Outer Banks. During the same year, forty-nine pirates were hanged in one month in South Carolina.

Six years earlier, the pirate Richard Worley harassed merchant vessels and fishing boats off the Jersey Coast, boarding them and demanding tribute. Operating from a small sailboat with a six-man crew, Worley hijacked a large sloop and christened it *New York's Revenge.* For six weeks he terrorized the seashore, until New York ship owners and the Governor of Pennsylvania sent out search parties to stop the marauder. Worley sailed down the coast to Charleston, where *New York's Revenge* was surprised by four armed merchant ships waiting outside the harbor. After a brief battle, the sloop was recaptured and the pirates put to the sword.

The Sword with the Golden Hilt

Tales of the pirates survived years after they disappeared from these shores. Reports of buried treasure became a part of Barnegat Bay folklore. One of these reports connects an old sword with a golden hilt to a mysterious treasure hunt. The sword was part of a collection of relics owned by Captain John Havens, of Point Pleasant. Havens was the first superintendent of the Life Saving Service, and his account of how the sword was found was recorded by Gustave Kobbé in his 1888 travelogue, *Jersey Coast and Pines*:

> *It is firmly believed to be a part of a treasure buried by pirates near the present site of Life Saving Station No. 22, about two and a quarter miles south of Beach Haven. The evening of Sunday, September 11, 1886, two men, representing themselves as surveyors, asked a surfman of the station to point out two cedars about one hundred yards northeast from the location of the old inlet. This the surfman was easily able to do, as the cedars were well known landmarks. Something in the manner of the men, who spent the night at the station, led the crew to suspect that their visitors were not what they represented themselves to be, and the next morning, after the men had left the station, one of the crew climbed up to the lookout and trained a spyglass on the cedars. He saw two men busily engaged in digging up the sand. One of them, happening to glance up toward the station became aware that they were being watched, and they departed in haste, bearing something with them. Several surfmen then hurrying over to the cedars, discovered that two holes had been dug there and found the valuable sword on the edge of one of the holes.*

Captain Havens' collection, including the sword with the golden hilt, was destroyed in a fire in 1905.

Treasure on the Manasquan

Another strange treasure tale was written by Richard Harding Davis, a well-known author and war correspondent who was a frequent summer visitor to the Point Pleasant area during the late 1890s. In 1911, he published a short story titled *My Buried Treasure*, in which a young writer agrees to help a shady character named Edgar dig for treasure in return for permission to write about the adventure one year later.

The narrator and Edgar travel by train from New York to Point Pleasant, where they follow an old map to a site southwest of the Manasquan Inlet, near three cedars behind the beachfront dunes:

> *From the north and south we were now hidden by the two high banks of sand; to the east lay the beach and the Atlantic Ocean, and to the west stretches of marshes that a mile away met a wood of pine trees and the railroad round-house. I began to dig . . . I took my comfort in anticipating the thrill that would be mine when the spade would ring on the iron-bound chest; when, with a blow of the axe, I would expose to view the hidden jewels, the pieces of eight, coated with verdigris, the string of pearls, the chains of yellow gold. Edgar had said a million dollars . . . the spade slipped through my cramped and perspiring fingers, and as it struck the bottom of the pit, something — a band of iron, a steel lock, an iron ring — gave forth a muffled sound. My heart stopped beating . . . With a swift kick I brushed away the sand. I found I was standing on a squat wooden box, bound with bands of rusty iron. I had only to stoop to touch it. It was so rotten that I could have torn it apart with my bare hands. Edgar was dancing on the edge of the pit, incidentally kicking sand into my mouth and nostrils.*

Unfortunately, in an ironic twist, Edgar then refused to let the writer view the uncovered treasure, in keeping with the agreement that his only reward would be to write about the hunt. Although it is not known whether the story is truly autobiographical or not, Davis's authentic descriptions of Point Pleasant and its natives lend realism to the tale.

Robert Louis Stevenson and Treasure Island

A short way up the Manasquan River is a small, uninhabited wooded island, which was originally owned by the Osborn family, but is traditionally known as Treasure Island, because it was once visited by Robert Louis Stevenson. The world famous author came to the shore in the summer of 1888 and stayed on the river's north bank at the Union House, opposite Gull Island. During this time, Stevenson was working on his final draft of *The Master of Ballentrae* and enjoyed sailing catboats with his companion, Will Low. Twenty years later, Low recounted the story of how Treasure Island got its name in his autobiography, *A Chronicle of Friend-ships*:

One afternoon we landed on an island a little way up the river, whose shore upon one side was protected by a bulkhead. As the island was nameless, we proceeded to repair the oversight and christened it Treasure Island, after which we fell to with our pocketknives to carve the name upon the bulkhead, together with our initials and the date. This inscription was there some years after, and if the winter tempests have spared it, I am pleased to signal it for some one in quest of a Stevenson autograph, as it might figure as a unique specimen in almost any collection.

According to another old tradition, the Lenape frequently left their squaws on this island when they gathered in the spring for major fishing expeditions. During the early days when Squan Village was a prosperous seaport, square-rigged ships and large schooners sailed in and out of the inlet. Because of strong-flowing alongshore currents, the mouth of the river moved more than a mile south over the years until it became completely closed to shipping in the late 1800s due to heavy shoaling. It remained closed for thirty years, until the Army Corps of Engineers began dredging to keep the inlet open.

Whether pirates ever visited Treasure Island may never be known, but it is a possibility, which might explain the origin of an old and mysterious deep pit that lies off the northern shore of the small island.

Charges of Piracy on the Barnegat Coast

The Barnegat Coast became most notorious during the first half of the nineteenth century. Shipwrecks were so common, and the loss of life so high from 1830 to 1850, that city newspapers and magazines frequently charged that piracy lay behind the disasters.

The *Sentinel of Freedom*, a Newark weekly, headlined a typical report on February 24,1835:

New Jersey Land Pirates Again! The Passengers, who were thrown upon our shore, on Tuesday last, from the wreck of the packet ship Sovereign, at the imminent peril of their lives, were, we are told, mostly robbed of their money and clothing. A lady passenger states that after being landed on the beach, the miscreant inhabitants stole her baggage, watch and money. The other passengers were also robbed and their trunks broken open and pilfered before their eyes. Other parties of those harpies, it is said, were lying off the wreck in their boats, ready to seize the prey, as soon as by the destruction of the vessel, it should come within their grasp. It is a burning shame, a deep disgrace that these pirates are suffered to live and plunder upon our shores.

A week later, the *Sentinel* printed an embarrassed retraction:

The New Jersey Pirates Acquited. We are very much gratified in being able to state explicitly that the story, which has gone abroad through the whole country of the plundering of the passengers of the ship Sovereign on the Jersey shore, has not the slightest color of truth. We learn from a conversation with the United States Marshall, whose name has been freely used on the occasion, that he has ascertained in the most authentic manner that the people in the neighborhood are not in the least degree culpable. The robberies appear to have been committed by the sailors and others belonging to the vessel, on the credit of the Jersey wreckers.

Four seamen were subsequently found guilty of robbery at a trial in Toms River. They were fined and sentenced to prison. Many other similar reports of pirates and plundering appeared in the popular press during the next twenty-five years. These charges were so persistent that a Toms River newspaper, the *Ocean Emblem,* took up the defense of local volunteer lifesavers in an editorial on December 17th, 1852:

It has been for a long time quite fashionable for the New York and Philadelphia press, with some honorable exceptions, to charge upon the shore inhabitants every species of crime and inhumanity. They lose sight of the disinterested benevolence of the poor surfmen, their noble daring to board a stranded wreck, and at the peril of their lives, to save the suffering crew and passengers. These acts are never mentioned, but if a pin's worth of property is lost it is charged upon the Barnegat Pirates!

Two early incidents that fueled these charges were the wrecks of the *Henry Franklin* and the *James Fisher*, which were both stranded near Barnegat Inlet in 1834. Six local residents were convicted of looting the vessels and jailed for that crime. Although no one was accused of attempting to decoy the ships closer to shore, the convictions gave credence to the rumors of Barnegat Pirates at work on the shore.

Barnegat Light and the Great Storm of 1846

The shoals around Barnegat Inlet made passage so hazardous that Congress authorized $6,000 to build a lighthouse. A forty-foot-tall brick beacon was erected on the northern tip of Long Beach, three hundred feet south of the

Late-night tavern tales told of ruthless pirates haunting the beaches on stormy nights, luring passing ships ashore. Some tales said they led a donkey down the beach with a lighted lantern tied to its neck, glowing in the windy darkness. ***(Engraving from*** **Harper's New Monthly Magazine*****, from the collection of the author)***

Interior of a Life Saving Station, 1878, depicts the surf boat, caronade, and breeches buoy commonly used during the late-nineteenth century.
(Engraving from* Frank Leslie's Illustrated News, *from the collection of the author)

Early settlers on the seashore lived in small shanties surrounded by wild dunes. Many made their living as "wreckers," salvaging stranded vessels. The Federal Government established Life Boat Houses on the New Jersey coast in 1841 and most wreckers served as volunteer lifesavers when ships came ashore. *(Print from* Harpers, *1878)*

inlet. But even a lighthouse could not prevent disaster from striking when a howling gale began to blow during one of the worst storms of the century.

Ten vessels were lost off the Monmouth Coast that night — from Sandy Hook to Squan Beach. They included the *Pioneer*, the *Register*, the *Arkansas*, the *Antares*, the *New Jersey*, the *Lotty*, the *Alabama*, the *Mary Ellen*, the *Van Zandt*, and the *John Minturn*. The bodies rolled in on the morning tide for many days after.

The *New York Herald* headlined "The Terrible Storm" on February 17th:

> *Many years have elapsed since we were called upon to describe the greatest calamity to life and property than that of the 14th. last and the morning of the 15th. About 60 lives have been lost in one wreckmasters district. The amount of property is not yet fully ascertained; but enough is known to say that from a quarter to half a million dollars will fall upon the insurers of Wall Street from this gale.*

The most controversial and tragic loss was the wreck of the *John Minturn*, an American packet ship that struck a sand bar off Squan Beach during the height of the storm. The *Minturn* and her sister ship, the *Orleans,* were sailing off the Jersey Shore bound for New York from New Orleans. They both carried passengers, mail, and express freight. The *Minturn*'s cargo added 459 tons of burden to her 398-ton weight, and was valued at $70,000. It included cotton, sugar, molasses, hemp, corn, wheat, hams, lead, merchandise, and a large sum of money in the strongbox.

A First Rate Packet Ship

Nearly one hundred feet long, the *John Minturn* was a first-rate three-masted packet ship, built at Stonington, Connecticut, in 1842. Painted dark green with a white stripe and thirteen gun ports on each side, the *Minturn* ploughed through high seas with all the sail she could carry, moving steadily ahead at twelve knots. More than 150 packet ships operated offshore during the mid-1800s. They were solidly built ships and very few of them were ever lost.

The *John Minturn* left New Orleans on January 28th, with a crew of twenty-two, sailing under Captain Stark, who brought his young wife and two small children along for the trip. Five passengers were on board, bound for New York. The weather was fine and the cruise was uneventful until she encountered the wreck of the *Cherokee* off the southern coast. Twenty terrified seamen were rescued from the foundered vessel and taken on the passing packet ship. They joined the voyage north, raising the number of people aboard the ill-fated *John Minturn* to 51.

The blue sky changed to gray as the *Minturn* sailed up the coast along New Jersey. The restless sea grew wild and a chilling wind began to howl. Suddenly, the storm was upon them, blowing across the water with a mounting rage. Less than four miles off the deadly shoals of the Barnegat Coast, the *Minturn* was approached by the pilot boat *Blossom.* Captain Stark at first refused service, but then changed his mind as the storm grew worse. Around five o'clock Saturday afternoon, he took the New York pilot, Thomas Freeborne, on board. Together they prepared to deal with the storm that threatened to blow the *Minturn* ashore.

The Wreck of the *John Minturn*

Steering into the gale, the *Minturn* attempted to ride out the "nor'easter" and avoid being rolled over by the wind on her reach. Gusting sleet and snow attacked the ship. Her mainsail caught the wind but quickly split from top to bottom, and the ship swung out of control on the surging swells. The fierce gale ripped through her fore-topsail and headsails, leaving them streaming from their spars as the ship plunged toward the shore like a ghost.

The captain and pilot struggled with the wheel, attempting to steer the *Minturn* head on to the beach. The ship slammed into the outer bar bow first, then lifted and struck again, cracking her keel. Relentless breakers pounded the *John Minturn*, flooding her deck and driving her broadside to the beach, tilting into the wind with her foremast and mainmast broken. Her tattered sails snapped like whips on the hard-driving gale.

Panic-stricken passengers and crew gathered in the forecastle at the head of the ship. The pilot cried out: "Hold fast, everybody! It will be daylight in a few minutes and the shoremen will come out for us!"

It was about three o'clock in the morning and the deserted, windswept beach lay three hundred yards away — with dark shadows of storm clouds dancing across the dunes in the flashing moonlight — separated from the ship by black, boiling seas and strong currents. A ramshackle, low-roofed tavern lay behind the sand hills a short distance south, its narrow windows shuttered against the cold, salty spray.

Uncle Tommy Cook never forgot that long night:

On the 14th. of February, 1846, I was awakened in the night by the shaking of my house. I could feel my bed trembling . . . and I arose and donned my clothes in the darkness. I told my wife that a dreadful storm was upon us and I feared it would make dreadful work.

Volunteer lifesavers were already busy with the wrecked schooner *Alabama*, stuck on a shoal a half-mile south of Manasquan Inlet. Somehow word of the *Minturn* spread quickly through Squan Beach, but the nearest boat was three-and-a-half miles away from the vessel, at the head of the bay. Wreckmaster Hugh Johnson was at the *Alabama.* Other shoremen raced to the *Minturn* — from West Mantoloking, Bayhead, and Point Pleasant — arriving before daybreak, running down the beach across the peaks of the dunes, wading through flooded glades the storm tide cut through the narrow sea islands. Seventy-mile-an-hour winds roared across the frozen reach, drenching the shoremen and blinding them with sleet and stinging sand. Yellow foam blew off the ocean and clung to their beards and clothing. The roaring sea surged against the beach, chewing a deep ragged cliff in the wet sand at the water's edge.

Tommy Cook was one of the first to arrive. Standing on a high sand dune, he saw the ship coming:

I scarcely raised my eyes when I saw 100 yards from shore the American bark John Minturn going by like a race horse. Every sail was blown away and her deck was crowded with passengers, many of them shouted to us as the current carried them so swiftly by . . . She soon struck, by which time hundreds of neighbors had gathered on the shore hoping that they might do something to help the women and children, who were gathered in the bow, the stern having quickly gone to pieces. Several attempts were made to launch the lifeboat, and finally two sailors got off in it, carrying a line to them, but the current swept them to the south as swift as an arrow.

John Maxson — a veteran lifesaver — hurried to the wreck, five miles north of his gunning lodge on the bay:

I never knew a worse storm than that in which the Minturn was wrecked. I was scared myself. The water was half-thigh deep all around my house, and between it and the top of the beach, on Sunday morning. The ocean broke through the sand hills between my house and the Minturn, and run over into the bay . . . When I arrived I found the Minturn turn fast on the outer bar, about one-third of her stern resting thereon. . . .

Inside a Life Saving Station, the men are playing poker around a lantern lit table when the door bursts open with a windy chill
(Print by Howard Pyle from **Harpers Weekly**, *1878, courtesy Frank J. Wilson.)*

To the rescue! Lifesavers bring a surf boat to the scene of a shipwreck. ***(Engraving from*** **Harper's Weekly,** ***from the collection of the author)***

On board the stranded ship, the terrified passengers and crew fought against the freezing rain. Two sailors launched a lifeboat, but it crashed against the port side of the big ship and foundered. The shoremen on the beach watched helplessly. Two more sailors launched a yawl with a lifeline. The swift current quickly pulled them away — and they had to cut loose or be sunk. Seeing this, the volunteers gave chase. According to the official *Report*:

> *The people on shore followed it, and familiar from daily practice with the precise point of danger, as the boat neared the land, instantly formed a rope of hands, and with one of their ends resting on the shore, the others pushed into the sea, into the very power of the undertow, and as the waves were curling over it, at its moment of extremest peril, seized the boat and brought it to shore — another moment and it would have been too late. .*

The surfmen brought the seamen up on the beach and quickly bailed out the rescued yawl. The wreckmaster, who had just arrived from the *Alabama*, offered any reward to anyone daring to launch the boat and attempt to bring a lifeline to the *Minturn*. No man accepted the offer and one spoke for all when he said: "We will go without money as soon as with . . ." But the wind was too fierce and the waves were too furious. The sea was a churning cauldron of broken timbers and spars. Even the two rescued seamen remained on the beach as the day dragged on. Some men tried to float barrels to the wreck, with lines attached, but they were swept away on the tide. The deathwatch continued as darkness fell, and all attempts to reach the stranded ship proved fruitless.

The Deathwatch

For eighteen hours the freezing passengers and crew numbly hung on for dear life on the wave-swept bow and ice-shrouded rigging. Around 10 P.M., the huddled people on the shore heard an awful sound as the *John Minturn* shuddered and broke apart on the outer bar. Men, women, and children were swept into the white-capped raging sea. Their screams were heard on the shoreline above the shrill whistling of the wind. The shoremen watched in horror.

Thirty-nine persons perished in the surf, and their bodies came ashore as far as eight miles away, including Captain Stark, his wife and children, and the pilot. The beaches were strewn with wreckage and cargo. Thirteen victims survived — having been rescued by volunteers or washed up on the beach clinging to broken timbers. One of the survivors, a young girl named Rebecca Jane, was saved by David Brower of West Mantoloking. They later married. Another castaway, a youth named Will George, was adopted by one of the witnesses, Joshua Polhemus.

Farther up the beach, off Point Pleasant, all hands were lost on the stranded schooner *Alabama*. Lifesavers made several attempts to reach the five doomed crewmen, but the vessel went to pieces just after sunrise. The seamen on board the *Arkansas*, off Deal, and the *Lotty* and the *New Jersey*, near Ocean Grove, were more fortunate. Each vessel suffered only one fatality. The rest of their crews were saved, as were the entire crews of the *Antares*, the *Mary Ellen*, the *Register*, and the *Van Zandt*, which all struck on Monmouth Beach.

Report of the Special Commission

The nation was stunned by the disasters. New Jersey Governor Charles Stratton appointed a special commission to investigate the *Minturn* tragedy and the many other wrecks that night. The commissioners journeyed down the coast to Squan Beach, and took testimony from thirty-six survivors and eyewitnesses. The gathered evidence was published a month later in the *Report of the Commissioners to Investigate the Charges Concerning the Wrecks on Monmouth Coast.* Their conclusion refuted sensational charges made by the city presses — which were frequently controlled by the underwriting companies — that local residents refused to come to the aid of the shipwrecked victims and that they looted the bodies of the dead.

William P. Chadwick, a seasoned lifesaver who had come to the aid of many shipwrecks in his long life — including the *Ayrshire*, the *New York*, and the *John Minturn* — was saddened by the charges:

> *No man, except my father-in-law (John Maxson), has done more to save drowning men than I have. I tell you it's an awful sight to see the poor creatures clinging to the rigging and bowsprit, to see them washed ashore before your eyes, sometimes close to you, without your being able to help them. And their dead bodies thrown up on the sand. You don't feel like stealing or murder at such times. And besides, I never knew a dead man come ashore that had anything in his pockets.*

Although some beached cargo did disappear, and some money was stolen from the captain's cabin — allegedly by the sailors — the *Report* praised the shoremen. Regarding the *John Minturn*, the Commission concluded:

> *. . . the records of the surf can show few more persevering, enduring and courageous efforts to save the perishing passengers and seamen than were shown by Monmouth surfmen on that occasion . . .*

The Life Saving Service

Because of the horror of the tragic wrecks along the beach, the public recognized the need for an organized Life Saving Service. Federal funding

Shore people on the beach cheer as the lifeline reaches the shipwreck and the first passengers are drawn ashore in the Life Car.
(Print from* Frank Leslie's Illustrated News, *1868, courtesy F.J.W.)

was first advocated in Congress by New Jersey Representative William A. Newell, who made a dramatic plea. As a result, $10,000 was granted in 1848 ". . . for providing surfboats, rockets, carronades and other necessary apparatus for the better protection of life and property on the coast of New Jersey." The following year, 14 small one-and-a-half story, cedar-shingled Life Boat Houses were built on the shore between Sandy Hook and Cape May. A bill passed by Congress in 1854 authorized 14 more stations, including new houses at Bay Head, Squan Beach, Island Beach, and Long Beach Island.

The first paid keepers, who received a $200 salary, were not selected until two years later. The keeper held the keys, maintained the equipment, kept records and summoned local experienced volunteer surfmen to assist in rescues when vessels were in distress offshore. The volunteers were compensated with a small share of the salvage. Although the houses were mainly in use during the cold weather months, the equipment was always kept ready during the summer in case of emergency. Major improvements in life saving were introduced in 1850 with the first use of a small mortar to fire a ball with a rescue line from the beach onto the rigging of stranded vessels. The development of an enclosed corrugated metal surfboat, known as a Life Car, also reduced casualties during rescue operations. A late innovation was the invention of the breeches buoy, which proved much safer than the Life Car in bringing people ashore.

201 Saved on the *Ayrshire*

The mortar and the life car were first used in action during a fierce snowstorm on January 12, 1850, when the immigrant ship *Ayrshire* was wrecked on Squan Beach, near the Chadwick House. John Maxson, Keeper of Station No. 5, discovered the wreck. With the help of his two daughters and William P. Chadwick, he successfully landed 201 passengers and crew from *Ayrshire*. Maxson and Chadwick both received gold medals from Congress for their heroism and resourcefulness.

340 Lost on the *Powhattan*

There were other times, however, when even courage and new methods of rescue could not overcome the terrible conditions that prevailed during fierce northeast storms. On the black night of April 18, 1854, the *Powhattan*, an immigrant ship outbound from Germany, struck a bar one hundred yards off

The Shipwrecks.

There was on the John Minturn, when she was wrecked, five cabin passengers, besides the captain's wife, son and daughter, with twenty seamen from the ship Cherokee, who were coming home after her loss. The vessel struck at about three A. M. She sheered broadside to the beach, and heeled off shore. The captain, his wife, children, five cabin passengers and others of the two crews, amounting in number to 28 persons, perished, and among them the second officer, Mr. Sturges. Seven persons escaped in the boat, but some of them have broken limbs. The following is a list of her cabin passengers :—Mr. Komer and lady, Mrs. Stark, Mr. J. Leeds, Capt. Babcock, Messrs. Levy and Baker. The ship immediately bilged. She is principally owned by Messrs. Stanton & Frost, of this city. She was a fine A 1 ship, five years old, 450 tons burthen, and is insured for thirty thousand dollars, as follows : at the Pelican, $7,500 ; Alliance Co., $3,750 ; at the New-York, $3,750.

General Mutual, ¼, Capt. Stark's interest.

Hartford Protection, ⅛, E. Faxson's interest.

Atlantic, N.Y., 1-16 or ⅛, E. & C. P. Williams's interest.

The following is a manifest of the cargo of the ship John Minturn :—283 bales cotton, 503 hhds. and bbls. sugar, 254 bbls. molasses, 3000 pigs lead, 100 bales hemp, 754 bags corn, 35 bbls. wheat, 5 casks hams, 106 tierces beef, 100 casks pork, 177 bbls. and 548 kegs lard, 42 bbls tallow, 44 do seed, 13 boxes merchandise, 16 bales skins, 9 tierces and 33 bbls. wax, 947 hides, 107 bags feathers, 4 bales, 30 bdls. and 3 casks hair, 17 bbls. and 1 cask bristles. She cleared from New-Orleans for New-York Jan. 24th.

Her freight money amounted to about $2,800.

The Journal of Commerce says :

The captain sent a rope ashore by the boat saved, and following immediately after in another boat, and with the rope as a guide endeavored to land all the crew and passengers in safety, but from some cause, as yet unknown, the rope gave way, and the boat containing the captain, it is believed, swamped, and all that remained thus perished. The cries of those on board were heard on the beach until about 10 o'clock the following day, when it is expected the vessel went to pieces.

Capt. Stark was close in shore, as is customary at this season of the year, expecting always a North-wester ; and as the wind very suddenly chopped round to the East, he had not time to get his vessel far enough off to be safe, and was thus driven ashore.

The persons saved in the boat reported that there was a ship lost about three miles from them ; and the ship Orleans, from New-Orleans, having been in company the day before, they supposed her to be the one ; but we are happy to say that the Orleans arrived safe at this port yesterday.

The John Minturn took a pilot on board on Saturday, and he has probably perished with the others.

The vessels which arrived this morning report the gale off the coast as very severe.

The Shipwrecks: News of the *John Minturn* tragedy was reported in *The New York Tribune* on February 19, 1846. *(From the collection of the author)*

Long Beach, near the present location of Surf City. Keeper Edward Jennings sighted the stranded ship before sunrise. He dispatched his three-man crew to haul the life saving apparatus down from Station No. 7, six miles north of the wreck. Heavy coastal flooding made it impossible to get the equipment through. The *Powhattan* broke up under the smashing breakers. Three hundred eleven passengers and twenty-nine crew men were lost at sea.

The *Powhattan* tragedy created a public demand that paid keepers with full-time crews be maintained during the winter, and resulted in fourteen more stations. During the next eighteen years, stations were built about five miles apart down the Jersey Coast. Nearly three years after the wreck of the *Powhattan*, volunteer life savers managed to save all hands on board the Black Ball packet ship *New York*, which ran aground off Island Beach. The December 31, 1856 issue of the *West Jerseyman*, a Camden newspaper, published a gripping account of the rescue:

> *The immigrant ship New York went ashore on the coast of Ocean County, near Wearstown (sic), on the 20th. inst., with 280 passengers and a crew numbering 23 . . . the New York lay a helpless wreck in the breakers, with her passengers in an almost perishing condition. The gallant New Jersey shoremen were on hand, periling their own lives for the rescue of their despairing fellow creatures. Towards midnight, the whole were landed, in a most deplorable condition, on a sandy, sterile beach, without food and destitute of shelter, save the scanty accommodations offered by the little life saving station, which was barely sufficient to shelter a tenth of their number: men, women and children of all ages, huddled together for warmth, and cowered upon the bare sand before the December blast.*

In the same year, William F. Brown, an Ocean County Assemblyman, praised shoremen in a passionate speech before the State Assembly. Brown concluded, "If the benevolent and heroic deeds of the men entitle them to be called 'Barnegat Pirates,' then may 'Barnegat Pirate' be inscribed on my brow!"

U.S. LIFE SAVING SERVICE
1848 – 1871

Old Barney

On the morning of November 2, 1857, the small beacon at Barnegat Inlet collapsed into the sea. The forces of erosion devoured more than three hundred feet from the shoreline in less than twenty-three years. Lt. George Meade, who was later a hero at the Battle of Gettysburg during the Civil War, designed a new lighthouse, which was built by the Army Corps of Engineers in 1858. It cost $60,000, ten times more than the first beacon, and was four times as large.

The new lighthouse, constructed of red brick, stands 172 feet high and is twenty-seven feet in diameter around the base. The red and white painted structure gently tapers upwards toward the seventeen-foot lamp chamber at the top, 217 steps up a long spiral staircase. Nearly 16,000 square-riggers and steamships sailed past Barnegat Light during its first year of operation.

The powerful beacon — with 80,000 candlepower — could be seen thirty miles out at sea. Henri Lepaute cast the lens in 1856 at the St. Gobian Works near Paris. The light weighed five tons and was composed of 1,024 crystal prisms, each nearly ten inches long, mounted in a sturdy brass frame. It was so perfectly balanced it could be turned with the touch of a finger. Flashing through the night every ten seconds, and projecting twenty-four flashes every four minutes, "Old Barney" became a major landmark on the Jersey Shore.

A Close Call on the *Costa Rica*

Although great improvements were made in lifesaving along the coast, rescue work remained an unpredictable and risky business. On the stormy evening of January 17, 1869, the brig *Costa Rica* ran aground off Squan Beach, near Bay Head. A volunteer crew led by Peter Sutphin launched a surf boat, and had just boarded the stranded vessel when a great wave smashed their boat against the ship. Trapped on the wreck, the volunteers joined the ship's crew in the rigging and waited through the icy night for rescue. Shortly before dawn, David Fleming assembled a crew at Station No. 7 in Bay Head. They launched through the furious surf and saved all hands on board the *Costa Rica*. None of the rescuers received or requested payment for their efforts, nor were they reimbursed for the loss of the surf boat.

The *Maid of the Mist* Meets the Barnegat Pirates

Nine years later, the tales of the Barnegat Pirates were so widely believed that when the *Maid of the Mist* came ashore off Point Pleasant, crew members armed themselves with pikes when they saw the lifesavers approaching in a surfboat. One of the rescued seamen, John Treworgy, of Maine, fell in love with a local girl, Miss Euretta Herbert. He settled in the area and gave up the sea for marriage. On another occasion, ten years later, the crew of a Chinese ship stranded off Seaside Park believed they were under attack when lifesavers on the beach fired rescue lines to the ship from their cannon-like Lyle guns.

The Tragic Tale of the *David H. Tolck*

There were times when nothing seemed to go right during rescue operations, when gale winds and rough surf refused to cooperate. The wreck of the *David H. Tolck* was one of those times. The *Tolck*, a three-masted schooner, was sailing north from Cuba with a cargo of sugar bound for New York. She struck a bar off Long Beach, near Loveladies, in the early morning hours of February 27, 1879.

The situation on board the *Tolck* was desperate. Captain Irving Sawyer tied himself and his wife and baby to the main mast, and prayed for rescue as the freezing wind ripped through the sails. Life Saving crews from Loveladies and Harvey Cedars rushed to the beach around dawn as the ship began breaking up on the bar. The gale was so fierce that surf boats were useless and the Lyle gun had to be fired four times before the lifeline reached the schooner's rigging.

Nearly frozen to death, Captain Sawyer and his wife gave their child, one-and-a-half-year-old Genevra, to the second mate, Emanuel Clausen, and ordered him ashore in the breeches buoy. The lifeline jammed halfway to shore, and the pair hung suspended over the tossing seas. The lifesavers acted quickly, backing up the beach and yanking the rope hard to break it between the buoy and the vessel. The desperate gamble succeeded, and they hauled in the seaman with the baby clutched numbly in his arms. Another line was fired to the ship and four more seamen were saved before the *Tolck* sank beneath the waves, taking Captain Sawyer and his wife, strapped to the mast. The girl survived and was adopted by a local family. The story of her tragic voyage and the wreck of the *David H. Tolck* was set down in an epic poem called *Saved Off Barnegat*, written by Ethel Beers in 1880.

Last Days of the Volunteer Crews

Volunteer crews served bravely from 1848 to 1870, when Congress authorized manning alternate stations with a paid keeper and six-man crew during the foul weather season. Superintendent Sumner Kimball named the re-organized force the United States Life Saving Service and by 1872 all of the stations on the Jersey Coast were fully manned. Finally, in 1886, the Federal Government began manning all stations with full-time paid crews. During the previous 15 years, 544 vessels were stranded or sunk off the shore of New Jersey, resulting in the loss of 78 lives. More than 1,093 mariners are known to have been lost due to shipwreck along this region from 1800 to 1871. The need for more stations was recognized and by the end of the century there were 42 of them erected between Sandy Hook and Cape May, standing approximately three miles apart.

For many years after, these well-built Victorian stations, with thirty-five-foot-high watchtowers and sharp gabled roofs, were landmarks on the coast, around which grew the towns of Bay Head, Mantoloking, Chadwick, and Seaside Park. Life Saving Station No. 14, now a historic site, still stands surrounded by wild dunes at Island Beach.

From the early days of the volunteer crews, local families contributed fathers and sons to the cause of saving lives. Service records chronicle the courage of the surfmen and document the old days when shipwrecks were common on the New Jersey coast. A long and colorful era ended when the Life Saving Service merged with the Marine Revenue Service in 1915 to form the United States Coast Guard.

Old Barney Saved from the Waves

Barnegat Light still stands by the edge of the sea, but only because of persistent and determined efforts to save her. By 1869, the strong ocean currents had eroded nearly all of the seventy-five-foot-wide beach between the light and the inlet. Once more the beacon was in danger of falling into the waves. After repeated efforts by the Army Corps of Engineers to construct protective barriers, the lighthouse was officially abandoned to the sea. She was decommissioned after sixty-eight years of service and replaced by a lightship twenty miles offshore.

But local residents refused to give up Old Barney and raised funds and devoted their time and energy to build a jetty to save the lighthouse. The Federal Government gave the land to the State of New Jersey, which now maintains the site as a State Park. Despite the new lightship, the Coast Guard maintained an automatic lamp, reduced to 11,000 candlepower, until 1944, when Barnegat Light was finally completely retired from service.

The Mystery Wreck at Mantoloking

Shipwrecks are few and far between now, and most of the old Life Saving Stations are long gone. They were usually built on leased land and torn down when the need for them had passed. Once in a while a mystery wreck is uncovered on the beach at Mantoloking in the wake of a strong storm tide — a reminder of the vanished era of sailing ships along these shores.

The old broken hulk lies capsized, sunken in the wet sand beside the foaming surf, a short distance away from where Life Saving Station No. 11 once stood. Her heavy keel and dark curving timbers are marked with barnacles and algae. Green-rusted fragments of old copper plate cling to the thirty-five-foot hull, which may once have been three times that length. Wooden trunnels and hand-forged bronze spikes hold the four-inch-thick planks together.

Although long rumored to be the wreck of an ancient Viking ship or the ruins of a lost Spanish galleon, local neighbors and boat builders believe her to be the stern section of an old coasting vessel that broke up in high seas and sank more than a century ago. It is possible the wreck is the stern of the *John Minturn*, known to have been lost off this shore 134 years ago. According to S.W. Thompson's deposition in the *Report*:

When I first came to the shore I discovered the stern part of the main deck with the house attached upon the beach, the house on the main deck very much broken, but not so much but what I did go into it . . .

It is possible that wreckers stripped the shattered cabin off the broken hulk. She lies buried bottom-up in the wet sand, and has never been fully excavated. Other testimony, by John Bannister and Frances Smith, identifies the location of the *Minturn* stranding with the site of the mystery wreck:

There was a house within 200 yards of the beach, to which we attempted to go, after sundown, having been wet all day and nearly perished.

The only house standing in the area was Uncle Jakey's tavern, which stood less than two hundred yards from the old battered stern. Finally, the text of the *Report* gives the location of the *Minturn*'s last resting place as follows:

The vessel . . . struck on the outer bar, nearly opposite James Herbert's shantee, the only tenement between that and the head of the bay.

Other sailing vessels known to have foundered off Mantoloking during the mid-1800s include the *Clara Brookman* (1857), the *Underwriter* (1854), the *Johanna* (1870), and the *George Taulane* (1880). The steamer *Creole* came ashore around 1868 more than a mile north of the mystery wreck. Or it is possible the hulk washed down the beach from one of the many wrecks off Bay Head that occurred around the same time: the *Alabama* (1846), the steamer *Queen* (1850), or from one of three vessels stranded in 1862 — the M*emento*, the *Hazard*, or the *Civita Carrara.*

All that is certain about the mystery wreck of Mantoloking is that her fittings and construction indicate she was built sometime after 1764. Where she came from — and how she was lost — may never be known. She remains a mystery, a dark relic from Davy Jones Locker, appearing and vanishing by the water's edge like a ghost ship lost in time.

Were There Really Barnegat Pirates?

In the same way, we may never know for sure whether Barnegat Pirates ever really roamed the dunes on stormy nights long ago. The Commissioner's *Report* denied such practices and most contemporary shoremen did as well. But one Osbornville old timer remembers things differently. Mrs. Lilah Gant Shultz, now 81 years old, remembers her grandfather, Abner Clayton, who earned a gold medal saving victims from the shipwrecked *George Taulane* a century ago. He sold the medal for its cash value. And she also remembers her great-grandmother, who told her the strange fate of her great-great-grandfather:

Now I couldn't bring you any proof of this, but my great-grandmother was a Pearce and she had a father and brother that was on the bay and down the waterways with the shipping. And they went to sea — it was about three months before she was born — and they never were heard of . . . and they say that the Barnegat Pirates got 'em and took the ship. And she never knew her father. Now I heard her tell that story 'cause I can remember it. So that's going back . . . but there were some pirates!

The mystery wreck at Mantoloking

A Busy Day at Barnegat: The Wreckers at Work. The raging storm drives the stricken ship over the bar, as passengers, cargo, and wreckage wash up on the beach. ***(Print by Granville Perkins, from* Frank Leslie's Illustrated News, *1868, courtesy of Frank J. Watson)***

The Pirates of Barnegat

Many of the beaches south of Bay Head retain their original wild and desolate character. One can wander for miles among the dunes without coming upon human habituation other than the Life-Saving stations or an occasional gunner's hut. These beaches were settled by whalers as early as 1640, whales being then plentiful off shore. Afterwards, and until the establishment of the Life-Saving Service, it was on these beaches that the "Barnegat Pirates" plied their infamy.

These miscreants had not the venturesome spirit to cruise the sea and attack every vessel they met, sometimes even accepting the risk of a fair battle. Their piratical acts were the more dastardly because they rarely involved peril to the lives of those who perpetrated them. A man who coldly shoots down his fellow-man from ambush is not more cowardly than were these Barnegat Pirates. Woe to the ship and crew which in those times found themselves off one of the Jersey beaches of a stormy night!

The elements were not half as pitiless as the wretch who trimmed the false beacon on the beach, while the band of wreckers stood among the dunes peering with straining eyes through the gale and sleet in eager expectation that some vessel would be lured out of her course and driven on to the shoals. It is easy to imagine the scene which was then enacted.

A Ghostly Heaving Form

Suddenly a ghostly, heaving form is discerned through the storm. A ship is plunging towards the breakers. There is a crash, a wail of despair, heard above the uproar of the tempest, and the false light has fulfilled its mission. The wreckers are now watching the surf. Suddenly a dark object is tossed up from the hollow of a wave and rolled ashore through the surf — the corpse of the first poor fellow to drop benumbed from the ice-coated rigging. The wreckers regard him with indifference — he is only a sailor with no money about him. Another is cast ashore and then another; and then they come rolling in faster. Some object larger than a man's body darkens the surf. It is a door from which one of the panels has been knocked out. A man has thrust an arm through the frame and hangs on to it, while with the other he clasps a woman so tightly that even the fury of the elements has not availed to separate them.

The wreckers pay more attention to these corpses. They search the captain's clothing till they find a wallet and then take his wife's ear-rings. The number of corpses washed ashore has confirmed what the crash with which the vessel went on the shoal told the wreckers — she is a large ship, a prime prize for the Barnegat Pirates in spars, timber and cargo. And the chances are she will break up before daylight, so that they can secure a good share of the plunder under cover of the night.

In League with the Demon of the Tempest

Such were some of the scenes once enacted on that desolate shore when the Pirates of Barnegat were in league with the demon of the tempest. When one reflects upon the terror of a storm at sea; the joy with which the tempest-tossed mariner must have beheld what seemed to him a familiar beacon; and the despair that must have come over him when he saw the line of hissing breakers ahead, and realized that he had been lured to certain death, one fails to find words strong enough to express one's sense of the villainy of the Pirates of Barnegat.

The natives of the coast are rather chary of information regarding these matters — they are too nearly contemporaneous to be freely spoken of. But sometimes, while sitting of a winter evening around the open fire-place of one or another of the old-fashioned inns on the coast, one can gather no uncertain details of these crimes, and old sportsmen will tell of taverns among the dunes where wines of the finest vintages of France and Germany could be had for a mere song.

A Dark Tradition of Wild Winter Nights

There is also a dark tradition that of wild winter nights a white female figure can be seen wandering up and down Long Beach, and suddenly falling upon her knees and bending over with clasped hands, as if over a corpse. This is said to be the specter of a young woman who was an active member of a band of wreckers of which her father was the leader. One night, when the corpses were beginning to roll in from a vessel which the band had lured on to the shoals the men heard their leader's daughter give a shriek and saw her throw herself over one of the bodies. It was the corpse of her sailor lover, who it was afterwards learned, had escaped from a wreck on the British coast and had then shipped for home in the very vessel she had helped lure to destruction.

Surfmen haul in the life car, filled with passengers, as other wreckers rejoice with their gifts from the sea. On the mainland, a shore family gives shelter to shipwrecked survivors. Many others were less fortunate. ***(Print from*** **Harper's*****, 1880, courtesy of Robert Reinert)***

The Service Has Put an End to Wrecking

Nowadays, the only men to be found on the beaches of a stormy winter night are the life-savers. The service has put an end to wrecking as a business. For a living the natives now "follow the bay" or provide entertainment for summer visitors and the sportsmen who are at all seasons attracted to this coast.

Of a winter night, instead of hoisting false signals on a stormswept beach, they draw up to the open fireplace or sit around the tap-room stove of their village inn, and their signalling is confined to "tipping the wink" to one another when to begin "loading up" some fresh, green youngster, down from the city on his first duck-shooting expedition, with stories of the wonderful sport to be had on the bay — stories in which the 52 broad-bills bagged in a day by one gunner at Wrangle Creek, or the 73 bagged in Sedge Islands thoroughfare, or the single haul of 200,000 pounds of fish in Metedeconk River in 1847, usually figure in the expressive native vernacular.

Another story is perhaps cut short by a gust of wind caused by the opening of the door. Three muffled figures seem to be fairly blown in. When they have thrown off their greatcoats the newcomers turn out to be an ex-sheriff from Toms River, with a spare, shrewd, gray-whiskered face, and two friends who have come down to have a quiet little game with the landlord.

Joining the Circle Around the Stove

They join the circle around the stove, and the ex-sheriff reminiscences for the benefit of the young sportsman of the days when he could beat every man in Ocean and adjoining counties at quoits. Then he invites all hands up to the bar. "Drink hearty, gentlemen! Drink hearty!" he says briskly, and tosses off three fingers of rye, after which he and his friends retire with the landlord. The next morning, at breakfast, the landlord and the ex-sheriff's two friends can hardly hold up their heads; he has long ago hitched up and is well on the road to Tom's River.

It may be judged from this brief sketch that life along Barnegat Bay is quite different from that at the resorts north of Bay Head. There the visitors do not mingle with the natives. But along Barnegat Bay one is brought into quite different relations with them. You feel like knowing more of the man who brings down his red-head every time, who knows every fishing ground, and who can steer his yacht unerringly through all the channels, thoroughfares and "slews," and an "entente cordiale," such as exists between the Adirondack hunter and his guide, is soon established between the sportsman on Barnegat Bay and his boatman or gunner.

— by Gustave Kobbe, from* Jersey Coast and Pines, *1889

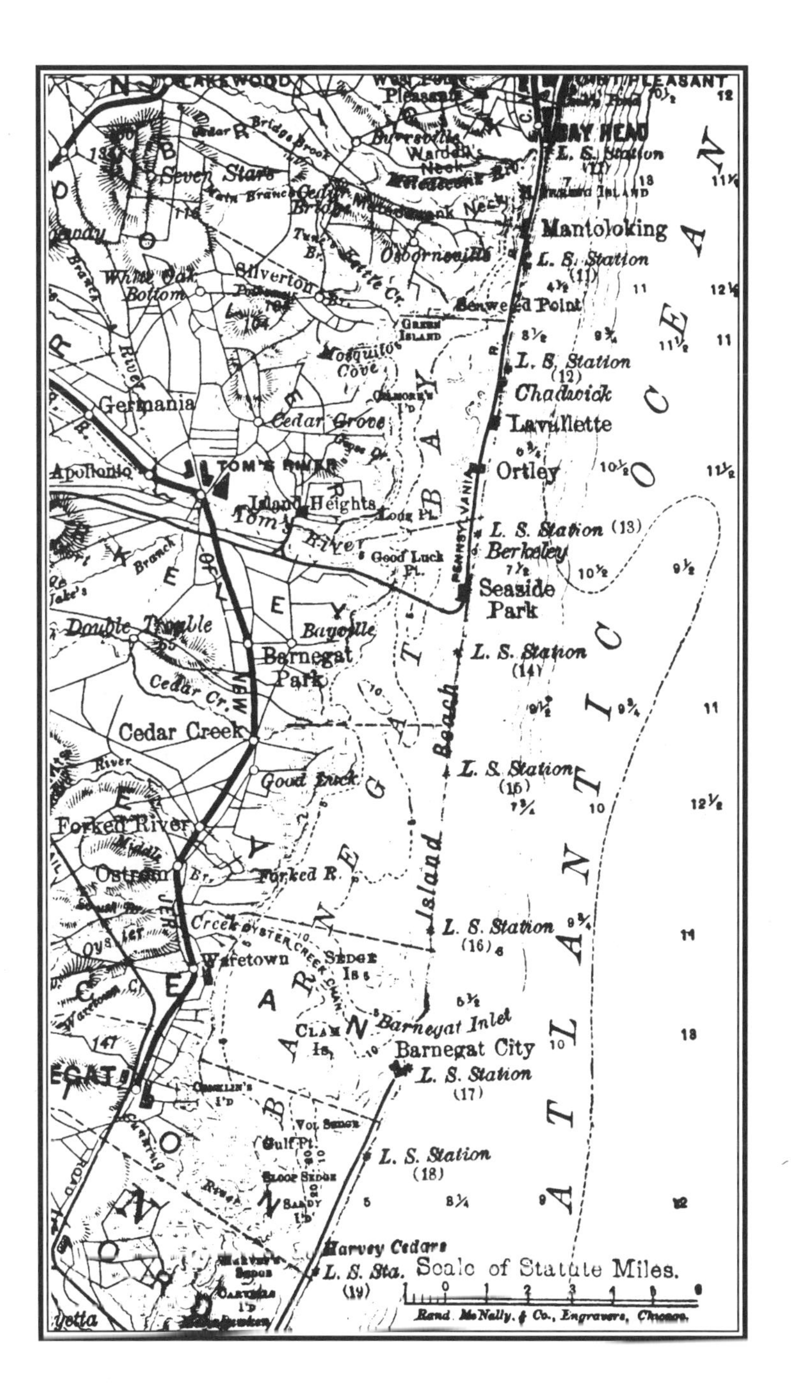

A map of Life Saving Stations on the Barnegat Coast.
(Map from* Jersey Coast and Pines, *1889)

A Night With The Life Saving Service

Patrolling the beach, a volunteer lifesaver spots the ship's distress rockets and signals the crew with a flare. ***(Print from* Harper's, *1878)***

Suppose it is a December night. It is sure to be cold. From the last of the equinoctials until the westward-bound steamers from England begin to make good voyages again, there is no warmth to speak of along the Jersey shore. Let us suppose too that it is dark and blustering, so that we may feel with full poignancy what a surfman's experiences sometimes are.

A big fire is blazing in the living-room of the station, and four of the men, with the keeper, are taking their ease around it, or lying in their bunks, while the two others are putting on their coats and mufflers, and looking longingly toward the hearth. The latter are going out on patrol, and as they are human, they delay as much as possible, re-adjusting their dress, pressing their pilot caps over their heads, pulling their gloves farther on, and giving their neck-cloths a final twitch. The duty is inexorable, and with a last regretful look at the fire, they shiveringly plunge into the outer night.

The wind is full of needle-points, and cuts them like a knife, and the darkness blinds them for a few moments, and extends in every direction, except around their feet, over which their lanterns cast a ring of white light, and in the window of the house, which glows with warmth. Above the moaning of the air is the loud beat of the sea, as the waves break on the shore and recede with sibilant sound; and the spray is lifted and driven inshore by the wind in feathering streaks.

Patrolling the Shore

The two patrolmen say "good-night," and separate; one looks back to see the lantern of the other swinging to and fro on the sands, and decreasing in brilliancy until it is altogether lost behind a projecting bluff, and he feels absolutely alone amid an unreal silence that would not be as awful were the waves and wind completely still.

The stars are remote and merciless in their crystalline splendor, seeming to be fixed in that black firmament only to show how distant a thing heaven is; and the sea — it is invisible; where the waves rush up the beach and leave a glazed surface on the sand, a few diamond points reflect the stars, and beyond these an impenetrable wall is built upward; there is no sea at all; but watching more closely, the patrolman discovers a vibrant cord of white, rhythmical in motion, like a taut string that is depressed near the middle and suddenly released, and that cord he knows to be, though he cannot see, the frothing crest of the successive waves.

The walk would have many terrors for a nervous or superstitious man, or for almost anyone of sensitive organization, and the patrolman is superstitious; but he is so familiar with the darkness, the loneliness, and the roar that he treads along the beach in a reverie — not a reverie of the deep secrets over which Nature is brooding, but so prosaic a matter as the care of a small family who are now asleep on the main-land — until he fancies he discovers a light fastened to the black wall. He stands still and looks again; it has disappeared. Before him, as he looks seaward, is that blackness, which seems so solid that one would expect a pebble thrown at it to rebound, and he resumes his march, thinking that his eyes have deceived him, or that the light has been a phosphorescent sparkle.

A Bark Close Inshore and in Extreme Peril

But there it is again! And now the first light, which has stood at the mast-head, is augmented by the flare of a rocket and the blue fire of a signal, which reveal a bark close inshore and in extreme peril.

According to his instructions, the patrolman instantly ignites his red light, which is done by striking the holder against his knee, that action exploding a percussion cap, and he is surrounded for several seconds by a flood of crimson so vivid and so vigorous that no wind or rain is strong enough to extinguish it. When the light expires, he hastens back to the station with the news, and that quiet outpost is suddenly put into as tumultuous a state as the storm outside. The life-boat is placed on a carriage, the carriage having very broad tires to its wheels, so that they can not sink in the loose sand, and the life-car, with other apparatus, is placed in another vehicle, both being drawn to the point nearest the wreck, where efforts are made to obtain communications with it.

Throwing a Life Line

There are three possible means of communication — by the life-boat, the life-car, and the life-raft. The first two are at use at all stations, and the last has been adopted at a few, but it is only under very favorable circumstances, or in extremities, that the boat is used. A line is thrown over the wreck either by a rocket or a mortar and shell, several efforts being made before success is attained, and the first line is attached to a stronger one that is secured to a mast of the vessel and to the shore.

Launching the Life-Car

The life car is suspended from the line and hauled on board the distressed ship; three or four persons are put inside it, and it is hauled back again, repeating the journey until all are safely landed. But the work is much easier in the description than in the performance. If the wind is blowing on shore, rocket after rocket flies on its meteorlike course through the tempest, falling miserably short, or being carried too far astern or ahead by the wind; sometimes the rocket fails altogether, and the boat or life-raft is the only resource left.

The life-car resembles a covered boat with a few air-holes in the top, the perforations having raised edges to prevent the water from entering, and a ring at each end, with a hawser attached, enables it to be drawn through the surf. The "boatswain's chair" and the "breeches buoy" are similar, though older and less efficious, devices.

The former is a simple loop of rope hung from a taut stout hawser that extends from the stranded vessel to the beach, and in the loop a person sits and is pulled ashore. The latter consists of a common circular life-preserver, made of cork, with short canvas breeches attached, through which a man thrusts his legs, and, thus suspended, is drawn ashore, as in a chair. Both of these expose the passenger to the fury of the waves, and in the case of women and children, they are not suitable on this account, while the life-car lands its occupants without wetting or exhausting them, unless it capsizes, in which extremity it is liable to prove fatal.

Having seen the signal-man's red light burning, the crew of the wrecked ship utter a glad cry of deliverance, and wait for the brilliant spurt of the rocket bearing the line to them — wait until the synonym of the word seems to be life-long agony. The ship lies heavily to the leeward, and grinds deeper into the sand as each sea strikes her and breaks over her decks, tearing away the houses and knocking the men off their feet. The sails hang loosely and in pitiable shreds from the yards, and the masts bend unwillingly in the fiercer blasts, and threaten to spring.

A Cheer in the Wind

The shore is invisible, but the thunder of the breakers tells the men that it is near; and presently a fire is lighted on the beach, which fitfully shows the dreary background of sand hills. A rocket is fired, and both those on shore and those on the ship watch it unfold its train of sparks; the wind sweeps it aside, and hopes go out like scintillations; another follows, and the breaths of all the watchers are held until it is seen to fall over the deck of the ship, when they are released in a cheer that the violent ill nature of the wind can not quell.

— *from* **Harper's New Monthly Magazine,** *1878*

Among the Wreckers: The U.S. Life Saving Service comes to the aid of shipwreck victims near Barnegat Lighthouse.
(Engraving by Granville Perkins from* Harper's Weekly, *June 25, 1868, from the collection of the author)

Shipwreck of the packet ship *Cornelius Grinnell*, on Squan Beach, February 14, 1853. A fine vessel of twelve hundred tons burthen, she was built at Boston in 1850. All 270 passengers were safely landed. ***(1853 engraving from*** **The Flag of Our Union,** ***courtesy of Dick Updike)***

Heroism Rewarded

The George Taulane Wreck

One of the most gallant rescues ever made by the United States Life Saving Service was fittingly commemorated at Tom's River on Thursday of last week, by the presentation of United States life saving medals of the first class.

On the afternoon of February 3, 1880, the men of stations 11 and 12 were alarmed by signal guns seaward. It was a bitter day, the sleet driving before an easterly gale so thickly that it was only by covering their heads with thick woolen mufflers that the men could face it. The apparatus was got out in readiness and then all hands strained their eyes seaward to catch a glimpse of the vessel.

At last through a break in the driving sleet they caught sight of a schooner with a rag of her forestaysail set, trying in vain to beat off the ice shore, whose breakers were even then close aboard her. She was too far out for the short lines to reach her, so the men of both stations joined forces, and a number of volunteers coming to their assistance they dragged the heavy apparatus over the sand dunes and through the inlets on the beach, taking advantage of every opportunity to throw a shot at her.

Several times the vessel struck, but the fierce gale drove her on again, and it was not until she had bumped along shore for three miles that the line could be got aboard of her. Within half an hour thereafter the crew of five men were landed, and the vessel soon went to pieces. Lieutenant W. C. De Hart, Assistant Inspector of the Fourth Life Saving District, reported the facts to Washington, and the men's conduct was thought worthy of the highest honors which the nation bestows for such heroic deeds.

On Tuesday, Lieutenant De Hart received the medals, eighteen in number, from S. I. Kimball, General Superintendent of the U.S. Life Saving Service, and Thursday he presented them to the men, in presence of a large number of spectators, accompanying each presentation with a few words expressive of his own appreciation of their gallantry.

The recipients are Keeper Lewis Truex of Station 11; Keeper William P. Chadwick, of Station 12; and Charles Seaman, Tyler C. Pearce, William Van Note, John Fleming, Benjamin Truex, Peter Sutfin, William H. Brower, Abram J. Jones, Demarest T. Herbert, Charles W. Fleming, David B. Clayton, Abner S. Clayton, Isaac Osborn, William L. Chadwick, Abner Herbert and David B. Fisher. Some of these men are not members of the life saving crews, but volunteered on this occasion.

The medals are two inches in diameter, three-sixteenths of an inch thick and their coin value is $80 each. On the obverse is a design in relief representing three men in a surfboat rescuing a drowning man from the waves. Around the margin are the words, "Life Saving Medal of the First Class, United States of America." On the reverse the Goddess of Liberty is represented resting her hand upon a shield upon which is inscribed the recipient's name and a brief statement of the heroic deed. Over the shield an eagle is soaring and around it are an anchor, cable, capstan and other nautical emblems. Around the margin in raised letters is inscribed: "In Testimony of Heroic Deeds in Saving Life from the Perils of the Sea. Act of Congress, June 20, 1874."

— *from* The Manasquan Sea Side, *1881*

West Creek. *(Print from* **Harper's Monthly,** *1878, from the collection of the author)*

Following the Bay

Ship and boat building prospered around the bay area in the nineteenth century. Small yards were established on creeks and streams, from Metedeconk and Toms River down to Little Egg Harbor. Most of them were short-lived operations, surviving for only a few seasons. Others lasted for several generations. The yards smelled of tar and fish and wood smoke. Their gray, weathered sheds stood on the marshes for many years, surrounded by stray spars, tangled rigging, and piles of scrap lumber. A bewildering assortment of small boats and large vessels lay scattered about, in varying stages of construction or decay, up on blocks or in the water. Makeshift docks lined the shore, made up of random timbers, leaning this way and that, creaking with the tide.

The Barnegat Bay boatman was a distinct breed, known for his easy-going manner and characteristic gait as he wandered the yard, in no apparent hurry or direction. He would work on a job for a while, then stop to go searching for exactly the right piece of lumber or brass fitting. Along the way he'd swap a few yarns, help launch a few vessels, come up with exactly the right method for raising an impossibly tall mast in proper position, double-check the continuously perking coffeepot, and finish another job he'd neglected the week before. Somewhere along the way he'd trip over exactly the right piece of lumber, or a boxful of fittings would fall off a shelf, delivering the exact brass fitting. He worked long days, from dawn until dusk, and the pay left a lot to be desired. But somehow the smell of the lumber and the sound of the lapping water and the sails snapping on the breeze made it all seem worthwhile.

In the old days all you needed for a boatyard was a big circular saw, a lot of lumber, and a steam box. A few teams of oxen or horses made the hauling much lighter, and a blacksmith produced all the hardware. Ships and boats were built by hand, using rule-of-thumb methods. Plans were unknown. Usually someone whittled a small model and after much discussion the lines of the vessel were agreed on and the job began. More than two hundred ships were launched during the century, usually built of white oak, pine, mulberry, chestnut, and cedar. Even a few square-rigged brigs were produced. But the largest ship came out of Forked River in 1856: the one-hundred-foot *Lydia Cowperthwaite*, a three-masted schooner that required a crew of seven to operate. Some ships took two or more summers to complete.

Sloops, Schooners, and Bluefish

And for many summers the bay teemed with locally built rowboats, catboats, and garveys. Heavy scows floated near the marshlands, piled high with salt hay for market. "Following the bay" was a time-honored tradition. Local captains — men like John Lott Dorsett of Beaver Dam — were admired for their knowledge of the water and weather. Many captains hired out their sloops and schooners to visiting sportsmen who were eager for a taste of outdoor life — and bluefish.

During the last decades of the century, Barnegat shipbuilding went into steady decline. The clearing of the forests as more vessels and homes were built helped exhaust the source of timber. The tall cedars and pine that once characterized the Barnegat shore became a memory. Local marshes bloomed with cranberries as their cultivation became a major source of income for men, women, and children, who trudged through the swampy bogs carrying wooden cranberry scoops and buckets of sour red berries. Wildflowers and orchids blossomed all over, and songbirds filled the pines with their music.

The first steamboat toured Barnegat Bay in 1809, belching black smoke and attracting much attention as it churned down the coast and entered her shallow tidal waters. No one guessed they would soon begin replacing the sturdy sloops and schooners that were the backbone of the coastal trade.

Sailboat Racing

Barnegat Bay's long tradition of sailboat racing came about as a result of the federal blockade of Southern ports during the Civil War. Local captains, with time on their hands, began racing each other in catboats. Their stirring weekend races chased away the doldrums created by the distant war and raised local spirits on long hot summer afternoons. Enthusiastic crowds of natives and visitors gathered on the shore as fishermen, traders, lifesavers, and city yachtsmen engaged in rousing competition at the bang of the starting gun. Everyone cheered the battling crews when the swift catboats raced across the shallow blue bay past Herring Island, Seaweed Point, and Kettle Creek. Hovering fishhawks circled above, watching with sharp eyes.

The first regatta was held in 1864 on Toms River. The Challenge Cup — the oldest racing trophy in the country — was introduced six years later when the Toms River Yacht Club formed and hosted the first club race. In the 1880s sneak-box racing was first organized by Henry J. West, a summer cottager at Seaside Park. The sport became very popular and inspired the formation of yacht clubs at Mantoloking, Bay Head, Lavallette, and Seaside Park.

The Barnegat Sneak-Box

The Barnegat sneak-box was a local invention — first built by Captain Hazelton Seaman, of West Creek, in 1836. He called her the "Devil's Coffin" because her small cockpit was just large enough to conceal one gunner. Lying in a prone position, the gunner camouflaged himself with salt hay and could easily sneak up on an unsuspecting flock of ducks or geese.

Light and low decked, early sneak-boxes were propelled by oars or poles and had a sharp bow. Usually around twelve feet long, the small craft was perfectly suited for the shallow tidal waters of the bay. They even had thin oak strips attached to the bottom so they could be used as sleds when the bay froze over in winter. Basic provisions, as well as small sails, oars, guns, and ammunition, were stowed snugly under the hatch.

Other boat builders improved on the original design, particularly John Crammer and Samuel Perine who perfected sails for the short mast. Nathaniel Bishop of Toms River sailed the *Centennial Republic* from Pittsburgh to Florida, by way of the Ohio and Mississippi Rivers. He published an account of the unusual voyage in 1875 called *Four Months in a Sneak-Box*. His book created a new interest in the unusual small craft, and they became very popular with summer visitors.

A Center for Sneak-Box Building

Bay Head became a center for sneak-box building when Ben Hance opened his boatyard in 1874. Morton Johnson started his shop in the 1890s and produced countless vessels. Twenty-two years later, his son, Hubert Johnson, established another yard here, and Charles Hankins began building rugged surf boats down in Lavallette. Dave Beaton founded his long-lived boatyard on a small cove by West Mantoloking many years later. He watched in wonder when Louise Edgar Colie — who lived across the bay on the beach in Mantoloking — built her own sneak-box in his yard.

Eighteen-foot gaff-rigged models were introduced before the turn of the century, and were a common sight sailing and racing around the bay. Later versions included a seventeen-foot sneak-box in 1902, and a twenty-foot class, called Sandbaggers, which required a six-man crew. One of the fastest sneak-boxes was the sixteen-footer introduced in 1914, which was later improved by adding marconi rigs. But the favorite of all was the fifteen-foot gaff-rigged sneak-box built by J. Howard Perrine of Barnegat.

The Coming of the Railroad

The coming of the railroad in the 1880s brought about a complete transformation of the nature of commerce and transport. The steel rails of the Iron Horse opened up the seashore for the rapid development of summer resorts around Barnegat Bay.

The change opened up new possibilities and markets — and the pace of life quickened as the old way of life, based on the bay and the sea, looked westward and saw that times were changing.

The Flowering of Summer Resorts

The flowering of summer resorts along the seashore before and after the turn of the century attracted many notable and unusual people to the bay area. U. S. Grant, Horace Greeley, and Teddy Roosevelt visited the Chadwick House during the 1880s. Writers seemed drawn to the Point Pleasant area, including Robert Louis Stevenson, Francis Hodgson Burnett, and, years later, Eugene O'Neil. One of the most unusual visitors was Mme. Helena Petrovna Blavatsky, the Russian spiritualist whose interests in Buddhism, alchemy, and the occult led to the founding of the Theosophical Society. Mrs. Jesse James was a popular summer visitor in Lovelandtown in the 1890s.

Richard Harding Davis spent many summers here with his family. His brother, Charles Belmont Davis, wrote of their childhood during the 1870s in his book *Adventures and Letters of Richard Harding Davis*, which was published in 1917:

> *Point Pleasant was then a collection of half a dozen big farms, which stretched from the Manasquan River to the ocean, half a mile distant. Nothing could have been more primitive in the pastoral loveliness or much more beautiful. Just beyond our cottage the river ran its silent, lazy course to the sea. With the exception of several farm houses, its banks were unsullied by human habitation of any sort, and on either side beyond the low green banks lay fields of wheat and corn and dense groves of pine and oak and chestnut trees. Between us and the ocean were more waving fields of corn, broken by little clumps of trees, and beyond these damp Nile-green pasture meadows, and then salty marshes that led to the glistening white sand dunes, and the great semi-circle of foaming breakers, and the broad blue sea.*

As summer cottages and hotels spread throughout the area, local "pineys" and "clamdiggers" witnessed a growing invasion of "city slickers" sweep down in the

Setting Decoys: In the old days, countless gunners roamed around the coves down the bay, on the water in catboats or sneak-boxes, or behind duck blinds near the shore. ***(Engraving from*** **Appleton's Journal*****, March 2, 1872, from the collection of the author)***

spring and depart in the fall. The New York and Philadelphia press forgot all about the Barnegat Bay Pirates and frequently sent journeymen correspondents to cover the fashionable watering places, as they were called, on the Jersey Shore.

These feature writers usually travelled by train and stagecoach to visit the gunning lodges and farmhouses that took on boarders in season. Their colorful, highly descriptive narratives of travels around the bay area appeared in a variety of publications during the 1870s and 1880s, including *Appleton's Journal*, *Frank Leslie's Illustrated News*, and *Harper's New Monthly Magazine*. The correspondents were often accompanied by staff artists such as Granville Perkins, whose sketches and drawings were transformed into steel engravings to illustrate the articles. These engravings usually focused on sailing, fishing, and gunning, and they provide a vivid glimpse of everyday life in the villages surrounding Barnegat Bay. Many of these pictures are reproduced in this volume.

Artists of the Seashore

Other artists also visited and lived around the area during this time, attracted by the natural beauty of the seashore and the solitude of the dunes. G. M. McCord, a New York City artist, lived in a shack along the deserted beach front of Mantoloking during the 1870s. His seascapes were highly regarded and included in the American Museum of Art collection. A. B. Frost was another major artist of the period, known for his realistic paintings of Barnegat

Barnegat Fisherman. *(Engraving from* **Frank Leslie's Illustrated News,** *1868, from the collection of the author)*

"The Bluffs" on the boardwalk at Bay Head — one of the first summer resort hotels.
(Sketch by E.J. Meeker, circa 1900, courtesy Mr. and Mrs. Alfred Johnson.)

marshes and beaches. Miss Lisa Downer, of Mantoloking, was a talented amateur who painted haunting watercolors of the bay in the 1890s.

Gerard R. Hardenbergh

One of the finest and least known local artists was Gerard R. Hardenbergh, who was born in New Brunswick in 1856 and studied at the Pennsylvania Academy of Fine Arts during the late 1880s. He lived in Ortley Beach during the early 1890s and later, in 1900, moved into a houseboat — which he called the *Pelican* — moored on Scow Ditch, near the Bay Head Yacht Club. For many years he lived by himself and wandered all over the bay area, painting the wild beauty of the creeks and salt marsh and sand dunes. He was a soft-spoken, wiry character with long white hair, and he was fond of wearing unfashionably old-fashioned clothing. Hardenbergh supported himself by trading his paintings for groceries and basic necessities. He was very popular with local children who often gathered around his battered easel to watch him at work.

Hardenbergh was an authority on birdlife, and some of his paintings of quail and marsh hens were reproduced in a limited series of color lithographs. His interest in local wildlife even extended to insects. One of his most unusual works is a study of three grasshoppers communing under towering stalks of beach grass. The picture features an attention to detail and sense of grace comparable to the finest Japanese painting.

But he is best remembered for his watercolors of seascapes and landscapes that delicately capture the subtle hues of Barnegat Bay sunrises and sunsets in pastel-like blue, gold, and pale green. Hardenbergh's classic turn-of-the-century views of Beaver Dam, Bay Head, Mantoloking, and Chadwick Beach, offer a clear vision of Barnegat Bay's natural beauty.

Hardenbergh married at the age of 49 in 1906, and painted very little after that. He died in Bay Head in 1915. Several of his paintings, perhaps more than fifty, have survived, but are rarely on public display. Some of them are included in the National Collection of Fine Art in Washington, D.C. Most of his surviving

Snipe shooting on Barnegat Bay. *(Illustration by A.B. Frost, circa 1906, from the collection of the author)*

watercolors are in private hands, treasured heirlooms of longtime Barnegat Bay families. A selection of these paintings is published for the first time in this book.

The Photographic Record

Photography rapidly grew from a cult-like alchemical art to a popular interest during the late nineteenth century, but during this period having your picture taken was still regarded with awe as a magical act that defied time and mortality. Sitting for a portrait was a serious matter that required a suitably somber expression as the subject contemplated the mystery of eternity. Not very many photographers wasted time or film attempting to document everyday life or local scenery.

One photographer who did pay attention to the outside world was Addison W. Bronson of Bay Head, who made a remarkable photographic record of local scenes during the 1890s and early 1900s. Bronson's eye captured the details of life along the seashore during those years of rapid change and development. His views of old farmsteads, salty old-timers, and coastal schooners passing offshore have a unique and timeless quality.

Some of his fine photographs, along with others taken by Slade Dale and amateur photographers over the years, appear in this book, selected from old family albums and private collections. These pictures offer an authentic view of the old days around Barnegat Bay — like peering through windows to a vanished era where the faces of the past gaze back at us through the looking glass of time.

Ducks, Geese, and Shore Birds

For thousands of years, great flocks of wild waterfowl filled the air in winter and nested in the marshlands around the bay in summer. When the head waters were still brackish — before the inland passage of the Point Pleasant canal connected the Manasquan River to Barnegat Bay and made the seacoast peninsula actually an island — nearly every species of bird could be found. Wild celery flourished along the marshes, and redheads and canvasback were common. Scaup, black duck, brant, yellowlegs, snipe, pheasant, and Canada geese thrived.

From the early days, baymen took to the sedges and streams. Musket fire echoed across the waters throughout the year. The fowling piece was an East Coast tradition dating back to the development of the muzzleloading double-barreled shotgun around 1800. These guns were sometimes six feet long and, using black powder and homemade shot, they required remarkable skill for wing shooting. The percussion cap models gave way to the hammer breech-loader in 1855, and the hammerless shotgun appeared in 1871.

Gunning on the Bay

In the old days, countless gunners roamed around the coves down the bay, on the water in their sneak-boxes or behind duck blinds near the shore. Duck blinds, made of reeds, salt hay, seaweed, tree branches, and scrap lumber, were designed to blend in with the background. Hunters built them six to ten feet offshore, facing out on the open water.

They usually arranged a large group of decoys in front of the blind, with a long string of them stretching out a few hundred yards to lead the birds in. Gunners often used "tollers" — live tame ducks or geese mingled among the wooden decoys — to lure down incoming flocks of wild waterfowl. Tollers who proved to be shy or uncooperative frequently ended up on the dinner table. Baiting the marsh or ice with corn or other feed commonly was practiced.

The old-time gunners were hardy characters, happy to lie still for several hours in cramped positions, indifferent to the cold and damp, waiting for precisely the right moment to call the first shot as a wavy line of black heads or a V of canvasback swung into the wind. Game was so plentiful that many local gunners made a good living guiding small parties of wealthy sportsmen. Others became full-time hunters for the city markets, and often fired five hundred shells a day.

The Market Hunters

These market hunters developed murderous methods for maximizing their kills. One of them was the battery gun, an array of five guns like outstretched fingers. Mounted on the bow of a skiff equipped with a kerosene lantern, they were generally used for night hunting. Shooting from behind a blinding light, birds were often slaughtered wholesale, or, "like sitting ducks." Another method was the use of the sink box, a square wood and canvas platform that was submerged to water level and camouflaged. The use of battery guns and sink boxes proved so lethal they were outlawed in New Jersey in 1879.

The ultimate weapon in the market hunter's arsenal was the punt gun, a homemade cannon-like device twelve feet long, often weighing more than one hundred pounds. It was fashioned by mounting a ten-foot section of seamless high-pressure steam pipe, with a two-inch bore, on a rough-hewn walnut stock. The punt gun was deadly at a range of fifty yards. As many as ten geese or thirty ducks could be killed by a single, well-aimed shot at a sitting flock. Using these guns, market hunters often had daily quotas of thirty-five geese and one hundred ducks.

An old-time Canada goose decoy

Punt guns were usually set in a skiff with the barrel pointing out over the bow, and the stock cushioned by several bags of oats to absorb the powerful recoil when the gun was fired. Over-charged guns frequently exploded, maiming or killing the hunter. The booming echo of these big guns rumbled through the pines late at night after the turn of the century around Metedeconk, Silverton, and Oyster Creek.

The wholesale slaughter of wild waterfowl became even more severe as a result of the development of the Browning automatic shotgun in 1900, and even larger kills became possible. The waterfowl flocks of Barnegat Bay were decimated in the following years. Finally, in 1918, the Federal Fish and Wildlife Service outlawed the use of big guns in this country, and, along with state agencies, established game limits and restrictions on hunting.

Barnegat Bay Decoys

The quaint wooden decoys that old-time gunners used are their greatest legacy. Hand carved and oddly evocative, these decoys are treasured relics long admired for their smooth and flowing lines. While local shorebird decoys, such as snipe, heron, and sandpiper, were whittled from solid wood, dugout duck decoys were generally made from two hollowed-out sections of Jersey white cedar. Barnegat decoys are noted for their lack of wing carving and their gently tapered tails. Generally round and hollow, they were weighted with lead for proper buoyancy and feature meticulous head carving and natural-looking plumage.

Decoy making was a popular pastime between seasons for those who followed the bay. Although there were talented individuals who were masters of the craft — such as Henry Shourdes of Tuckerton — making decoys was often a joint effort, with some natives skilled in carving heads while others specialized in decoy painting.

Fortunately, many decoys created by old-time baymen have survived the rigors of shot and time. Among the finest were those made by Ben Hance and Taylor Johnson, of Bay Head; Ezra Hankins and the Birdsalls, of Point Pleasant; the Lovelands, of Lovelandtown; Will Hall, of West Mantoloking; Tom Gaskill, of Toms River; and the Grant, Soper, and Kilpatrick decoys, of Barnegat. Their life-like ducks, geese, and shorebirds continue to captivate the eye with natural, muted colors and timeless simplicity. Barnegat Bay decoys are New Jersey's contribution to an authentic American folk art, dating back to the feathered mud-and-reed lures of the Lenape. Later generations carry on the tradition of carving wooden decoys by hand, as well as gunning and fishing and sailing the bay.

ALL THE

SUMMER RESORTS

ON THE

NEW JERSEY COAST

ARE REACHED

VIA THE PENNSYLVANIA R.R.

OR THE WEST JERSEY R.R.

THE MOST PROMINENT ARE:

Atlantic City, Asbury Park, Atlanticville, Absecon, Anglesea, Barnegat, Beach Haven, Brighton, Beasley's Point, Cape May, Cape May Point, Deal Beach, Elberon, Forked River, Highlands, Island Heights, Long Branch, Lavalette City, Monmouth Beach, Manasquan, Manahawkin, New Branch, Ocean Grove, Ocean Beach, Ocean City, Point Pleasant, Port Republic, Pleasantville, Spring Lake, Sea Girt, Sea Side Park, Sandy Hook, Sea Bright. Sea Plain, Somers' Point, Sea Isle City, Seaville, Sewell's Point, Tom's River, Tuckerton, West End, Waretown, West Creek,

Travelers via these Lines enjoy ALL THE COMFORTS KNOWN TO MODERN RAILWAY SCIENCE.

Splendid Passenger Equipment. Perfect Road-bed. All Known Safety Applianccs.

Steel Rails. **NO DUST.** Stone Ballast.

Pennsylvania Railroad Stations in New York: Courtlandt Street Ferry and Desbrosses Street Ferry. Brooklyn. Brooklyn Annex Station, Foot of Fulton Street. Philadelphia: 32d and Market Sts.; Front and Berks Sts.; Germantown Junction; West Jersey Railroad Station, Foot of Market St.

FRANK THOMSON, General Manager. L. P. FARMER, General Passenger Agent.

The coming of the railroad in the 1880s brought about a complete transformation of the Jersey Shore. ***(Print, circa 1882, courtesy of George Williams)***

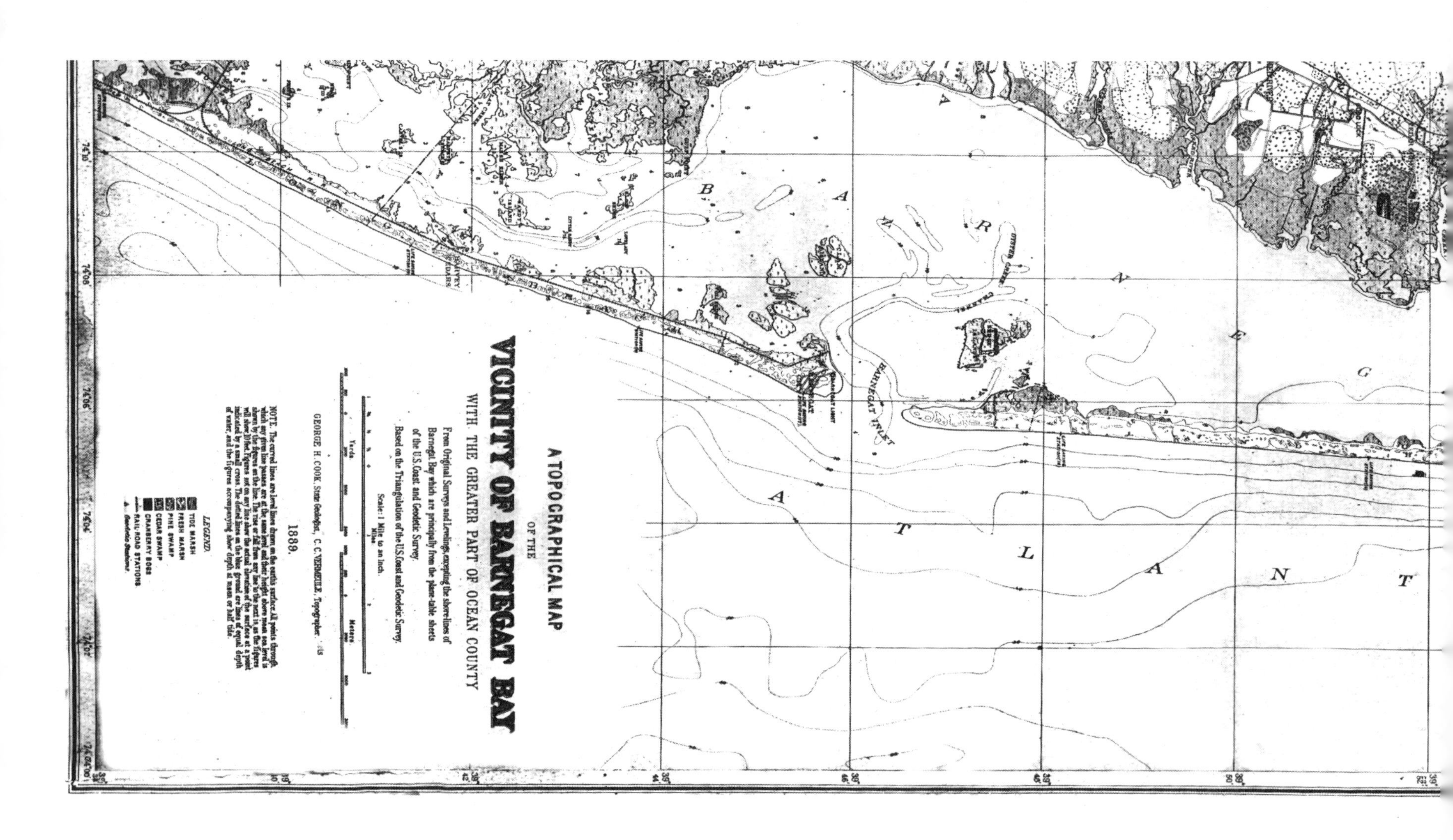

The Vicinity of Barnegat Bay, 1889. ***(Map courtesy of Jerry Woolley)***

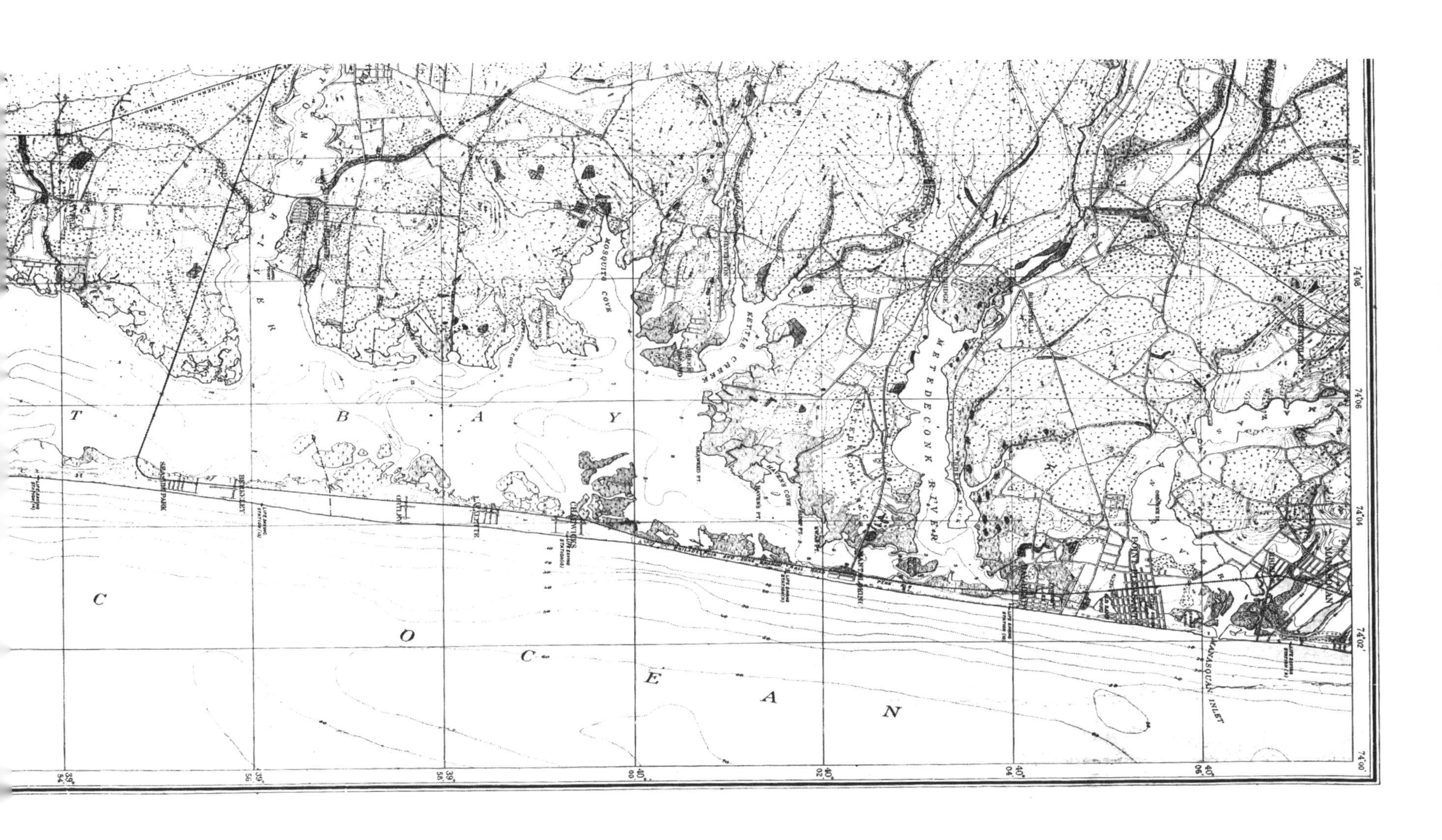
B A Y
C O C E A N
MOSQUITO COVE
KETTLE CREEK
METEDECONK RIVER
MANASQUAN INLET

Salt Water Day

Let's head for the beach,
let's get away,
let's celebrate summer
before it's too late!

Salt Water Day,
let the old fiddler play,
let's dance and be merry
on Salt Water Day!

Let's have a clam-bake
like the Indians did,
let's catch crab and stripers,
let's bring all the kids!

On the golden beach,
by the deep blue sea,
where the gulls fly free,
we want to be!

Let's sail on the breeze,
let's roll in the hay,
let's watch the sun set
down on Barnegat Bay!

Salt Water Day,
let the old fiddler play,
the sweet summer song
of Salt Water Day!

Salt Water Day: Families came in droves from the farms and villages on the mainland for the annual mid-summer celebration.
(Engraving by E. W. Kemble from* Harper's Weekly, *August 13, 1887, from the collection of the author)

The Barnegat Hotel
A Tavern by the Sea

It was near the evening of a fine spring day when our young officer and his aged mother found themselves at a hotel, overlooking the sea, in a most wild and picturesque portion of New Jersey. The house was a low, old fashioned red building, covering considerable ground; and was very comfortably filled up for a country establishment of the period; but there was one peculiarity about it which could not fail to strike a stranger with surprise.

The furniture and appendages seemed to have been gathered from the four quarters of the globe, and with a very small reference to propriety of fitness. Broken masts and spars, ropes and torn sails, anchors and pieces of ordnance, lay scattered around; and a marble figure of Apollo, of respectable workmanship, kept guard over a water-trough in the courtyard.

Within, the contrast was equally remarkable. Rich sofas and chairs, Turkey carpets of disproportionate size to the floors they covered, and spread about without order; pier-lasses, vases, marble tables, pictures, and damask curtains were mixed in with wooden benches, deal stools and tables, and other rustic furniture.

This incongruity at once attracted the notice of our travelers, came to the conclusion that many of the articles in question had been rescued from the deep; and that each, could it speak, might tell a story involving something beyond insensible matter — a tale of human vicissitudes and sorrow.

After supper, Mistress Warwick and her son walked out upon the hills overlooking the ocean. The verdure of the region seemed principally confined to the acclivity occupied by the hotel. There was a background of stunted trees and distant hills, interspersed with occasional cleared patches and mean huts.

In front, at the first of a ragged line of cliffs, was a broken beach, and the interminable and deceptive sea, which sufficiently indicated the dangers of the coast. To the right, the shore curved inland; and in the distance, as far as the eye could reach, presented to the view a sandy plain slightly varied by elevations, and devoid of vegetation, save an occasional shrub oak or yellow pine.

The history of that coast has long been written in storms and human disasters. Now, however, it was at the close of a calm day; the gulls floated in the air, and fearlessly dropped down and dipped their white breasts in the measured waves, as they rolled in ceaseless succession against the shore.

— *from* **Camp Fires of the Red Men** *or*
A Hundred Years Ago, ***by J.R. Orton.***
(J. C. Derby, Publisher, New York, 1855)

Seaweed on the shore of Barnegat Bay.

The wilderness beach meets Barnegat Bay.

On Board Captain Dorsett's Schooner

Barnegat Bay extends from Bay Head away down on the face of New Jersey. It is long and shallow, and there is only a narrow strip of land between it and the great Atlantic. Its channels are tortuous and its fishermen and sail-boat captains are a rather exclusive set, who pull up the channel stakes so that they can keep the knowledge of the water way out of the reach of amateurs.

But for all of this, they are a clever, good-hearted class of men, and "Captain John" Dorsett is about the best of them. They are not zealous, as a rule, to "go outside," and are, in fact, poorly equipped for ocean work, either as to experience or safety. So they come and go, about the bay, to and from the various fishing and shooting grounds.

Provisions for the Trip

To be well provided for such a trip, one ought to have a rough flannel shirt, a pair of old trousers, comfortable shoes, and a canvas hat. He ought to be free from prejudice and predilections in regard to his personal appearance, and the redder his nose burns, and the browner his hands grow, and the more fish he catches, or birds he kills, the better is he to be esteemed. A rubber overcoat and an extra coat and heavy undershirt are quite essential additions to his comfort.

For ourselves, we have had delightful weather. I am writing on the cabin table while the party outside are catching fish. Fragments of conversation, principally touching the game laws, come drifting in through the open companionway, and the boat gently pitches at her anchor in the teeth of a northwest wind. We have had no sickness and no casualties.

The Boat and the Crew

I may as well describe the *Dorsett* more in detail. The *Dorsett* is comfortably arranged and carries a crew of three — Captain John Dorsett, Johnny, his son, and Joseph Chessman, the cook. She is the largest vessel on the Bay, and measures about twenty-five tons burden, being forty-five feet from stem to stern and over fourteen feet beam. She is owned by parties in Point Pleasant and Philadelphia, and being fitted for this especial service she has accommodations and conveniences beyond those of any other craft.

Her cabin is just high enough for a moderately tall person to hit the deck-beams once or twice a day. These and the main boom have suffered several contusions, to which all hands, including "Captain John," have contributed their share. The cabin is also supplied with other modern improvements which make life on board not altogether a torment.

The humors of such a congenial party are numerous and amusing. The meals always commence with the proper blessing, and then follows a chorus "Where's seven?" "Who's got two?" "Here's three," until the napkin rings are well distributed. They never come to the right plate to begin with, and these clearing-house performances are both necessary and comical.

Then, there's another feature of the fun, which consists in the gradual absorbtion of the Uncle Remus nomenclature. The law firm of Whitehead & Gallagher is metamorphosed into the partnership of Brer Wolf and Brer Fox. The managing editor of this journal has demonstrated his staying powers and persistence in fishing sufficiently to be styled Brer Tarrypin. Brer Bar is the Philadelphia member of the party. It is Brer Rabbit who pens these lines.

The Fish of the Bay

The fish to be had in the bay are of several sorts, as might easily be supposed. Weak-fish seem to be the principal attraction and shrimp is the natural bait, though crab is often used. Our party have taken some that were very large and fine, and Joe has cooked them for us in a way to let us enjoy them before their novelty and freshness was gone. We had sea bass and porgies that went on the table this morning within half an hour of their being caught. These sea bass are to my taste — and I think I could get a unanimous endorsement of that opinion — the best of all our catch, except perhaps the "debbies" sometimes called "Cape May goodies," which have a most delicious flavor, and are known by the dark spot on each side of the head.

For these and for sand porgies, and for sea bass, the bait is clam. You drop your hook to the bottom and then fish not more than a foot above it for all these varieties. We have contrived to eat what we took in, except once or twice, when we gave away a large catch to those who made a business of what is our pleasure. We can safely assert that we have not wantonly wasted and destroyed.

Launched on the Fourth of July, 1883, this schooner was originally named after her builder and captain, John Lott Dorsett, of Beaver Dam, Point Pleasant. She was later renamed the *Rosamond* and sailed the bay for many years. *(Photograph circa 1895, courtesy of W.C.S.)*

The Favorite Old Schooner Yacht.

The favorite old Schooner Yacht, sailed by Captain J. L. Dorsett, is again in commission this summer and can accommodate some of his patrons. To all who know her, a description is unnecessary. **Her record is established.** To those who never enjoyed an outing on her this will suffice. She is forty-six feet long, fourteen feet four inches wide; has sleeping and table room for eight passengers, with spring beds and clean linen. Carries a first class cook. Supplied with the best food the market affords.

Three dollars a day each for a party of five or over; includes all expenses except bait for fishing. Special accommodations for ladies.

For particulars address

JOHN L. DORSETT,
Point Pleasant, New Jersey.

"The Captain, straight as an arrow, old fashioned yet keenly alive to the doings of the outer world, is in full harmony with his surroundings. A lover of antiquities; a hoarder of relics of by gone days." —*from* The Manasquan Sea Side, *1888. (Photograph circa 1895, courtesy of A.J.)*

Captain Dorsett by his back porch with the figurehead from the shipwrecked *Duke of Argyle*. (Photograph, circa 1908, courtesy of Arthur J. Birdsall)

When your hook is at the bottom and you are waiting for the quick snatch of the weak-fish or the gobbling tug of the bass, here comes a gentle, tentative nibble, then a grappling pull, and now this is Sir John Crab who appears reluctant at the surface, clasped around the bait, and is dragged out with a landing net. Arrived on board he sides savagely into a corner, and nips at any one who stirs him up.

Or perhaps you have a queer, odd sort of jerk, and this is now a toad-fish, a nasty, bulbous little beast who is so vicious among his subaqueous neighbors that he is summarily executed and then tossed overboard. Or it may be that here comes a "bloater," and then we have a trifle of amusement. He has a white belly and a dark, spotted back. His eyes are changeable from a brown to a green, and his face is really a face, and comically human.

Tipped over, and his stomach scratched, he becomes indignant and works his inside arrangements until he pumps himself full of air, and is as round as a ball and as rough as a hedgehog. This is probably his means of defense, and the amazed and pompous appearance of him when he is full enough to burst generally starts a laugh. Then he, too, is pitched over and floats for a second, when, with a sudden collapse, he sinks and flashes out of sight.

We have also caught the "black-fish," and the "gall," a somewhat similar but uneatable variety. By the way, while I was counting up my fish, I ought to have named the "sea-robin," a very peculiar small beast with two wings and several tentacles for fins. This fish emits a musical note, and is said — though not by any experienced person of the party — to be a first-rate article of diet. We generally let the pretty things go back into the sea.

Crabs, Oysters, and Clams

We are also becoming cognizant, but not very scientifically, of the variations followed by the crab in his brief career. We discover that he can be "hard" or "soft," or a "shedder" or a "comer," or that he may be apparent under other forms and fashions. But we dislike him, for he is very abundant and very troublesome.

The harvest of these waters also embraces oysters and clams — black and white — and you can see the clammers at work "treading" the sand, wet to their waists, in order to find them. When one is found, the right hand goes down and picks it up, and it is cast into a small, floating "car," which is drawn about by the left hand. It is a hard way to get a living, but not so tedious as that of the sheepshead fishermen, who sit in their "sneak boxes," or small gunning boats, and bait and fish and fish and bait all day long, and perhaps get one, and perhaps get none whatever. The hotels pay these men by the day, and take their catch, large or small, as an equivalent.

The Bones of Lost Ships

Barnegat Bar is a wild tumble of tossing waters. The inlet is the worst on the coast, and the shore is strewn with vestiges of wreck. We can see the boiler of the *Idaho*, still in mid-channel, where she went down. The last vestiges of the *Mediator*, a Southern vessel, lies on the North Point. Other ships have left their bones hereabouts, and "Captain John," who was in the wrecking service, spins us a good many yarns about his experiences of storm and tempest. We would ourselves have gone "outside," but the wind was against us, and the surf was so high on the bar that we could not well go about, and so fall off into the trough of the sea with any safety. As it was, we had a taste of the rollers, which showed us how a little more of the same would make a difference in the equilibrium of our stomachs.

Beating down the Bay, now to right and now to left, we at last reached "Harvey's Cedars," where we found Mr. Puffer and his family, and the Misses Beam, who reported life to be worth living, and whom we met just returning from the surf, looking picturesque. The Judge and I consequently went and had a bath, and a good one it was, and on a fine, hard, safe shore, but not so good as one on the North Beach.

Bathing in the Ocean

There we were away from everybody, and had no guide or clue to the coast which is constantly changing. So we joined hands, and waded in against a vast rush of breakers, which picked us up and pitched us down, and thumped and bumped and half-strangled us, filling us with their own vigor and sparkle, and making us glow with the fresh energy of their strength.

Here, too, we saw many shells, but of no great variety, and the work of the wind in carving the beach and sand hills. A thoughtful man can spend many a contemplative hour there, if the mosquitoes and green-headed flies will only let him alone. We, ourselves, have escaped nicely. The wind has been unfavorable for these pests, and our cabin is well protected by wire netting. But these coast-guards, who patrol every night from station to station, covering the three or four miles between the life-saving houses, must have a hard time of it!

The long line of telegraph poles which rises above the sand hills is a grim reminder of their duty and the United States Government ought to be both generous and intelligent — and intelligence here amounts, let me tell you, to generosity in their enrollment and support. They are a most valuable and little appreciated body of men. It is difficult for the uninitiated to derive from such a rude sketch as this the true picture of such out of door life.

The Wind Whistling in the Sails

When you sit with the wind whistling down upon you out of the hollows of the sails; when the distant coast stands green and lonely, only marked now and then by a house or a fishing village; when the white-caps come running along with lines of foam in their track; when you see the gulls and the snipe flying, and when the water at night sparkles with phosphorescence; when you sit aft, in the evening, chatting or smoking or singing; when you can doze or read, or talk, or amuse yourself otherwise as you choose, then, perhaps, this

Captain Dorsett, with his grandchildren, on the front porch.
(Photograph courtesy of Arthur Johnson)

The Dorsett House: "Nestled snugly among the pines in Ocean County, and standing back about 500 yards from Beaver Dam Creek, is one of those old fashioned houses whose cornerstone was laid sometime during the Revolutionary period. Its quaint look and utter loneliness cause the traveller to pause. There is something about the place that makes him forget about the present and wander into the past. . . ." ***(Photograph circa 1895, courtesy of George Morris)***

THE PLEASURE YACHT

"JOHN L. DORSETT,"

OFFERS extra facilities to Sportsmen for duckshooting on Barnegat Bay.

THE best shore gunners are in her service with extra sneak-boxes and plenty of decoyes.

AMPLE cabin room, spring beds, a well supplied table and all the comforts on a modern yacht.

SHE can be chartered on liberal terms, by addressing,

Captn. JOHN L. DORSETT.
POINT PLEASANT,
OCEAN COUNTY, N.J.

existence may assume a new advantage in the eyes of those who care for the breath of the salt air and that "contemplative man's recreation," angling. Nor is it an expensive luxury to enjoy, compared with some of those summer discomforts miscalled "watering places."

The puns and jokes of this present cruise are both numerous and frightful. It is to be hoped that we shall all survive these tortures of the English language to which our ears have listened. It is probable that a "burneder" set of men are not often to be met. And doubtless, long after this voyage is over, we shall bear in memory the frequent slogan which generally precedes a "new" departure, namely, this: "It's a long time between smokes," or "It's a short time between bites." But whatever may be the resolution, the preamble remains the same.

Questions from the Quarter-Deck

There now arises from the quarter-deck a demand to know what a fellow means by writing when he ought to be doing something else; what a fellow intends to do with what he writes; what a fellow proposes to give away to *The Citizen*, in the matter of personalities; in short, what, in the name of decency and fitness, ought to be done about it anyhow? So, to avoid heart-burning and bitterness, and to use again his favorite line and sinker, this scribe must conclude this story.

He would like to write up "Captain John's" tale of the stranded emigrant ship; he would like to refer particularly to Joe's chowder and Johnny's saturnine enjoyment of the casualties of life; but he must forbear. He has merely to add that Brer Tarrypin's catch of fish is complete, and a legal document is now made out in due form to authenticate it.

Our evening has ended with a most wonderfully beautiful sunset — the west kindled into amazing loveliness, and the water as smooth as glass. These sunsets are themselves among the rarest pleasures of the Bay.

P.S. — This letter has been read to the company around the cabin lamp, and has passed criticism, everybody standing out stoutly to retain whatever joke has been made on any one else!

— by S.W.D.

from* The Citizen, *1883

Point Pleasant, June 21, 1910 — Captain John Lott Dorsett, an aged waterman, poet, yacht designer and builder, and for many years Keeper in the Life Saving Service in the days of the volunteer crews, died last night at the Dorsett homestead, near Beaver Dam, on the outskirts of this resort. He was about 80 years of age.

Captain Dorsett was one of the best known men along the Jersey Coast. As a young man he lived on Squan Beach, about five miles south of Point Pleasant, and was Keeper of the Life Saving Station at that place, before the Government put in paid crews. After he left this service, he designed and built, as well as sailed, large pleasure craft.

Captain Dorsett was a man of cultured taste and wide reading. He was the author of a number of poems that had wide circulation, and had many friends in all walks of life, including not a few of prominence in the nation. His home at Beaver Dam was a museum of relics of the sea including figureheads, quarter and stern boards from wrecked vessels, and many curios from all over the world, as well as those picked up on the beach during his long life.

— *from* The New Jersey Courier

Her Eightieth Birthday

— poem by Captain John Lott Dorsett.

Lines written by John L. Dorsett on the meeting of his brothers and sisters to celebrate their mother's eightieth birthday, April 7th, 1889.

Once more again we all have met, around our mother dear;
Her children, five are all alive at this her eightieth year.
Though time has laid its hand on us our locks are turning grey —
Let us be children once again while we are here to-day.

Our childhood home and early life, by her protecting arm,
Was made secure from care and strife — it shielded us from harm;
With every cross we ran to her, no other voice could soothe
Our troubled minds or aching heads, or angry passions smoothe.

Let us remember how she worked, the family to supply —
She cooked our food and made our clothes which then she could not buy;
No clothing stores, with suits all made, could then be found near home,
But with her needle and her shears, and product of her loom

She spun the wool and wove the cloth, and cut and made by hand
With thread she also spun from flax (I'll have you understand),
The coats and pants and underclothes that all the family wore;
Our stockings, too, were knit by hand, and not bought at the store.

Her household cares were manifold — so many things to do,
That now are never done at home, but bought, and cheaply too;
She always made the family yeast, from hops grown on the place,
And boiled great kettles of soft soap in the open fire place.

The apples dried and gathered herbs, like sage and mint and thyme,
And, O, those doughnuts that she made at merry christmas time;
No one can tell the many things that she has found to do,
Words cannot make the picture plain or form an idea true,

Of what she had done in eighty years, those four score years of care,
Have left her hale and hearty yet: a blessing very rare;
Her mind is firm, her eye is bright, her hand is steady too —
Such fancy needle-work as her's, there's very few can do.

God bless our mother: may she live through many years to come,
All free from pain, and cares, and fears, within her happy home.

(Courtesy of Wayne Scholl)

Mrs. Chamberlain reading in her rocking chair at the Cook Farm, Point Pleasant.
(Photograph by Addison W. Bronson, circa 1895, courtesy of Arthur Johnson)

Mayor Aaron S. Pennington, fixing lunch in the kitchen of his Bay Head home. ***(Photograph, circa 1900, courtesy of William C. Schoettle)***

A summer day at the head of the bay around 1908. ***(Postcard from the author's collection.)***

Surf Fishing

Down I ran along the banks of the Manasquan until I came to its inlet. There, on coming to the beach, I found an excited, eager crowd of some thirty or forty boys and men running up and down it, and stopping every now and then to throw their line into the roiling surf, as yet, however, without success.

I stood on a sand-bank at the mouth of the Manasquan River and watched. Presently there was a loud shout from the opposite bank, and I saw them running. There was a strange sort of boiling appearance in the water, and then a whole host of small fish, moss-bunkers, flung themselves wildly on the sandy beach, flopped about thereon, gasped hysterically, and then, after a few more fruitless leaps, lay still, choked by the hot air and burning sun. The men and the boys were meanwhile swinging as fast as they could their squids, and sending them, some of the best throwers, fifty yards into the surf. No sooner did the squid touch and disappear beneath the water than they ran up the sand-hills, and lo! a large bluefish came leaping and tumbling out of the sea.

—*from* **Harper's New Monthly Magazine,** ***1868***

From the Manasquan River to Barnegat Inlet

The cove at Brielle on the Manasquan River. ***(Photograph, circa 1910, courtesy of Dick Updike)***

1900. ***(Postcard from the collection of the author)***

1900. ***(Postcard from the collection of the author)***

Squan Beach, 1897 — The road leading to Manasquan Inlet and the beachfront from Uncle Tommy Cook's Farm, Point Pleasant.
(Photograph by A.W.B., courtesy of A.J.)

Uncle Tommy Cook's Farm. ***(Photograph by A.W.B., courtesy of A.J.)***

The Birdsalls: Father Eugene Birdsall (top right) with his three sons: Arthur (bottom right), James (bottom left), and Edward (top left) in Lovelandtown. ***(Photograph, circa 1900, courtesy of Arthur J. Birdsall)***

Susan Johnson, Mrs. Van Note, and Charlotte Van Note, on the front porch at Dorsett Dock Road, Point Pleasant. ***(Photograph, circa 1890, courtesy of Mrs. E.K.)***

The railroad station at Point Pleasant Beach, looking south. *(Photograph, circa 1895, courtesy of Arthur Johnson)*

Thirty years after the conclusion of the Civil War, Ocean County veterans gathered at Clark's Landing in Point Pleasant to parade and pay tribute to fallen comrades at the nearby Methodist cemetery in Point Pleasant. Many local men between the ages of 12 to 45 were drafted or enlisted during the five-year-long conflict. The U.S. Navy recruited many baymen while others were assigned to the infantry with the Ninth, Fourteenth, and Twenty-Ninth New Jersey Volunteers, and some became horse soldiers with the First, Second, and Third New Jersey Cavalry Regiments. ***(Photograph, circa 1895, courtesy of George Morris)***

Ocean County soldiers saw bloody fighting at Cold Harbor, South Mountain, Spottsylvania, Rapidan, Brice's Cross Roads, and in Sherman's march through Alabama. As many as one out of four men died in combat or due to wounds and disease. On the local front, fortunes were made by shipbuilders and by masters of vessels with contracts to carry government cargo. ***(Photograph, circa 1895, courtesy of George Morris)***

Mrs. and Capt. John Loveland, of Lovelandtown.
(Photograph, circa 1900, courtesy of Mrs. Esther Kinsley)

Mr. and Mrs. Harry W. Hazard, of Bay Head, canoeing on Beaver Dam Creek.
(Photograph, circa 1895, courtesy of William C. Schoettle)

A sandy trail through the pines in the summertime. Such roads connected the early villages scattered along the shores of Barnegat Bay. ***(Photograph courtesy of Axel Carlson)***

A Man Who Has Cheated the Sea of Many Lives

The keeper of the life saving station at Bay Head is a fine example of the heroic skill possessed by those men along the Atlantic coast who annually save millions of dollars of property and hundreds of lives. He is a little above fifty years of age, iron-limbed, active, cool-headed, and with a knowledge of his duties which render his services beyond value.

David Fleming was one of those who, nearly forty years ago, stood on the snowy Squan Beach when the *John Minturn* was driven ashore, and who helped drag the dead bodies beyond reach of the roaring waves. He was then only a boy, but he was a boy extra-ordinarily active, and with a powerful skill in swimming or managing a boat in the surf. When I. C. Merriman, of New York, more than thirty years ago engaged seven men as a crew of wreckers from among the very best men he could find along the Jersey shore, young Fleming was one of the first selected. . . .

David Fleming has been keep of this station for eleven years and for three years previous to that he was a member of the crew. During his term as keeper he has taken off thirteen vessels without the loss of a life. The amount of property cannot be calculated. From September to May 1st. the beach is patrolled every night from a point three miles to the north to one and a half miles south, and during that time the fire in the station is never allowed to go out.

—*from* **The New York World,** *1885*

Down the Beach

Seashore

On the beach at Bay Head: Mr. and Mrs. Clarence Loveland with Mrs. Lee Loveland.
(Photograph courtesy of Mrs. Esther Kinsley)

The beachfront, 1895, looking south from Bay Head to Mantoloking. *(Photograph by A W B , courtesy of A.J.)*

A three-masted coastal schooner sailing past Squan Beach. *(Photograph by Addison W. Bronson, courtesy of Arthur Johnson)*

The schooner *Mark Grey*, 304 tons, built in Massachusetts in 1882. She wrecked off Seaside Park nineteen years later.
(Photograph, circa 1890, courtesy of the Mariner's Museum, Virginia)

An early Life Saving Station at Island Beach around 1890. Joseph Reed was the keeper.
(Photograph courtesy of I.B.S.P.)

At the wheel of the *Herbert Rawding* off the Jersey Shore. A four-masted cargo schooner, she was later lost at sea near the Azores. *(Photograph by F. Slade Dale, courtesy of John Van Horn Jr.)*

The wreck of the *Antioch*, Squan Beach, 1913. *(Postcard from the collection of the author)*

Opposite page: One of the largest sailing vessels to ever come ashore on the Jersey Coast, the *County of Edinburgh* stranded at Point Pleasant one-third of a mile south of Manasquan Inlet on the icy winter night of February 12, 1900. Sailing under Captain F. W. Tode, with a crew of twenty-nine, she was a four-masted square-rigged ship carrying 2,160 tons and valued at $100,000. Built in 1885, she was re-floated after her stranding and disappeared on the high seas thirteen years later. *(Photograph courtesy of the Mariner's Museum, Virginia)*

675
Ship "County of Edinburgh"
Stranded at Pt. Pleasant N.J. Feb.

The View from the Life Saving Station Tower

Taking leave of the Bluffs, I went straight to the U.S. Life Saving Station. To attempt to eulogize what the group of men who were housed here did, not only in the saving of lives under the most unimaginable weather conditions but for their long agonizing hours of patrolling the beach in storms almost beyond endurance, is an impossibility. Outside of these duties, to top it all off, they were Bay Head's first firefighters.

For this trip, the tower was my objective. Imagine how pleased I was when surfman Albert Forsyth offered to escort me. If only he could know how great he was going to be to me, on my many visits, when we would sit by the hour and he would talk about all those tales and anecdotes that were helpful when I was writing my book.

There is no one alive today who could possibly describe the view from that tower. It was breathtaking. Looking south, the strip looked so bare with the ocean on one side, Barnegat Bay on the other. The towns resembled mere specks as the distances between them were so great in 1903.

One could plainly see all the gunning ditches and, at the tip, Barnegat Light. To the southwest was the Metedeconk River, Parkers Neck, and the Beaver Dam with nary a farm or house in sight and, beyond the Mantoloking bridge, Haven's Cove, Kettle Creek, and Mosquito Cove. To the northwest was Twilight Lake and then, towards Point Pleasant, Maxons Pond, Little Silver Lake, Cooks Pond, the Manasquan River, and the inlet. Behind this whole western scene was nothing but heavily dense woods — and then in turning about, there was the great blue-green Atlantic Ocean!

While up there, I was most fortunate to see the Philadelphia train coming down the tracks. It is easy to see why the Pennsylvania Railroad, when they first opened this line in the summer of 1882, advertised with pride that this was one of the most scenic train trips in this country. Thanking Mr. Forsyth for his kindness, I departed . . .

— by William C. Schoettle

(Reprinted with kind permission of the author. Excerpted from "A Personal Memoir of a Magical Journey," an unpublished short story about a time travel visit to the Bay Head of 1903, written by Mr. Schoettle for family and friends in 1998. Schoettle is also the author of "Bay Head 1879–1911," and for many years he operated the Bay Head Book House. He currently resides in Williamsburg, Virginia.)

The Bay Head Life Saving Station, 1889. *(Photograph by A.W.B., courtesy of A.J. and W.C.S.)*

Lady in black on the beach at the fish pound as storm winds toss the sea.
(Photograph by Harry W. Hazard, circa 1892, courtesy of W.C.S.)

The six Fleming brothers of Point Pleasant: Top — John, Alfred, Joseph; bottom — James, David, and Charles.
(Photograph, 1916, courtesy of Nancy and Sean Fleming)

Henry Ware **surf fishing.**
(Photograph, circa 1900, courtesy of Anna Brower)

Late 1880s — at the Atlantic Avenue Pavilion, Point Pleasant Beach. *(Photograph by H.W.H., courtesy of W.[illegible] S.)*

Life at the Sea Shore

Point Pleasant is an old village, on the south side of Manasquan River, near the head of Barnegat Bay, and about one mile back from the beach. Between it and the head of the bay, and the beach and the river, has been laid out a resort in streets and lots. Several of the lots have been sold; and some cottages built. A hotel also has been erected, first class, accommodating 150 guests, and a horse railway laid between it and the beach. This region has long been frequented by strangers during the summer months. There is a fine carriage bridge across the river connecting it with Manasquan. Stages run over it between the depot, the hotel, and the head of the bay. The lack of a railroad until now has been a serious drawback to its prosperity. It is now supplied. There are several good hotels, or boarding houses. The principal are the: Arnold House; Curtis House; Falkenburg's; Maxon's; Osborn's; and the Resort House.

Bay Head. In 1879 a party of gentlemen, belonging to Princeton, purchased a considerable tract, on the sea at the head of Barnegat Bay, and gave it the above name. They at once built houses for themselves, and now invite others to join them. They adjoin Point Pleasant: and the facilities for reaching that place belong to them.

St. Elmo. This place is seven miles below the head of Barnegat Bay, on Squan Beach. A party of Princeton gentlemen were its originators. It has been laid out in broad streets, and lots 50 feet by 100 feet, running parallel with the sea and bay, and at right angles. The company also own an adjacent tract, on which are lots of larger size. The beach here is good, the sand firm, and the surf bathing fine. Excellent water abounds, and the place is very healthy. The adjacent waters of the bay, which is three miles wide here, afford rarest opportunity for boating, sailing, fishing, still water bathing, gathering ice for summer use, etc.; and so is an invaluable adjunct of a sea side resort. The company's lands adjoin Chadwick's, a famous, and long established, hostelry, especially for sportsmen; game, in its season, being very abundant.

Lavallette City. This place is immediately south of St. Elmo. Its characteristics are similar. The company own more land than does the St. Elmo. They have sold a great number of lots. A large fine hotel, fronting the sea, has been built upon the property. Cottages are being erected.

Seaside Park. This place is about one mile below Lavallette. It was the pioneer of sea side resorts, on this beach. Two large hotels, Seaside Park and Franklin, have been erected; which, ever since they have been finished, have been well filled with summer visitors. It lies about opposite the mouth of Toms River, and is a pleasant sail from Toms River village, the county seat of Ocean, or from Island Heights, a new and thriving summer resort, on the river two miles below. The distance from Toms River is about six miles. Connection is made at this village with Philadelphia and New York, by means of the New Jersey Southern, and Central, and Pennsylvania railroads. A steamer runs from the depot to the beach in summer time.

The above places, St. Elmo, Lavallette and Seaside Park, with some tracts between, owned by individuals; but who are in accord with the companies, contain some 1,500 acres, and a sea front of some five miles. Some day, they will form one large and popular, perhaps the most popular, of all cities by the sea.

Barnegat Bay, on the inside, raises these places above all others, for the purposes of a sea side resort. The bay is from two to five miles wide. Its length is almost thirty. It is the largest body of water, of its kind, in New Jersey. Fish, oysters, clams and game abound in it. The railroad being built will fully develop these places. Still, to those who have leisure for the purpose, a steamboat or yacht ride, across, or down, or up, the bay, as the case may be, is not to be deprecated — It is, indeed, one of the pleasant experiences of a trip to the shore that a sail is necessary or possible.

— by William C. Ulyat,
from **Life at the Sea Shore,** ***1880***

The Metedeconk Tribe No. 166, Improved Order of Red Men, meeting at the Arnold House in Point Pleasant in 1911. ***(Photograph courtesy Nancy and Sean Fleming)***

Sneakbox Racing

Racing the 20-foot sneakboxes has been the favorite, one might say, the typical Summer sport on Barnegat Bay of late years. These racing sneakboxes though evolved from the original gunning box, are of very different design. They are mostly extreme scows of light draught, and all cat-rigged. A few, however, are narrower and deeper, approaching more nearly the form of the ordinary catboat.

All important races are held under the auspices of the Barnegat Bay Yacht Racing Association, a federation of eight yacht clubs on the upper bay. Prizes are given to the first, second and third boat in each race by the club over whose course the race is held. In addition, the Association awards points, five to the first, three to the second, and one to the third boat, with a championship pennant at the end of the season to the boat winning the largest number of points. During the season just past, eleven men's races were sailed, the first on July 3d, the last on September 6th. A series of four ladies' races were also held, points and a championship pennant being awarded the same as for the men's races.

In the recent series, *Frolic*, of the Mantoloking Club, sailed by her owner, J. R. Such, captured first place, with 23 points; *Resolute*, of the Island Heights Club, sailed by Thompson Brooks, was a close second with 22; and *Picaroon*, of Mantoloking, S. J. Meeker, Jr., skipper, third with 14.

In the ladies' series *Frolic*, sailed by Mrs. Runyon Colie, was first with 13 points; *Goodnuff*, of Bay Head, sailed by Miss Cattus, was second with 8, and *Mystery*, also of Bay Head, sailed by Miss Ver Planck, was third with 6. These three ladies are all splendid skippers, able to hold their own with the best of the men in handling racing craft.

Frolic, the winner of the two championships, is a much deeper boat than any of the rest of the fleet, and combines in an unusual degree the qualities of racer and all-around boat. She is at her best turning to windward, and is an excellent little sea-boat, as she proved on a trip from Sandy Hook to Barnegat Inlet, part of the tie is a three-reef breeze from Southeast. She was designed and built by J. H. Perrine, of Barnegat, N.J. *Resolute*, the winner of second place, is one of five boats, practically alike, built in 1914, for Island Heights and Seaside Park yachtsmen, from designs by C. D. Mower. They are narrower and carry somewhat smaller and lighter rigs than the older type of scows, and unlike them, do not use shifting ballast.

The Mantoloking and Bay Head yachtsmen were inclined to underestimate the capabilities of these boats at first, believing that they did not have the power to compete with the old boats with their bigger rigs. They soon found that they were wrong, however. The new boats proved to be remarkably good, and fully able to hold their own in average racing weather. *Resolute* is at her best reaching in nice whole-sail breezes, but is a good performer on all points of sailing, and was extremely well handled throughout the season. *Picaroon*, the third boat, is one of the older, or Bay Head type of scows. She seems to do relatively better in a fresh breeze, but is a good all-around performer, and was very well handled by her young skipper.

No account of sneakbox racing would be complete without mention of the *Arran*, last year's champion, and acknowledged crack for several seasons. Also *Quickstep*, of Forked River, which did not race this year, but won many prizes in her day.

Yachtsmen seeing the sneakboxes for the first time are not always favorably impressed, but are apt to experience a change of heart on further acquaintance. As a matter of fact, these boats with their large rigs are veritable flyers. Though limited in length to 20 feet over all, there are no restrictions as to sail area, crew or ballast. A skipper may carry as much or as little weight as he pleases, depending on his estimate of what the weather is likely to be during the race. This has resulted in the production of a boat about as fast as it is possible for a 20-footer to be, and under conditions which suit them, it is doubtful if faster boats of their size than the sneakboxes can be found anywhere.

The leading boats in some of last Summer's races covered the course at an average speed of about 7 miles an hour, and the general average in all the races was high enough to have done credit to much larger yachts. Taking them in all, the sneakboxes are a very interesting and sporting class of racers, and being peculiarly well adapted to Barnegat Bay conditions, they are likely to retain their popularity for a long time to come.

—from* The Rudder Magazine, *1915

On the Bay

The Main Dock of the Bay Head Yacht Club, around 1900. ***(Photograph courtesy of W.C.S.)***

A Barnegat Bay catboat coming around Herring Point and heading west along the Metedeconk River.
(Photograph, circa 1890, courtesy of William C. Schoettle)

"The Yacht Club House stands at the head of Barnegat Bay, ten minutes walk from all the hotels. Summer visitors are welcome to join the club and enjoy its many benefits, athletic sports, sailing, tennis, social functions and the famous 'Afternoon Teas.' " — from G. R. Hardenbergh's *Bay Head*, 1909.
(Photograph an early view of the Bay Head Yacht Club around 1890, courtesy of W.C.S.)

The *Osprey* — one of the biggest sailing yachts ever built at Morton Johnson's yard — lies at anchor in Bay Head. *(Photograph, courtesy of Axel Carlson)*

A catboat under construction in the workshop at Morton Johnson's boatyard in the early 1900s. ***(Photograph by F.S.D.)***

Joe Stillwell standing on the platform at the Mantoloking railway station, around 1900. *(Photograph, courtesy of Mr. and Mrs. C.J.H.)*

The wild sand dunes of Mantoloking, early 1900s. *(Postcard from the collection of the author)*

"April 12, 1915 — The British bark *Invermay*, from Dublin to New York in Ballast came on the beach at Mantoloking on Sunday morning in clear weather. She struck head on, but her Captain kept her sails on her during Sunday's southerly gale, and she swung around, her bow pointing southward . . . The general impression on the coast seemed to be that she must have beached purposely — if so, the job was not done very well." — *from* The New Jersey Courier.

Life Saving Station No. 11, around 1900, at Mantoloking: "There are at least 11 men whose homes are in the West Mantoloking vicinity who are in various Life Saving Stations between Sandy Hook and Beach Haven. Their names are Joel Hulse, Forman Hulse, Henry Ware, Edward Rogers, Theodore Sculthrope, Ephram Brower, W. E. Falkenburgh, Alex Brower and Lewis Brower." —*from* The New Jersey Courier.

"June 1, 1901 — The club house dock has been built out 250' with a 'T' on the end. One of the features of the Mantoloking beach is a number of pavilions, the roofs of which are formed from pine boughs." —*from*
The New Jersey Courier. *(Photograph of the Mantoloking Yacht Club by H.W.H., circa 1895, courtesy W.C.S.)*

A merchant's wagon stopping by the Mantoloking General Store in the summer of 1900.
(Photograph from the collection of the author)

"November 22, 1894 — Jacob B. Herbert of Mantoloking, better known by the name of 'Uncle Jakey Harbor,' will become an octogenarian on January 15, 1895, if his present good health continues. For many years Uncle Jakey kept a famous tavern on the beach at Mantoloking, the resort of sportsmen from the cities, of visitors from the main shore towns, and which blossomed out into a blaze of glory on 'Salt Water Day.' " —*from* The New Jersey Courier.
(Photograph courtesy of W.C.S.)

Built in the early 1880s, the bridge connecting Mantoloking to the Metedeconk Neck provided easy access to the barrier beach at the head of the bay. *(Postcard, circa 1910, from the collection of the author)*

Established in 1899, the Seaside Park Yacht Club recently celebrated its centennial anniversary.
(Postcard, circa 1910, from the collection of the author)

Getting ready for the races, Seaside Park Yacht Club. ***(Postcard, circa 1910, from the collection of the author)***

Sand dunes and bayberry between Bay Head and Mantoloking. *(Watercolor by G. R. Hardenbergh, 1905, courtesy of Mr. and Mrs. Alfred Johnson)*

One Time the Beach Was Beautiful

At one time the beach was beautiful with many sand dunes covered with purple wild sweet peas in summer. Sand dunes were very important during storms, to keep the ocean from flowing under the boardwalks, over the roads and destroying the houses. It would flow on across to the bay and destroy the bay docks. Some docks had benches and covered roofs so people could sit and watch while their children were happily catching crabs.

The beaches also had real high beach grass with long roots that kept the sand from blowing away. Even wild kale grew on the dunes and could be eaten in salads. After several years had passed many people wanted the sand dunes leveled because they interfered with their view of the beach and the ocean from their beach front houses. So they were removed, much to the sorrow of the people who live year round at the seashore.

Beachcombing

People who lived along the beaches were called "Beach-combers." They would walk along the beaches trying to find things. Sometimes you would find pineapples, clothes pins, pencils, and toys. I remember after a heavy storm all kinds of fruit would wash ashore. Oranges, lemons, bananas, crates of grapes and figs, and 50 lb. bags of sugar or flour. Bananas were always green and people would put them under their porches to ripen. The flour and sugar was good too, because it used to harden on the outside of the bag, but it was good and dry inside. A baker I knew gathered lots of lemons and made pies and sold them in his bakery shop.

Drums of oil and gasoline could sometimes be found. The men who found gasoline would sell it. All of these things that washed ashore were either washed off the decks or thrown over the sides to lighten the vessels to prevent sinking during violent storms.

I remember a little schooner that came ashore all by herself near the South Seaside Park fish pounds. Her cargo was beautiful bolts of silk and other kinds of material. Some of the bolts washed overboard and people swam out in the ocean and got much of it. When the guards of the boat found out about it, they demanded its return.

Warm Summer Days

On warm summer days, once in a while a sloop or smack would sail close to the shore if the wind was from the west. These are small sailboats and would come so close you could see all on board. I have often seen the lovely white sails from my porch and would go down to watch them. They knew they could come in close on a west wind, because if the wind increased it would blow them back into deeper water. In a strong east wind they could be blown into the shore and be beached, and perhaps damaged by waves.

Before my father joined the Life Saving Service, he and several other young men owned a sea skiff together and went fishing every day. They made a good living, as they had a ready market for the fish they caught. A sea skiff is a very seaworthy boat.

Squalls and Gale Force Winds

Barnegat Bay is beautiful when in a calm mood, but it can be terribly dangerous when aroused by squalls and gale force winds and rain storms. I have seen it in both stages many times. In summer strong winds are usually from the south.

My husband, who was also in the Life Saving Service, once had to report back for duty at his station in Island Beach after being home on liberty. There was a bad wind and rain storm raging and he had to cross the bridge across Barnegat Bay to get to his station. The wind was so strong the only way he could cross it was to tack like a sail boat as it blew him from one side of the bridge to another.

After the storm was over a lot of lumber had been washed up on the beach. My husband got enough lumber to build a small house for me not far from his station on Island Beach. I used to go on early patrol with him in summer. We used to see beautiful moonlit nights. One time the ocean was all phosphorescent, and the waves looked like gold when they broke. Sometimes thunder-showers started coming up and we would run to keep from getting wet. We most always made it back before the rain came.

On My Grandparents' Farm

My grandparents had a farm in Osbornville. I loved spending my school vacations with them and I used to help grandfather plant his garden. He used to grow a small, round, green melon called a "vine peach," which tasted like a cantalope. After grandfather's day I could never find them again.

They had a large grape arbor and also a large hen house and yard with plenty of chickens. Grandmother always had chicken every Sunday for dinner. They had a large corn field too. I learned to husk corn grown for chickens and horses as well as grandfather could. I did it with an empty corn cob. I just pushed it up and down on the filled corn cob and that loosened the corn so it fell out.

No Ice-Boxes in Those Days

We always had a large pig for meat in the winter, and what they called a "smokehouse" to keep it from spoiling. No ice-boxes in those days. We always had a large potato and turnip hole filled with hay to keep them from freezing in winter, and had a large corn crib screened in for corn for the horse and chickens.

Ice houses were made for summer so food would keep. A large square hole was made real deep in the ground in the woods and filled with plenty of sawdust and hay to keep the ice from melting. Ice was sawed in large cakes or squares from the river and bay. Some winters Barnegat Bay will freeze over but it is hard to know how deep it is frozen. The water is salty and the motion of the tides under the ice make it difficult to estimate its thickness. A top was built over the ice house so no one could fall into it, and to keep out rain and snow.

Home Remedies

We had to go to Lakewood for winter supplies. Flour by the barrel and also sugar. It took a day to go there and back. Folks made many kinds of medicines from plants that grew in abundance in the woods. They even made salve from different plants to cure burns. Grandfather once had a wart on his finger, so he cut one of the horse's hairs off her tail and tied it real tight around the wart. It cut off the wart some time later. Pepper was used to stop bad bleeding from a wound, big or small. It formed a tight web so air could not get in. Peppermint leaves were useful and also roots of sassafrass were used for tea as a medicine. Salt was used to stop nosebleeds. People had many ways of helping themselves in those days.

Exploring the Attic

On one of my Christmas visits I went into the attic to explore. Strings of crowder in their skins were hanging in colors of red, blue and black. They tasted so good when cooked. Slices of dried peaches on strings were also in the attic. Hops were there for colds. That's how things were kept for winter use. A very useful attic. Trunks of old clothing and even an accordian. I took that downstairs and made some awful noises on it.

Cranberries and Blueberries

Grandfather owned a cranberry bog and hired pickers when the berries were ripe. Everyone wore mitts so hands wouldn't get sore. Ends of the fingers were cut off so you could feel the berries. But mostly cranberry scoops were used, which were the size of a dust pan with a wooden handle and prongs that you pushed through the vines and scooped up the berries. It was faster than picking singlehanded.

In summer he hired blueberry pickers, all of them women. They decided where they would pick and let him know what time to meet them at a certain time in the afternoon. He was always there on time with his big and small measures. He would measure the berries and weigh them. That went on all summer. They were crated and sent to the New York market. He filled his wagon and next morning drove to the Mantoloking railroad station and met the train. His wagon was called a carry-all, with curtains on the side which could roll up.

The Urge to Tramp

One day grandfather and I had been out riding and on our return he unhooked Nell from the wagon, as usual, and she started to go into the barn. But she would not go in. She just put down her head and sniffed and sniffed. Grandfather knew someone was in the barn. He patted Nell and went on in and found a man in the stall next to Nell's, all snuggled up in the hay to spend the night. Grandfather brought him out, then Nell went in. Grandfather offered him supper but he had gotten food somewhere else. Then he left and was on his way. There were plenty of tramps in those days who just got tired of working all year. Good workers until the spring, then they got the urge to tramp until fall again.

Nothing Was Easy

Grandfather's land covered a large meadow, which was used to feed Nell and also to make a good comfortable bed to lay on. One day grandmother and I went to the meadow to pick wild grapes and strawberries for jelly. Believe it or not, there were real snapping turtles there hissing. We didn't see them but we sure heard them hissing.

It was hard getting to sleep some nights. So many whip-poor-wills calling all night, and spiders buzzing, and katydids calling "katydid" and "katydidn't." And frogs in the pond sounding off too.

The water pump was on the front porch and it was hard keeping it from freezing in winter. We had plenty of water on hand and tipped the pump at night by lifting the handle. We had to pour water to get it working again.

Nothing was easy in those days.

— by Anna Brower, 1979

Pound fishing at Normandy beach. *(Photograph, circa 1920, courtesy of Herman Bennett)*

One of the Heroes of the Jersey Coast

Running down the old familiar landmarks of "Squan Beach" a few days ago, I was surprised to note from the car window the forlorn aspect of Captain Chadwick's house and prompt inquiry soon brought a copy of the *Courier* confirming my fears that he had passed away.

I cannot spare the time, nor you the space to recount his many rescues and feats of seamanship but it is to be regretted that men like Chadwick and Dorsett pass away with but a line to commemorate their daring deeds as surfmen and lifesavers.

William P. Chadwick was eighty-five years of age and had been in the Life Saving Service for thirty-one years, most of that period in charge of the Chadwick house, known at various times as Nos. 5, 9 and 12; upon the death of John Maxson, volunteer keeper of No. 5 in 1855, he volunteered his services, and served two years without pay and as a paid keeper until 1862, being succeeded by the late John Lott Dorsett. Captain Chadwick was reappointed in 1868 and remained in charge for eighteen years.

During this time, with the assistance of volunteer or paid crews he performed many acts of conspicuous bravery, for his were the days of the old cedar surf-boats which were kept right side up by main strength and good judgment and but little reliance was placed on the crude mortar apparatus. This may have been due to the unsuccessful efforts of Capain Burton and the crew of the bark *Argyle* who were unable to haul the gear through the heavy set of the current, although a shot line had been placed in their hands by the effort of Chadwick, C. W. Maxson and other volunteers.

This tragic disaster was vivid memory to Captain Chadwick and his description of the long day of toil, contesting with the sleet laden gale and wild surges for the lives of the doomed crew was a sombre story, lighted only by the rescue of the sailor, Paul deCast, by David Fleming, and the magnificent effort of Captain Burton to breast the racing current with his powerful double overhand stroke, an effort that brought him straight into the beach, but broke his heart as he was dead as they raised him out of the surf.

Unfortunately the deeds of our coastmen do not live in song or story and that he and others with unfaltering courage and a splendid devotion to duty were instrumental in saving the passengers and crews of the *Jerome*, *Samuel Willets*, *Clara Brookman*, *William Patten*, *Princeton*, *DeWitt Clinton*, *Governor Bull*, *B. C. Scribner*, and many others, is as completely forgotten as the deeds of their grandfathers.

— by Charles Macauley

from* The New Jersey Courier*, July 25, 1914

"August 1, 1896 — Capt. William Chadwick ate 49 clams, drank six bottles of beer & gave three cheers for the Hon. William McKinley, the next President. Captain Bill, although just under 100 years old, executed a complicated double shuffle lasting two hours, to juba time, in a manner that could not be duplicated by anybody half his age." — from the *Chadwick House Register. (Photograph courtesy of William Gregor)*

The Italian bark *Fortuna* came ashore on January 18, 1910, near Barnegat Light on Long Beach Island.
(Photograph by Lewis D. Crowell, courtesy of Janice Wheeler)

The Chadwick Life Saving Station was one of the eight original stations along the Jersey Coast. Surfmen there came to the rescue of many historic shipwrecks, including the *Aryshire* in 1850 and the *George Taulane* in 1880. Pictured above: front — Howard Platt, Captain Bill Simpson, John Osborn; back row — Ed Rogers and John Hulse. The other crewmen are unidentified. ***(Photograph, circa 1900, courtesy of Stanley Hulse)***

The yacht race at Lavallette. *(Photograph, circa 1910, courtesy of Chris Myers)*

Philadelphia Avenue, Lavallette. *(Postcard, circa 1910, courtesy of Chris Myers)*

Michael Ortley's House was a popular fishing and gunning lodge during the 1800s.
(Postcard, circa 1900, courtesy of Anna Brower)

This 1897 view of Seaside Park captures the frontier spirit of the old seashore. Note the railroad station behind the early boarding houses.
(Photograph by A.W.B., courtesy of W.C.S.)

Summer tourists arriving at the Barnegat Pier railroad station at Seaside Park.
(Photograph, circa 1900, from the collection of Joel Rosenbaum)

The first bridge from Seaside Park to Toms River, completed in 1915, helped bring the new invention of the automobile to the barrier island. ***(Postcard, circa 1915, from the author's collection)***

A Barnegat Bay old-timer and his dog on the front porch.
(Photograph courtesy of Axel Carison)

Sneak-box race on the Toms River at Island Heights.
(Photograph, circa 1910, from the **collection of the author*)***

Visitors sailed across Barnegat Bay in the 1890s to enjoy fishing and gunning at the Reed Hotel, on Island Beach. Note the Life Saving Station in right background. ***(Photograph, circa 1900, courtesy of Island Beach State Park)***

Bound from Glascow, Scotland, the Norwegian ship *Artensis* came ashore on June 8, 1916, at Seaside Park. All the crew members were safely rescued.
(Photograph by Lewis D. Crowell, courtesy of Janice Wheeler)

Barnegat Ways

Uncle Charlie Broad

When the sea-wind from the northeast fell upon the beach and its folk, came snow in the time of winter. Then the yellow spume was rolled together in heaps ere it was lifted and thrown against the sand hills, to be scattered in a thousand fragments of brine.

Great gulls screamed and tumbled over the undertow, and when heavier gusts carried them inland, struggled desperately back to the surf. Then empty houses, built along the shore where no native of the soil would dwell, shook and swayed to the music of the gale, lattices rattled a hollow tatoo, and once in a while a shutter, torn from its hinges, swung for a moment before it crashed away to destruction.

On the dunes the beach grass drew its keen blades from sheaths of snow only to be battened down again by weight of the wind. In the little valleys which we called "the glades" coarse heather and bayberry rested, snug under cover, against the return of the sun. The more timid of the water birds assembled in spreading flocks on the open bay behind the line of beach. Summer visitors, whose temporary homes along the seaside were in danger at every flood-tide, were all away; but after the storm we should see some of them for a day or two looking about their places and making count of leaks and losses.

Gathering at the General Store

While tempests raged, the men who called Barnegat "the bay" were wont to congregate undisturbed by invaders from the towns. Wherever was a grocery or a general store one might find them sitting in old wooden chairs or on soap boxes. They sat from middle of the morning to dinner-time — which was and is still what it should be, noon — and again from dinner-time to dark.

Sometimes, if the stories were good and the women at home have been inclined to scold, they sat until ten o'clock at night, but so late a session was rare. Work was not constant in those days, and what there was could not be

done when the furied breath of the Atlantic swept the coast. So the women kept the fires alight in the kitchen and, if it had been a fairly prosperous year, in "the room" as well, while the men breasted snow and wind to the genial atmosphere of the store, where a white-bellied stove glowed scarlet under the ministrations of some admitted leader of the community.

Those days of friendly fellowship are gone. Storms come and vent their wrath against the land. People migrate, as they did, from city to shore and back again to city, but we have advanced away from much that the elders among us love to remember. The motor car has done its part; new ways have come into use; the boys and girls go from home, and if ever they do return it is with novel manners and thoughts which conflict with our traditions. Yet it will not be well if those men and women who have left a name among us be forgotten when we have followed to the Better Country — a glorious country indeed if it be better than this lovely land which Barnegat divides.

Shelter from the Nor'east Storm

It was in the time of rending nor'easters that one might learn to know the big men. When they began to speak every one else became silent. They had the authority of the tribe. A few of them had been accorded by common consent the honorable title "Uncle" — one must have lived a long life and lived it well, one must have earned the respect of his neighbors by unbroken abiding in one place and the affection of his friends by kindliness, to receive this honorary award. And almost always the title was followed by a nickname.

There was, it was true, Uncle John Johnson, but that was more euphonious than Jack would have been. On the other side of the stove there was Uncle Jimmie Moreland and Uncle Bill Henry Layton. In front of the stove where he could reach the poker and stir up the fire, sat Uncle Charlie Broad. He was the most remarkable of our folk, not only for what he thought himself to be, but also for what, all unconsciously, he was.

Uncle Charlie Broad: Born of Barnegat

He was born of Barnegat. A little cottage still stands by a corner of sandy roads between pine wood and cranberry bog. The house top droops toward the center of the ridge-pole, and at each end a chimney of moss-grown brick stands rigid and gives the front elevation, as the architects say, the appearance of a fish-tail roof in China. Along the south side runs a porch, darkened in summer by red trumpet vines and letting into the lower story only dim and mournful light. The floor is of thick, hewn boards and a foot or so of space separates it from the damp black sand which is the terrain there.

In that sagging structure Charlie Broad first saw the filtered glow of day. Thence in the after years he set out and thither he returned daily, and there at last he closed his eyes. He had no schooling, as he used to say. There were doubting Thomases who said he was illiterate, but that was not true. I have seen him on the porch dozing over his Bible, when the brief October sun brought older people out of doors to bask an hour or two.

From the Head of the Bay to the Inlet

The record does not tell that he ever traveled more than a hundred miles from home. Yet his name was known from the head of the bay to the inlet and even beyond. He did things that every bay-man does — dug clams, raked oysters in the old free days, shot and fished and sailed. All these he did no better than his fellows, but his fame was carried from man to man because of the deep and trenchant wit of his sayings and the faculty which he had, and knew he had, of expressing a whole volume of thought in a single terse sentence. Sometimes this gift of sententious utterance carried him to the verge of the unintelligible, but because he had said a thing we knew it must be worth consideration and so we came to its meaning.

His appearance was appropriate in one who habitually spoke from the fane — a mass of dense, shaggy hair, all white in the later years, heavy eyebrows over sharp but merry eyes, and a bushy beard, which swept his chest and made his one attempt to adorn his neck with the customary wear of common men an act of difficulty and final accomplishment a waste. The beard was white but tinged with gold at the edges. Below the corners of his mouth traces of tobacco lingered. His shoulders were platonic and his girth was ponderous. When he walked it was always without haste.

All the beach knew of his wisdom. Men would stop other men to ask if they had heard what Uncle Charlie had said. Even to this day one who is close to the hearts of the people can raise up pictures of the past by mentioning Uncle Charlie's name to some old fellow who sat at his feet long ago. To his memory let us consecrate this retrospection.

– by A.P. Richardson, from **Barnegat Ways**, *1931, The Century Co., N.Y*

"February 8, 1905 — George Brower has his boat finished, and is about to give it its first coat of paint. He says he will set some of our boys guessing this coming summer, as he intends to have a very large sail and bring all the racing cups at Mantoloking." — from *The New Jersey Courier*.
(Photograph courtesy of Annie Brower)

Opposite page: A Chesapeake "Pungy" with a load of lumber passing offshore. Coastal schooners were the last major use of sail for commercial purposes along the Eastern seaboard. Perfectly suited for coastwise sailing, their fore and aft rig made it possible for them to sail close to the wind and easily navigate shallow inlets and coves. Although their use peaked from 1825 to 1880, such schooners served the coastal trade well into the 1920s. *(Photograph by F.S.D., courtesy J.V.H., Jr.)*

A Barnegat Bay fisherwoman.
(Photograph courtesy of Anna Brower)

Tides of Barnegat

To the left of where she stood curved the coast, glistening like a scimitar, and the strip of yellow beach which divided the narrow bay from the open sea; to the right, thrust out into the sheen of silver, lay the spit of sand narrowing the inlet, its edges scalloped with lace foam, its extreme point dominated by the grim tower of Barnegat Light; aloft, high into the blue, soared the gulls, flashing like jewels as they lifted their breasts to the sun, while away and beyond the sails of the fishing boats, gray or silver in their shifting tacks, crawled over the wrinkled sea.

— by F. Hopkinson Smith, 1924

The sloop *Dryiad*, captained by Mark Schoettle of Bay Head, sailing off Barnegat Lighthouse.
(Photograph, 1898, courtesy of William C. Schoettle)

On the creek at Lanoka Harbor, with an Islander yawl in right foreground. *(Photograph, circa early 1900s, courtesy of A.B.)*

A Song of Its Own

Sneakbox, sloop
and cranberry scoop,
those days are long gone,

if you listen
you'll hear the bay
still has its song —

the whip-poor-will
calls from the willow
while you fall asleep,

and katydids chant,
frogs croak in the bog,
fish leap in the creek —

cattails sway gently,
the blue heron
splashes at dawn,

the lines chime
on the sailboats
tomorrow has come...

the bay sings
with the sea wind
a song of its own.

At Seaweed Point — a Barnegat Bay gunner and his dog.
(Photograph courtesy of Mr. and Mrs. A.J.)

The *Emma C. Berry* on Barnegat Bay. *(Photograph by F.S.D., courtesy of J.V.H. Jr. and W.C.S.)*

Swapping Tales Around a Red-Hot Stove

Barnegat Baymen and Fresh-Water Salts

Barnegat Bay is essentially salty, and it belongs to the sea as much by tradition as by the never-ceasing flow of its tidal waters. Over the breaking bar of its inlet many a vessel has chanced her way into shelter since the days of Henry Hudson, and although history tells us that this worthy explorer himself took but one brief look at the breakers on the bar and then headed the *Half Moon* offshore again with all haste, humbler sailors came in his wake to conquer the surf and make Barnegat their home. So down in the lower end of the bay, near the inlet, the baymen are salty by nature, born in the salt meadows with the boom of the surf in their ears.

But farther up, where Peter Jenness and I got our start, and developed a weakness for old hulks, around Bayhead, Kettle Creek and Metedeconk River, the water isn't quite so salty, and the baymen are only brackish too. Indeed, if it weren't for the vivid imagination and glib tongue of every true Metedeconker many of the upper bay's recognized salts would never have acquired their seagoing reputations. But swapping tales is a highly developed art in Barnegat's headwaters, and by the time he's sixty nearly every Metedeconker has talked himself into enviable standing as an old sea-dog, even though his only offshore experience was pound-fishing off the beach.

Deep Sea Thrillers at the General Store

Up until a few years ago you could drop into Hulse's general store almost any winter's evening, 'way up the sheltered river, and listen to deep-sea thrillers that would make you seasick — for the Metedeconker begins his tale where Captain Voss leaves off.

Being fresh-water salts ourselves, Peter and I used to listen to these colorful tales year after year with all the rapture of which small boys are capable. We enjoyed them all, and we didn't try to distinguish fact from fiction, nor ask embarrassing questions when a particularly thrilling incident, which we had come to know by heart, was recounted with glaring discrepancies from time to time. We grew to love the old boats which we heard so much about, and we gloried in their triumphs over the elements. We gave rapt attention to the valiant Metedeconker whose skillful hand brought his vessel safely through it all — and not a little thanks to Providence for sparing him so that he could tell us all about it.

Spitting on the Red-Hot Stove

We had our favorite stories, of course, and one of them was Uncle Charlie Loveland's tale about a pooping sea that all but swept his vessel clean. This was a vivid yarn about a deckload of green water and railroad ties, and it required unusual exertion in the telling; often it was hard to get Uncle Charlie launched upon it. But let someone spit generously on the red-hot stove at just the proper time, and the next moment you'd hear Uncle Charlie starting in to tell about the big sea that hissed just like that under the stern of the *Annabelle* — only louder.

With a background like this it was only natural that we should begin to lead fantastic lives ourselves, and when we went sailing in the summer time we weren't just two boys sailing our sneakboxes; we were lordly captains of vessels made famous by the red-stove of Metedeconk.

Over and over again we sailed the old *Pauline* up the bay in a howling northeaster, with fifty thousand hard clams on deck and nary a one washed overboard. We drove the *Jessie G.* against a green-eyed souther and put her across the bar in the Mud Channel with less than three feet of water on it, and she drawing every bit of four. We scuttled the *Celestine* off Brigantine to quench a fire in her hold, then patched her up, bailed her out, and sailed her into port on time, and never got a drop of water on the cargo. When we began to sink in the old *Harriet S. Brooks* off Sea Girt Light in 1866 we set her down on the beach at the top o' high water, and so gently that we never cracked a timber; and we cursed the cook for being a fool and breaking an ankle when he jumped to the hard sand.

Dreams of Sailing Around the Horn

All these things and countless others we accomplished in our sneakboxes in the summer time, after rehearsals around Mr. Hulse's stove. We decided that

Howard Rogers, a Barnegat bayman

Howard Rogers' Observation

"Along in the fore part o' last week I was on my bicycle goin' acrost the Mantolokin' bridge on my way home when I seen the draw was swung open to let Mr. Bronson through. It wan't wide open though and jest as the 'Bo Peep' got in the middle, her toppin' caught and give her boom a right smart pull. 'You scoundrel you,' yelled Mr. Bronson to the drawtender: 'You'll swing for this!'

"Right pert, I thot . . ."

all old boats had heroic pasts in keeping with Metedeconk traditions, and we soon acquired warped ideas about the virtues of every old hulk which we came upon. Even Captain Dorsett's old hay schooner up Beaverdam Crick took our fancy for a season or two, and it was our ambition for a long time to fix her up and sail her around the horn — a dangerous part of the coast which we knew lay somewhere south of Barnegat, probably below Atlantic City.

A Wonderful Vessel: The Emma C. Berry

But for all our love of the bouncing *Jessie G.*, the flaming *Celestine*, the gurgling *Harriet S. Brooks*, and Captain Dorsett's *Rosamond*, it was the *Emma C. Berry* which we especially revered. As fine a little smack as ever worked the banks, we had heard them say, with more than her share of seagoing virtues. If the performance of our sneakboxes was particularly praiseworthy on a windy day it wasn't in them that we went sailing home that night, it was in the *Emma C.* herself, all dry and comfortable just like your own parlor. But where she hailed from, or what she was, or where she was built, we never knew; she was just a name around the Metedeconk stove. But she was a wonderful vessel of course, for Captain Joe Tilton had been her skipper and Captain Joe never went to sea in anything but the best vessels afloat; he said so himself.

Then gradually the years began to deal harshly with our idols of Metedeconk and we found ourselves exploring new seas, with only vague memories of such companions as the old *Pauline* and the *Jessie G.* Uncle Charlie Loveland, Captain Joe Tilton, and the *Emma C.* all seemed to grow indistinct together, and like Santa Claus finally disappeared over the horizon of our realistic world. We were left disillusioned, with a growing suspicion that we could never find a yacht capable of doing everything that real Metedeconkers might expect of their boats. We knew that some day we'd have to find an old fishing smack or a cargo vessel or some sort of venerable hulk that could live up to the traditions of our boyhood days. We'd be on the lookout for some kindly old ship in which we could round the Horn again with Uncle Charlie and Captain Joe, even though we might have to do it all at anchor — or hauled out on shore beyond the reach of hungry worms and seeping water.

— by F. Slade Dale, from "Old Emma Comes to Barnegat,"

courtesy **Yachting Magazine,** ***June 1933***

Slade Dale finally found the *Emma C. Berry* and brought her back to Barnegat Bay where she was a familiar sight for many years. Dale eventually donated the smack to the maritime center at Mystic Seaport, Connecticut, where she was restored and is now on exhibit.
(This photograph, and the front cover photo of the* Emma C.*, by F.S.D., courtesy of John Van Horn Jr.)

Jenkinson's Pavilion, on the boardwalk at Point Pleasant Beach and on the south shore of Manasquan Inlet, proudly billed as "A Nice Place for Nice People." *(Photograph, circa 1927, courtesy of Dick Updike)*

Here One Forgets the Outside World

Barnegat Bay has ever been one of the wildest, most romantic of waters in the world. Certainly, there is nothing in America to compare with it and I have visited and angled in all of the national waters. Shortly after a boat passes southward from Seaside Park Bridge, all dwellings are left behind or obscured, with exceptions possibly at Waretown and Old Barnegat. Ever looming up in front, with an almost ever shining sun overhead, is the tall tower of the lighthouse at the inlet.

On the left hand are miles of the tallest, whitest sand dunes, between bay and ocean. On the right hand are the rising banks of varied hued greens of marshland, fading into tall forests of pines and oaks.

In that body of water from Cedar Creek oyster beds to the inlet, in season, are gathered all known edible fish which makes angling worth while at all costs, which make recreation so fascinating that all outside influences are out of place and all memories of elsewhere blotted out. Here one forgets the outside world nor cares what is happening to business or home or events.

It is obvious that every change, every new building put up bordering on this enchanted water, makes to the destruction of just so much scenic effect. Civilization, progress, improvements — all destroy nature. Such spots as Barnegat Bay are the sole recreative reliefs from the intensity of civilization, the enticing escape from office and home, from heat of summer and pestilence of unsavory smells of manufactories and crowded populations.

The recreative rest here, which no crowded coast resort can give, is of a type hard to find elsewhere, in fact cannot be duplicated elsewhere. I challenge the world to name any like body of salt water of like environment and fascinations, of like rest, boating recreations and angling, elsewhere on the face of the earth. Believe me, there is no bay or water so situated, so placed that in a few moments one so desiring can get back into the whirl of civilization.

Gradually, encroachments are approaching Barnegat Bay which will, if continued, surely change its character for the worst. Slowly a canal is being cut at the head of the bay to connect with outside waters. On that moment when such connection is made, all that is described above will go by the board in an instant.

The sewage of great cities and populations will come down through the new channel together with larger vessels of commerce, driving out the coveted species of fish, and making the present pleasure boating and angling as odious as it was formerly enjoyable and exclusive. In addition, buildings, wharves and populations will quickly arise around the whole bay. Where automobile parties at present find long stretches of enjoyable breaths of pine air, a continuous line of streets will as surely take the place of pleasure bearing roadways as they have elsewhere from Cape May to Portland.

Instead of the reasonable number of autos now passing to and fro between Lakewood and Atlantic City, there will be the same massed formations as make such great and costly highways as the Merrick Road of Long Island dangerous for travel and void of recreation. All the blossoms and greens along both sides of such massed highways are obliterated by ever floating storms of dust sent up by millions of grinding wheels.

Such is the history of other coast bays and waters and such will surely be the fate of Barnegat Bay, soon to become a mere memory of dead and buried pleasures of boating and angling, when the fatal connection by canal with outside navigation is completed.

— by Dr. H. H. Ballou, Editor — **New York Science News**

from* The New Jersey Courier, *1921

The Seaside Heights Boardwalk: Generations of teens came of age on the boards, working at the penny arcades, fun houses, and beaches. They caroused the electrically illuminated attractions through the night, riding the Ferris wheel and roller coaster, and seeking summer romance. ***(Postcard, circa 1930, from the author's collection)***

J.
FREEMAN'S
BATH
INSIDE
Abbotts Ice Cream
BERT'S
RESTAURANT
SODA
Abbotts Ice Cream
18 HOLES
PLAY GOLF
25¢
SKEE
BALL
34946

The historic 1910 carousel at Casino Pier on the Seaside Heights boardwalk features fifty-eight colorful, hand-painted wooden animals and the calliope music of an authentic Wurlitzer Military Band Organ, restored by Dr. Floyd Moreland and friends in 1989.

The Boardwalk

"One win choice!" cries the barker at the game of chance stand, as the clicking "wheel of fortune" winds down to the lucky, or unlucky, number. The barker sweeps the losing coins down the slot as eager gamblers put more money down to try again for the prize of choice — a stuffed animal or shiny toy — to take home as a shore vacation souvenir. The old local traditions of Salt Water Day and Big Sea Day became institutionalized when the carnival came to town and stayed after the turn of the century. Implementing the business philosophy of P. T. Barnum combined with the salesmanship of W. C. Fields, airy resort pavilions and penny arcades were built along the beachfront boardwalk promenades at Point Pleasant Beach and Seaside Heights before and after 1920.

While neighboring towns such as Bay Head, Mantoloking, and Lavallette sported noncommercial, residential boardwalks, Point and Seaside were The Boardwalks most people wanted to visit in the summertime. Generations of teens came of age on the boards, working at the arcades, fun houses, and beaches. They caroused the electrically illuminated attractions through the night, riding the Ferris wheel and roller coaster, visiting the gypsy fortune teller, seeking summer romance on slow beach strolls to the inlet and occasionally waking up sandy and rumpled in the morning shade under the boardwalk.

During the sunny summer days with turquoise skies, the surf and sand were home away from home, with tanned lifeguards on their stands, freshly painted white rescue skiffs, roped-in bathing areas filled with cheering children and multicolored beach umbrellas sprouting like mushrooms to protect the delicate ladies. Despite periodic jellyfish and shark scares, and the occasional surprise appearance of schools of dolphins passing by offshore, days on the beach sometimes slowed to a sleepy daze in the humid August heat.

Up on the boards were all the necessities around the bathhouses, such as french fries, hot dogs, lemonade, soda, caramel corn, cotton candy, and salt water taffy — and, of course, frozen custard, a popular new confection. The old folks were content to while away the hours in the rocking chairs freely available in the shaded pavilions overlooking the beach. The boys and girls were magnetically attracted to the penny arcades and the magical merry-go-round with its endless calliope music.

Although Point's old carousel was broken up and sold decades ago, you can still visit the two traditional menageries at Seaside. The 1910 carousel at Casino Pier is one of two surviving American-made classics in the state. Once the only attraction on the north end of the boardwalk and at its present location for nearly seventy years, it features fifty-eight colorful, hand-carved wooden animals, including a lion, a tiger, a horse, a donkey, and even a sea serpent, many of them moving up and down. Restored by Dr. Floyd Moreland and friends in 1989, and recently named in honor of the former professor of classics, the carousel received a historic preservation award in 1991. Children of all ages thrill to the intoxicating music produced by the authentic Wurlitzer Military Band Organ. The world spins when you're riding a merry-go-round surrounded by laughing children and happy parents. The universe of the boardwalk seems to center on the wheel of life we call a carousel, where we all have a chance to catch the brass ring and where everyone can revisit his childhood.

After Labor Day weekend, the summer crowds gradually disappear, leaving the windy, paper-strewn boardwalk to the long, lonely winter freeze, with boarded up arcades and solitary strollers. The bright days of summer seem far away on chilly winter nights as the eerie desolation conjures visions of passing time as the cycle of seasons turns on the Jersey Shore.

Weather Eye

Geese fly south across gray skies,
as daylight fades and evening sighs:
seasons change for everyone,
one more run around the sun,
looking back to where we've been,
old times seem to live again . . .

Sailing on a bay like glass,
things to come become the past —
lightning over summer seas,
a leaf loose on an autumn breeze,
snowflakes in the winter freeze,
lilacs that bloom then leave —
the seasons surely pass,
they say only love will last . . .

We'll set sail soon on rocking tide,
when geese fly north across blue skies,
times may change but we're still free
to live the way we want to be —
we'll greet lost friends at Fiddler's Green,
head out to where the wind will rise,
where mermaids sing and dolphins gleam,
and this world seems but a dream —
keep a weather eye till then,
we'll soon be sailing home again!

Winter ice on Barnegat Bay

The Great Nor'easter of 1992

Afterword

Last Summer

The white sails of nearly three hundred "lasers" billowed in the wind during the early days of the last summer of the 1970s, as the largest fleet of sailboats ever launched on the bay raced the Green Island course. Barnegat Bay continues its proud tradition as a major East Coast racing center. The Barnegat Bay Yacht Racing Association — founded in 1913 — frequently hosts national and North American championship regattas as well as regional races.

In the long history of the bay area, few periods have held as much promise or peril as the 1980s. After nearly four centuries of population expansion along the seashore, Barnegat Bay is threatened by an onslaught of development whose byproducts — sewage, petrochemicals, and dredging — have altered her natural balance.

The Sea and the Bay

Public concern about preserving the environmental quality of the bay area is growing stronger. The waters and tidal marshes of the Barnegat are a vital but fragile natural resource, the home of an intricate chain of life where thousands of creatures — including man — must breed and feed. Even a large percentage of local sea life depends on the beaches and wetlands of Barnegat Bay. For many reasons — economic, esthetic, and recreational — preservation of these natural resources is essential.

The ban on poisonous pesticides has resulted in long vanished species of birds returning to the area, including falcons, white egrets, brant, and red-winged blackbirds. The wildlife of the bay seems to be thriving. President Carter has declared 1980 to be "The Year of the Coast," and promises to initiate Federal legislation aimed at preserving the National Seashore. State and county authorities also recognize the need for protecting our coastal lands and waters.

Antique engraving. ***(From the collection of the author)***

Omens on the Horizon

Other omens on the local horizon are more paradoxical. The ocean has become a major dumping ground for everything from raw sewage to explosives, toxic metals, and radioactive waste.

Eighty percent of offshore dumping in the United States is carried out off the Jersey Shore. Commercial fishermen and party boat captains report increasing degradation of the ocean's waters and marine life. The situation remains critical. On the land, rampant development is turning the seashore into the city, while beach buggies are destroying vital sand dunes and foliage, tracking the beaches with ruts and using them as parking lots. The pines are being stripped for firewood and the illegal dumping of carcinogenic chemicals threatens our water supply.

In the midst of a mounting worldwide energy crisis, environmental protection legislation is being challenged. Oil and gas have been discovered off the central Jersey Coast, and fields three miles off Point Pleasant Beach will be leased to major companies for exploration. The possible environmental threat presented by offshore drilling — with its accepted risk of oil spills and runaway wells — has aroused local opposition.

And finally, in the wake of the near meltdown at Three Mile Island in 1979, continuing problems at the Oyster Creek nuclear plant have forced bay area residents to ponder the invisible threat of radiation — and the grim possibility of a local nuclear disaster in one of the fastest-growing counties in the nation.

Other recent events during the past year have been equally perplexing. Mysterious sonic booms have thundered across the shore, rattling windows and nerves. Scientists have been unable to explain the booming. Local newspapers have reported strange, colorful lights hovering in the nighttime skies over Barnegat Bay. One large silvery object was seen by three witnesses falling into the bay off Kettle Creek. All attempts at recovering the object proved futile.

A Homegrown Renaissance?

Popular interest in preserving the bay and its heritage has been steadily growing during the past ten years. The Ocean County Historical Society has long been a leading force in this effort and continues to expand its programs. Other groups, such as the Brick Township and Shore Harbor Historical Societies, have been doing valuable local work and research.

For the past five years, the Toms River Seaport Society has been striving to realize its dream of restoring the old seaport area as well as preserving the maritime heritage of the bay. Their dedication and enthusiasm have encouraged plans for a similar project in the old town of Barnegat, which hosts garvey races on the bay every summer. Other worthy local efforts include the travelling history exhibits, which are both enjoyable and educational, sponsored by the Ocean County Cultural Commission; and the growth of the SEA Alliance, a grassroots environmental group dedicated to protecting our natural resources and developing alternate energy systems.

Each summer, Bay Head holds a celebration called "Barnegat Day," and the spirit of the old-time Salt Water Day has been revived by the annual Seafood Festival in Point Pleasant Beach. Down in Waretown, the Albert Hall has been the focus of a rebirth of native music and poetry, a movement that appeals to both newcomers and old-timers. Albert Hall has also inspired the innovative programs of the Pinelands Cultural Society, as well as the teaching of local lore and arts and crafts at Central Regional High School.

It seems as though a homegrown renaissance is at hand, one that may be witnessed at the Ocean County Folk Festival, which draws enthusiastic crowds each September. As folk artist Merce Ridgway of Waretown sings, "It's a beautiful day, out on Barnegat Bay . . ."

The Spirit of Old Barnegat Bay

The preservation of Island Beach as a state park has provided a sanctuary for the spirit of old Barnegat Bay. Throughout the summer, people visit for swimming, fishing, jogging, surfing, and bird-watching. Some even hike all the way down the beach to the inlet for a glimpse of Old Barney, still standing proudly across the water, overlooking the bay and the foaming breakers.

People of all ages take the Nature Trail, and find themselves spellbound by the silent beauty of the windswept dunes and beaches. At Island Beach it is easy to return to the time when the sands belonged to the frogs and turtles and horseshoe crab — when the air was alive with the cries of sea eagles, and clouds of butterflies swarmed in the spring among the holly, bayberry, and white blossoming beach plums.

Some people return to the water like dolphins, enjoying the pure energy of a perfect wave turning as it glides into the shore. Sometimes they get lost in the dunes and make private discoveries: smooth shells, strange tracks, the bones of a seagull, or the dark timbers of an old sloop nearly covered with sand. And sometimes they simply lie back and melt into the beach, watching the clouds roll by under a hot summer sun, breathing with the whispers of wind and surf, drinking in the golden light that flowers in the mind.

The Ocean County Barnegat Bay Decoy and Gunning Show in Tuckerton, sponsored by Ocean County Parks and Recreation Department, draws over forty thousand people in September.

Acknowledgments

The Mantoloking Mystery Wreck. ***(Asbury Park Press Photo)***

Like any good vessel, this book has had a will of her own. She sailed where she would, before the wind and sometimes against it, according to her own schedule and inclination. When she was ready to arrive in port, she did, after a long and winding journey.

Down Barnegat Bay would not have been possible without the generous support and enthusiasm of those who shared the voyage of discovery. The seemingly endless process of research, writing and editing was made much more bearable by the interest of those who helped provide the many pieces of the puzzle that came together to form this book.

The pieces came from all over: from libraries and museums, from attics and dusty trunks, from vivid flashes of memories of long-vanished days. They came from the Barnegat Bay area as well as Virginia, New York, Connecticut, Massachusetts, and all over New Jersey. The project took much longer than expected. Weeks, months, and years went by, and the end seemed always just around the corner. Words met pictures and maps, and a portrait of a time and place began to emerge.

One find led to another and yet another, sometimes in the most mysterious ways. In the midst of researching Captain John Lott Dorsett, his ancient, battered scrapbook appeared out of the blue, filled with old stories, drawings, and the spirit of the man (thanks, Cap'n John), courtesy Rick Gefkin of the Toms River Seaport Society. Rick also shared his scuba diving experiences and relics that he brought up from the English privateer *Thistle* and other offshore wrecks.

The wreck of the *John Minturn* was a central event in Barnegat Bay history. After a long search for a picture of the vessel I accidentally stumbled onto a reference to the existence of the rare Currier print. It was listed in a small brochure stuck in an old book on a wrong shelf at the Point Pleasant Library. Later that night, while working on the manuscript, I found myself writing, "The *John Minturn* left New Orleans on January 28th . . ." (heading out on the last voyage) and strangely realized that that had been exactly 134 years before to the day. Although I knew the picture existed, I didn't know where it could be found. Alan Frazer, curator of the New Jersey Historical Society, had never heard of the print but gave me several good leads to check on. Finally, a few weeks later, I tracked down a very rare copy in the archives of the Museum of the City of New York. The date: February 15th, the anniversary of the tragic wreck on Squan Beach.

The circle was completed. The last piece of the puzzle was located just in time for publication in this book. Nathaniel Currier's print — made six years before Mr. Currier met Mr. Ives and began a famous partnership that was to last for more than half a century — returned to the Jersey Shore and gave a face to a name from the past. *The Wreck of the Ship* John Minturn *on the Coast of New Jersey* connects a nearly forgotten piece of local history with the mainstream of Americana documented by the legendary printmakers of the nineteenth century. It evokes the era of the coastal trade and places a local tragedy in a national context.

In the course of research, such coincidences became almost commonplace, subtle signs that the spirits seemed to be enjoying my dig into the past. Whenever the well seemed to be running dry, a new spring would appear: Bill Gregor (William P. Chadwick's grandson) would bring out the massive, leather-bound, gilt-edged *Chadwick House Register* — with its thirty years of daily notations of common occurrences before the turn of the century — complete with mummified mosquitoes pressed between the yellowed pages, saltwater stained from old storms. Visits by U. S. Grant and Teddy Roosevelt were duly noted, as well as the day Captain Loveland sighted a large "Sea Serpent" off North West Point and Captain Bozier "gave chase and succeeded in capturing it, Captain Loveland being completely paralyzed with fright. . . ." No further reference is mentioned, except perhaps in the piece of doggerel inscribed by Capt. Bunk on the inside back cover:

"And there are many captains bold,
much whiskey they can swig,
the biggest stories ever told
are not for them too big. . . ."

On other days Arthur Johnson would rummage through his incredible collection of local history and artifacts — the accumulated storehouse of a lifetime of collecting — and come up with a piece of the *Hindenburg*, or Captain Dorsett's ship's bell, or a cannonball dug out of the sands on the Cook Farm that was fired at Yankee privateers during the War of 1812. Up in northern Massachusetts, Frank Watson would invite me into his library of maritime history, which includes thirty-five years of research on shipwrecks off the Jersey Shore — much of it handwritten in countless black loose-leaf notebooks, containing all available references in print to each known wreck. But the notebooks were not nearly as impressive as Mr. Watson's memory: He had most of the facts on the tip of his tongue, and time flew by as we talked for many hours.

Louise Edgar Colie shared a lifetime of remembrances of Mantoloking and Barnegat Bay lore. Sitting at the dining room table of her old beachfront home, which has weathered many storms through the years, we drank many cups of tea as she went over her scrapbooks and pictures with a magnifying glass, her memory clear as crystal. Bill Schoettle gave willingly of his time with boundless enthusiasm, opening up his archives of Bay Head history and his personal

A Landmark on the Jersey Shore

treasury of local memorabilia. Whenever there was a fact to check on or a question to ask, Mr. Schoettle usually had the answer.

And there were many others whose help was invaluable. Mr. and Mrs. Joseph Forsyth and Mr. and Mrs. Alfred Johnson generously shared their Hardenbergh paintings and reminiscences. Mrs. Esther Kinsley, Axel Carlson, and Jimmy Polhemus shared family pictures and stories, and offered good leads to follow up on. Mr. and Mrs. John Van Horn Jr. contributed their timeless Slade Dale photographs and recounted tales of his exploits, including how Mr. Dale finally found the *Emma C. Berry*, fixed her up, and sailed her for many years on the bay and along the coast. Shortly before his death, he donated the *Emma C.* to Mystic Seaport, Connecticut, where she was restored to her original design as a one-masted vessel. Back in the water now, the *Emma C. Berry* is a central feature of Mystic's incredible maritime collection. Special thanks also to Donald P. Robinson, Director Ship Preservation at the Seaport, and to the Seaport's knowledgeable library staff.

Winfield "Scotty" Scott met me at the Bluffs and renewed an old friendship. We talked about his years of sailing, and he gave me some of the fine points on making boat models. He pointed me in the right directions, then insisted on picking up the tab for the drinks! And we laughed when I reminded him of what he said the time a yacht's head backfired catastrophically when we were working at Dale Yacht Basin.

Commander John Verdier welcomed me back to Island Beach State Park, where I once worked as a ranger, and he contributed his time and knowledge to this project, along with head naturalist Bud Cooper. Mac Beaton, Lolly Beaton, and Charles Hankins helped out on the history of Barnegat Bay boat building. And at least one old priceless photograph ("At the Normandy Beach Fish Pound") was saved from the trash bin for this book, by Mrs. Charles Hankins, while she was visiting a neighbor one day who was cleaning out the attic. (Thanks, Mrs. Hankins!)

And many others deserve thanks: Mr. and Mrs. Robert Morris, Ralph Autorino, Herbie Rogers, Howard Rogers, Mr. and Mrs. John Benedict, and the late Fred Shaw, who contributed the inside front cover tidal chart. He predicted twenty years ago that someday I'd get around to doing this book! At the age of ninety-two, he finally saw the galleys.

Patricia Burke and Fred Cramer of the Ocean County Historical Society, Toms River, offered valuable assistance and advice, as well as did Society Director Pauline Miller. Kevin McGorty, of the Ocean County Cultural Commission, was equally helpful. He doggedly tracked down the *Appleton's Journal* article and prints, and spent a day going to Trenton to dig them out of the files where they had rested for over a century.

Dr. Andrew Moreland welcomed me back to Ocean County College and gave me free access to the Rare Book Room of the College Library, where, with the able assistance of Dr. Alexander Garelick and Dr. James McGinty, I was able to locate ancient local maps.

Ken Sheinbaum, of the Monmouth County Library at Freehold, unlocked the vaults and even gave me a guided tour of the town. The staffs at the Ocean County Library and the Rutgers University Library were equally impressive and dedicated. Philip F. Purrington, curator of the New Bedford Whaling Museum, New Bedford, Massachusetts, was extremely helpful in his assistance in locating information on the *John Minturn* as well as his personal instruction on how to restore a weathered clipper ship bowsprit.

And thanks also to the Barnegat Light Museum staff, Gary Struncius of the Pinelands Cultural Society, and the library staff at the amazing Mariner's Museum, Newport News, Virginia.

Very special mention must be made of my great aunt, Mrs. Anna Brower of Seaside Park, who started preparing for this book as a young girl. She grew up in and around Life Saving Stations, hearing tales of shipwrecks and rescues. Her father, Henry Ware, and her husband, Lester Brower, dedicated their lives to the Service, and Aunt Anna chronicled their times in essays and photographs. We spent many long afternoons going through her scrapbooks and exploring her memories. When the hour grew late, she'd sit down at the piano and prove once again that, at the age of eighty-five, she can still play pretty quick ragtime!

To Wayne L. Hartman, who introduced me to Walt Whitman, *Moby Dick*, and sardines with horseradish (and who worked overtime proofreading and advising); to my parents, who let their dining room be turned into a workroom and suffered long-term typewriting in the early morning hours (and who helped in every way they could); and to Gail Reese, for her patience, motivation, and love.

And finally, *Down Barnegat Bay* might never have happened without the help of my friend, Don DuMont, who joined the search for the pieces of the past and shared the long-term burning of the midnight oil, as well as the strange synchronicity of events. His energy, perseverance, and insight helped keep the project on course. We hope you've enjoyed the voyage as much as we have.

— Robert Jahn
Mantoloking, N.J.
June 1, 1980
First Edition

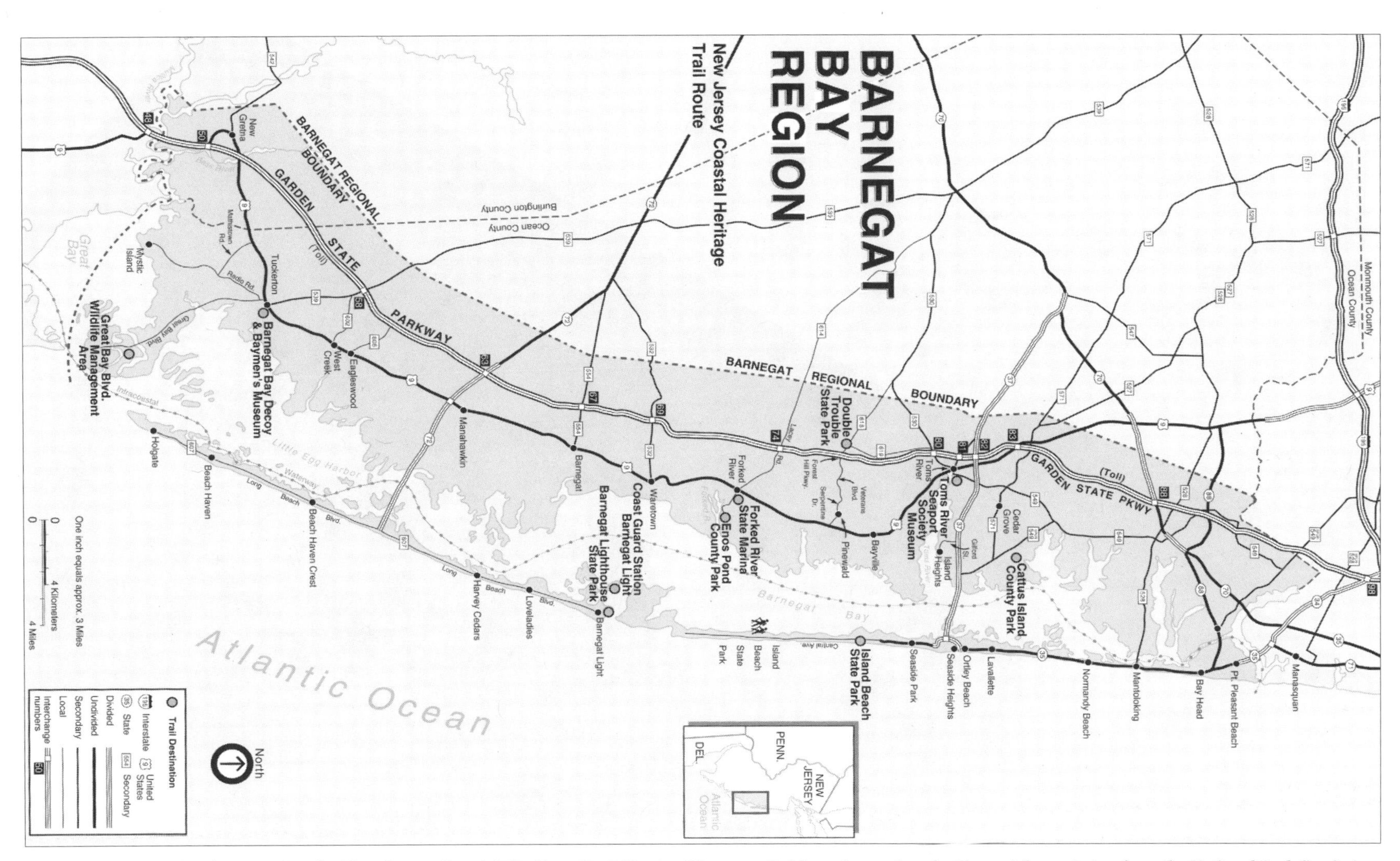

The Barnegat Bay Region map for the New Jersey Coastal Heritage Trail Route. *(Map compiled by and reproduced with special permission from the National Park Service)*

Aerial view of Barnegat Lighthouse and inlet, looking north across Island Beach State Park to the head of the bay.
(Photograph reproduced by permission of Studio 9 Photo Center Aerial Photography, Waretown, N.J.)

Travelling Through Time

Postscript to the Sesquicentennial Edition

There were more than ten thousand people living in the Barnegat Bay region when Ocean County was founded 150 years ago. With the twentieth century now thought of by some as "the good old days," and a new millennium at hand, the local population exceeds 450,000, a number that mushrooms to more than one million people during the annual summer tourist invasion of the Jersey Shore.

A Time Traveller

A time traveller from the present arriving by steam locomotive at the wooden railroad station in Point Pleasant Beach over one hundred years ago would be astonished by the transformation of a farming and fishing seashore village into a bustling summer resort about to enter the modern age.

According to the *Census of the Borough of Point Pleasant Beach*, compiled by Abraham Lower in 1898, our visitor would discover that sixteen passenger trains were scheduled daily in winter and twice that number in summer, with a daily average of 276 people arriving and departing! Even more amazing, sixteen mails were received each working day, and seventeen mails were sent out.

Our visitor could board a modern trolley car and tour the town over three-and-a-half miles of track and find a year-round population of 686 people living among 297 buildings, which included two pool rooms, three restaurants, four churches, and twenty-four hotels and boarding houses. Down on the beach, four hundred bathhouses waited to serve summer tourists eager for a taste of salt air and lemonade at the inlet pavilion.

Even electric lighting had recently arrived in town, with seven arc lights and 450 incandescent lights in service, as well as fifty-three telephone boxes and two long-distance stations.

Visiting the new cedar-shingled Public Library, our traveler could check out *Soldiers of Fortune*, the new novel by literary lion and local celebrity Richard Harding Davis, or wonder about the possibility of time travel as depicted in H. G. Wells' science fiction tale *The Time Machine*, which tells of a visit to an amazingly flawed utopia of the future.

If he stopped by the Post Office, he might encounter Captain John Lott Dorsett mailing a penny postcard depicting a local scene to his son Albert down in Toms River. At the only tavern around, he might overhear the town policeman chatting with the town clergyman, perhaps debating whether or not President William McKinley would be re-elected if he involved the United States in a war with Spain over the bloody revolution in Cuba. Would the Spanish fleet be audacious enough to bombard America's eastern seaboard? Meanwhile, the piano player in the parlor might be trying out a new ragtime tune about to take the country by storm, called "There'll Be a Hot Time in the Old Town Tonight!"

If he wished, our time traveller could catch the next train south down the barrier beach rail line and stop at any of the other stations along the way in the developing resort towns of Bay Head, Mantoloking, Chadwick, Lavallette, Ortley, and Seaside Park. Afterward he could continue west over the Barnegat Bay railroad trestle to Toms River and on to Philadelphia. Life at the Jersey Shore at the turn of the century was full of modern wonders!

Unexpected Moments

Today we can experience time travel at unexpected moments. A few summers back, something shining underwater caught the eye of nine-year-old Grace Malley as she waded knee deep along the southern sandy shore of the Manasquan River. Reaching down quickly, she retrieved an old, worn silver coin about one inch in diameter with squared corners, embossed with a Royal cross and the date "1736." She had found a Spanish real, a legendary "piece of eight" lost long ago by someone who had passed by generations before she was born. Her mind blazed with images of pirates and buried treasure. Her life was touched by the magical awareness that we are surrounded by history and the legends that connect us to the past.

On a cold, moonlit winter night in the same year, Gail Kinney was walking her black Labrador retriever, "Tar," along the Mantoloking beach when suddenly a distinct, vaporous mist drifted in off the ocean surf about fifty feet ahead of them. Tar's hackles rose in fright, and Gail felt an eerie, ghostly presence — something she had never experienced before in a long life of evening beach walks. Before her she saw the shimmering, silvery white figure of a woman in a long gown. Spooked by the extraordinary moment, she and Tar made a quick turn and headed home, off the sands that still shelter timbers from the wreck of the *John Minturn* over 150 years ago. The vivid image still mystifies her, and she wonders if it was an encounter with the legendary Maid of the Mist, long rumored to wander this beach, or perhaps some strange natural phenomenon that inspired such tales. "It wasn't that I was so scared, but I didn't want to get in the way of this lonely, haunting figure," she recalls.

Such reports are not all that unusual in an area rich in history. The Mauro family of Manasquan believes that their 1840s home, which is framed with trees and has interior walls that are insulated with river-mud adobe, is haunted by the ghost of Osborn Curtis, a local merchant who built the place and occasionally still visits late at night. After twenty years of living there, the Mauros have become accustomed to spirit footsteps in the dark, rattling doorknobs, and apparitions on the stairway.

Readers whom I've met at lectures and book signings have shared many amazing personal stories. There is the Silverton man who, as a teenager in the 1950s, discovered a gold doubloon inside a clump of bay mud while he was swimming in a local lagoon. There is the Waretown clammer who dragged up an antique deep-sea diver's helmet near Barnegat inlet. Inside the barnacle-encrusted, mud-filled helmet he found the diver's skull!

A Normandy Beach bait-and-tackle shop owner picked up a rusted flintlock pistol in the marshes near Curtis Point many years ago. Beachcombers still find arrowheads, spear points, rings, belt buckles, bottles, pottery, and even prehistoric mastodon teeth. Members of Ocean Wreck Divers and the N.J. Historical Wreck Divers salvage ships' bells, cargo, and anchors from old, sunken offshore vessels. We are surrounded by history still awaiting discovery.

Living History

Much of that history can be found in local bookstores, which carry many of the excellent regional volumes that have been published in recent years. Rare, out-of-print editions of shore classics are often available at nearby used and antiquarian book shops. Ocean County Library has expanded to twenty branches and is celebrating its seventy-fifth anniversary. It has a superb New Jersey collection at the Toms River headquarters Bishop Building, and hard-to-find books can often be obtained through interlibrary loan.

Area museums also have a wealth of coastal archives available for research and enjoyment. The Ocean County Historical Museum and Research Center, based in the stately, Victorian-era Birdsall house, offers maps, fossils, Native American artifacts, genealogy files, agricultural implements, and elaborate display rooms full of period décor, clothing, and family history. It also presents lectures and major exhibits, and publishes many excellent books and monographs available in its well-stocked gift shop.

Down the street and around the corner, the Toms River Seaport Maritime Museum has collected and restored 35 local vessels, including a Beardslee rowboat, a Hankins sea skiff, a Barnegat Bay garvey, and the *Sheldrake*, a twelve-foot sneak-box that F. Slade Dale sailed from New York City to Florida, via the inland waterway, back in 1925. There are also handmade boat models, charts, photographs, and marine records in its extensive nautical library.

The museum sponsors the Wooden Boat Festival every summer in July, which draws over fifteen thousand people to the riverside at Huddy Park for a two-day event. Now in its twentieth year, the festival is a refreshing experience. It is always wonderful to spend a day around so many fine wooden vessels, gleaming with polished brass work and smelling of fresh varnish. Recently seventy-seven boats participated, among them several vintage catboats and the 115-foot *A. J. Meerwald*, a 1929 oyster schooner, which has been designated the official State of New Jersey tall ship.

You can watch sailboats in action on the water every Saturday from late-June through Labor Day, as the Barnegat Bay Yacht Racing Association hosts races for sneak-boxes and "A-cats," as well as "E-scows" and "lasers" at various yacht clubs around the estuary.

Down on Little Egg Harbor in Tuckerton, the Barnegat Bay Decoy and Baymen's Museum has been established, housed in an authentic replica of a hunting shanty. The value of venerable decoys hand carved by local old-timers has skyrocketed over the past two decades, due in large part to the astronomical prices the old birds have fetched. A mallard drake carved by Rowley Horner of West Creek, and a swimming Canada goose made by Harry V. Shourdes of Tuckerton, *each* sold for $60,500 at separate recent major auctions. Not too bad for relics that not so long ago were used for firewood when they became too shot up for hunting. A mallard decoy carved back in 1900 by Percy Gant of Osbornville was pictured on a twenty-two-cent postage stamp issued in 1985 as part of the Folk Art U.S.A. series, according to Arthur J. Birdsall.

The museum boasts over one hundred antique decoys and shorebirds. Here are also exhibits of traditional crafts in woodcarving, toolmaking, boat building, clamming, fishing, and gunning. Maritime records and a vast collection of photographs document the lives of the baymen. Special exhibits include a Seaman sneak-box, a Hankins sea skiff, and U.S. Life Saving Service displays.

Next door, "Tip" Seaman Country Park hosts the Ocean County Decoy and Gunning Show, formerly known as the Barnegat Bay Decoy and Gunning Show, which has been drawing over forty-thousand people for the two-day event celebrating bay culture, music, and seafood. Sponsored by the Ocean County Parks and Recreation Department and organized by Mike Mangum for the past 20 years, the festival has become one of the largest free public events in New Jersey.

Nearby, along the creek, the $8.6 million Tuckerton Seaport project is underway on forty acres, which will hold twenty-five replica buildings, including a boat works, saw mill, decoy shop, clam and oyster houses, and even the long lost Tucker's Island Lighthouse. The N.J. State Council on the Arts and the National Endowment for the Arts have awarded a Leadership Initiative Grant and officially designated the area as the Jersey Coast Folklife Center, establishing a folk-arts program that will be promoted as a cultural tourist destination. The N.J. Department of Transportation issues custom "Baymen's Heritage" automobile license plates featuring Tucker's Island Lighthouse and a Shourdes Canada goose decoy, with revenue supporting the museum and seaport. Also available are plates bearing the image of the Barnegat Lighthouse and the slogan "Shore to Please."

Pinelands regional culture is alive and kicking every Saturday night at the Albert Hall in Waretown, which has been reborn in a new facility after a devastating fire several years ago. The traditional music performed by local and visiting pickers playing acoustic guitar, mandolin, fiddle, and banjo continues the folk, bluegrass, and country legacy of the Pinehawkers, the Albert brothers, and the Pineconers.

Honoring the Past

The Jersey Shore's past is also honored at many fine local museums that mirror the unique character of their communities. Historic buildings with period furnishings, including two 1800's homes, a barber and a butcher shop, along with an old-fashioned outhouse, are lovingly restored at the Barnegat Heritage Center. The salty old bay town also celebrates Pirate's Day in the summer.

A rich variety of nautical memorabilia, photographs, decoys, and tools can be found at Stafford Township Heritage Center, which offers a creative cultural program including Native American encampments and U.S. Life Saving Service tributes. Maritime artifacts, an original old post office, and the 1860 two-room Forked River school distinguish the Lacey Township Schoolhouse Museum. A vintage hand-pump fire engine is a rare item at the original 1909 railroad station, which houses the Ocean Gate Historical Museum. And a turn

Captain John Lott Dorsett's 1880 "Historical Cabinet Made from Pieces of 26 Shipwrecks" has been a centerpiece exhibit during the "Travelling Through Time" program at Ocean County Library. ***(Courtesy of his great-grandson Coleman Brice)***

The Bay Head Recreation Commission Presents

DOWN BARNEGAT BAY:
A SYMPOSIUM

Speakers • Slide Shows • Special Displays
Jersey Shore Art, Culture, Ecology and History!
Relics, Artifacts and Memorabilia!

Hosted by:
Robert Jahn
"Down Barnegat Bay"

Featuring:
Runyon Colie, Jr., with "Ned" Swain
"Sailing On Barnegat Bay in the 1920's"

A Barnegat Bay Ecology Symposium with:
Robert Anstett, O.C. Citizen's Conservation Council
William de Camp, Jr., Izaak Walton League
Terry Fowler, Div. Coastal Resources - N.J.D.E.P.
Robert (Graywolf) Hamilton, N.J. Native American Assn.
Shaun O'Rourke & Staff, O.C. Parks and Recreation
Evan Spalt, Save Barnegat Bay Coalition
John Tiedemann, Coastal Environmental Services

Waterfowl Carvings and Barnegat Bay Decoys by:
Herman Bennett
Arthur Birdsall
Bob Brown
Gene Hendricks
Ken Loveland
Ray Reid

Barnegat Bay Paintings by:
Al Barker
Patty Niebling
Virginia Perle

Special Displays by:
Brick Historical Society
Island Heights Cultural Assn.
N.J. Native American Assn.
O.C. Historical Society
Save Barnegat Bay Coalition
Shore Harbor Historical Society
Toms River Seaport Society
Mr. and Mrs. William J. Allsop II
Joseph Van Horn
Jerry Woolley

July 25 and August 22, 1991
Thursday, 7-9:30 p.m., at the Bay Head School, Grove Street

Also:
A Special Jersey Shore Book Exhibit this Summer at the
Bay Head Reading Center/Ocean County Library, Meadow Street

For Further Information, Please Contact:
Chairman Evalyn Shippee, (908) 892-0223
or Dave Pearson, (908) 295-8774

Free and Open to the Public!

of the century kitchen, with heirloom dishes, pots, and pans, makes us appreciate the skill that went into Grannie's homemade meals so long ago.

Across the bay, nautical antiques, fishing memorabilia, shipwreck artifacts, and the lens from the original lighthouse are unique exhibits at Barnegat Light Museum, which occupies a 1904 one-room school. Resort history, antiquarian toys, local decoys and sneak-boxes, and even a whale skeleton evoke the old days at the Long Beach Island Museum.

Up around the head of the bay, the Brick Township Historical Museum is located in the old 1800s-era Haven's farmhouse, which has been restored and includes outbuildings and a wishing well, along with a treasury of local lore and family records. The N.J. Lighthouse Association is also active in the community.

The newly formed Bay Head Historical Society, which includes Mantoloking in its domain, is hard at work restoring the 1880s-era Loveland family homestead, which will honor local sailing and boat-building traditions. Down the beach, Lavallette residents host the Heritage Day in September, and there are hopes of forming a local historical society. Seaside Park has formed an organization recently that is planning to develop a museum and cultural center. Seaside Heights hosts the annual Barnegat Bay Crab Race in late summer, a very popular event that also includes educational estuary exhibits and boat tours.

Point Pleasant Historical Society has established a new museum in the town hall to hold its extensive collections of photographs, postcards, scrapbooks, boardwalk memorabilia, and colorful artifacts of the resort's long history. Each September, the Festival of the Sea draws over 50,000 people to a downtown block party celebrating seafood and fishing. Nearby, on Route 88, stands a monument with a ship's anchor and a plaque reading: "In memoriam to the victims of the packet *Minturn* lost at sea in a storm off our coast, February 15, 1846." On the south shore of the river near Manasquan inlet, a bronze statue of a commercial fisherman will soon be erected to honor local mariners. Last year eight men from the area died when two clam boats sank offshore.

Across the inlet on the north shore, one of the last remaining undeveloped tracts on the river, long known as Fisherman's Cove, was recently saved as a Monmouth County park after a vigorous public campaign defeated a planned condominium project.

Squan Village Historical Museum, which recently found a new home after fire destroyed the Victorian railroad station it had faithfully restored, maintains an impressive collection of river history, as does the Union Landing Historical Museum in Brielle. Maps, documents, newspapers, photographs, and a treasury of local tradition can be found at both museums. Finally, descendants of the region's founding families have established the Monmouth

Settler's Association, which holds annual meetings in the fall to share family history, heirlooms, and genealogical information.

Historic Sites

The Ocean County Cultural and Heritage Commission, which is the official sponsor of the year-long Sesquicentennial celebration, has produced a remarkable variety of publications on the region's past. One of the most significant is the *Ocean County Historic Sites Inventory* published in 1982. A monumental four-volume study — each volume the size and thickness of a telephone directory — the work is a landmark in primary shore history research.

The *Inventory* documents the growth and development of the area from early settlement to the 1930s. During fifteen months of research, project director Kevin McGorty and architectural historians Marilyn Kralik and Michael May recorded and photographed 2,188 buildings, thirty-two historical sites, twelve historic roads, and five historic bridges. They were assisted by Heritage Studies, Inc. of Princeton and by staff members of the commission, which sponsored the effort. Funding was provided by the Board of Freeholders, with a matching federal grant from the U.S. Department of the Interior.

The final 1,765-page report presents a comprehensive portrait of Ocean County, from its rural farmhouses and historic attractions to its mansions, resort hotels, and boardwalk amusements. Thirty-three municipalities are represented, each with a section including area background and followed by several pages of significant local structures or sites documented with photographs. Introductory sections on natural features along with historical and architectural overviews are also included. They provide a solid foundation for the survey.

Anyone reasonably knowledgeable with county landmarks will find an abundance of familiar places and a wealth of fascinating background history. Most readers are amazed at the number of secluded, off-the-beaten-path places they have never noticed before. The *Inventory* is available at local libraries, historical museums, and planning boards.

"The survey gives residents, government leaders, and business communities a chance to take stock of the country's rich architectural heritage and consider what is worth preserving. It illustrates the importance of the historical environment in giving a neighborhood, town, or country a specific sense of identify," said project director McGorty when the report was first published.

Indeed, as the National Trust for Historic Preservation has noted, ". . . analysis has found that historic preservation is one of the highest job-generating economic development options available. It is the unique heritage, culture, wildlife, or natural beauty of a region that attracts sightseers in the first place. Visiting scenic and historic sites are two of the top reasons why people travel. We should make every effort to preserve the authentic aspects of local heritage and culture. The true story of an area is worth telling."

Tourists brought in over $1.6 billion to the region's economy last year, according to the N.J. Office of Travel and Tourism. Ocean and Monmouth counties have led the Northeast in recent annual *Money* magazine lists of "best places to live" in the United States, based on job growth, quality schools, and healthcare. These two statistics are directly connected to the central importance of Ocean County's natural resources and cultural heritage.

Our Coastal Heritage

The Ocean County Parks and Recreation Department manages over twenty parks and conservation areas with a combined total of more than four thousand acres in the Barnegat Bay watershed, including sites at Gull Island, Beaver Dam Creek, Metedeconk River, Wells Mills, Riverfront Landing, Berkeley Island, and "Tip" Seaman Park.

Cattus Island County Park, a crown jewel of the system, encompasses over six hundred acres of woodlands, marshes, and bayside. Big "C" Day celebrates the park's natural wonders in October with guided field trips, boat tours of Silver Bay, and slide-show talks at the elaborate Cooper Environmental Center. Many live creatures found in the habitat including snakes, turtles, and fish are displayed in natural settings. There are also excellent environmental education exhibits and the resources of the Vivian Nature Reference Library, according to chief naturalist Shaun O'Rourke.

Standing at the inlet on the north tip of Long Beach Island, the 142-year-old Barnegat Lighthouse attracts over a half million people each year and has become the most visited historic site in the state park system, according to superintendent Cynthia Coritz. The landmark red and white painted beacon is open to the public on special nights during the summer when a trip up the spiral staircase to the 172-foot tall lighthouse offers a spectacular view of the bay and the sea. The park is open daily throughout the year. New additions include a shady maritime forest trail, which is great for bird-watching, and there are plans for an official visiting center in the future.

Looking north across the churning, constantly changing Barnegat inlet, which remains one of the most hazardous passages on the coast for mariners, you will see the southern tip of Island Beach State Park. Ten miles of wilderness beach, towering thirty-foot sand dunes, woodlands, and sedges, the park draws over a million visitors a year, according to superintendent William C. Vibbert. Home to the osprey, black duck, otter, red fox, fiddler crab, and striped bass, among numerous other species, the 2,694-acre preserve was recently added to the list of Critical and Unique Habitats in the Northeast by the U.S. Fish and Wildlife Service.

At the south end of the park, the old boat house of former U.S. Coast Guard Station 112 has been transformed into a beautifully designed Interpretive Center with wonderful, natural displays and colorful, illustrated exhibits on the island's long history. Established with assistance from the Trust for Public Land and staffed with volunteers from the Friends of Island Beach and Save Barnegat Bay, the center also houses the Emily de Camp Herbarium.

There are hopes of restoring the nearby U.S. Life Saving Service Station, which is one of the last surviving unchanged stations along the coast of New Jersey. As Captain Robert F. Bennett, U.S.C.G. (Retired) has noted in his 1998 book *Sandpounders: An Interpretation of the History of the U.S. Life Saving Service*, published by the U.S. Coast Guard Historians Office, Washington, D.C.: "In retrospect, the U.S. Life Saving Service was a noble institution. From 1871 to 1914, while in incidents involving 28,121 vessels, the Service saved 178,741 individuals. And though they lost 1,455, this total is very nearly equaled by the current annual toll on recreational vessels alone."

The legendary motto of the surfmen was "You have to go out but you don't have to come back." It is time to pay tribute to these heroic lifesavers, who have been nearly forgotten, by restoring the Island Beach station to honor their memory. (Anyone interested in supporting this project should contact superintendent William C. Vibbert at the park.)

The U.S. Life Saving Service Heritage Act, co-sponsored by New Jersey representatives Frank Pallone Jr. and Frank LoBiondo, introduced in 1999, would provide federal funding to research and preserve some of the 140 surviving historic stations that still stand along our national coastline. If the act is implemented, it would authorize the National Park Service to carry out surveys in conjunction with the U.S. Life Saving Service Heritage Association, a nonprofit organization dedicated to preserving historic stations and currently working to obtain Congressional approval for federal support.

For further information on the subject, I also recommend *The U.S. Life Saving Service* by Ralph Shanks and Wick York and edited by Lisa Woo, an epic study published in 1996 by Costano Books.

Barnegat Bay is one of five regions officially designated part of the New Jersey Coastal Heritage Trail Route connecting important Jersey Shore natural and cultural sites. Established in 1988 by Congressional legislation, the trail was developed by the National Park Service in conjunction with state government and several participating organizations. Following existing roads, people are encouraged to visit Regional Welcome Centers, which offer information, brochures, video, and exhibits on maritime history, coastal habitat, wildlife migration, early settlements, and recreation at full service sites that are open five days a week, including weekends. Wayside exhibits at special sites and scenic views offer excellent background on the rich heritage of the region. For New Jersey Coastal Heritage Trail Route maps, contact the New Jersey Office of Travel and Tourism, P.O. Box 826, Trenton, NJ 08625-7418, or consult the Internet at http://www.nps.gov/neje.

The Past Remains

The past remains with us in unexpected ways. In recent years the Delaware Indians of Oklahoma, descendants of the Lenape who were displaced by the European invasion, have been actively engaged in a lawsuit to reclaim ancestral lands in New Jersey that the tribe believes were seized in violation of a 1790 federal law. Their goal is not to re-establish the long lost Lenapehoking, but to build a new gambling casino on the Jersey Shore.

Traces of the vanished Native American presence still exist along the bay at the mouth of Oyster Creek, where their ancient shell mounds, perhaps more than one thousand years old, bear witness to the passing of time. Further inland stands a monument to our passing civilization, Oyster Creek Nuclear Generating Facility, which one thousand years from now — and perhaps ten millennia from now — may only be remembered for the lethal radioactive waste stored there during the late-twentieth century. The spent fuel, which was used to light our homes and power our electric conveniences, will be deadly to living things for a period of time twice as long as our human civilization on Earth. In the face of mounting public opposition from local citizens' groups, such as Oyster Creek Nuclear Watch, and also because maintaining the plant is no longer a profit-making proposition, the facility is scheduled to be decommissioned in 2009. The threat of a local catastrophe on the order of Three Mile Island or Chernobyl has inflamed public fears about the aging, brittle reactor that cycles much of the waters of Barnegat Bay through its cooling system every twenty-four hours.

The impact of mass development on the watershed has become increasingly apparent over the past twenty years. Brown algae blooms have been more frequent and clam yields have been declining due to pollution from chemical wastes, pesticides, and heavy metals. The Congressional ban on ocean dumping and the closing of the Ciba Geigy pipeline, which poured millions of gallons of treated waste into the sea, were major environmental victories during the 1980s. Threats to surface and drinking water remain, however. Mysterious cancer clusters in the area have alarmed many residents. Deformed, mutant toads with extra or missing limbs have been found along the banks of the Metedeconk River, which provides nearly seventy-five percent of the tap water people drink in north Ocean County.

The Ocean County Soil Conservation District sponsors the annual Barnegat Bay Environmental Educators Roundtable, which features field trips and activities to encourage teachers to bring watershed topics into the curriculum. Other sponsors include Clean Ocean Action, N.J. Audubon Society, N.J. Marine Sciences Consortium, O.C. Parks and Recreation Department, and Rutgers Institute of Marine and Coastal Sciences.

The Ocean County Environmental Conference brings together many of these organizations to meet with concerned citizens at Ocean County College every October, organized by Alan Avery Jr., of the O.C. Planning Department and sponsored by the Board of Freeholders and the Association of N.J. Environmental Commissions.

At a recent conference a spokesman from the Office of Regulatory Policy of the N.J.D.E.P. emphasized the threat posed to the bay by boaters propelling their craft through shallow waters over submerged aquatic vegetation beds, landing at waterfowl nesting sites, and flushing the heads of their vessels directly into the estuary. The first two problems are being dealt with by continuing educational efforts, while the last problem is being addressed by "The Circle of Life," a twenty-foot-skiff with a three-hundred-gallon tank operated by Seaside Park. Currently the only pollution-control boat in the region, purchased with funds from the Clean Vessels Act, it pumps out as many as five hundred boats a day in the summer.

Save Barnegat Bay

Perhaps the most significant ecological progress regionally has been accomplished by the persevering work of Save Barnegat Bay (SBB), a nonprofit citizen's action organization. Spearheaded by the Izaak Walton League, a national environmental group, SBB was founded in 1986 to protect the bay, promote clean water, and oppose any threat to the health of the estuary. Working together with the Barnegat Bay Preservation Coalition, charter members included the American Littoral Society, Citizen's Conservation Council, Commercial Fisherman's Association, Congress of Concerned Citizens of Brick Township, Ducks Unlimited, Federation of Beach Associations, N.J. Conservation Foundation, N.J. Shore Audubon Society, Normandy Beach

TRAVELLING THROUGH TIME : DECADE

10th. Anniversary Celebration
Point Pleasant Branch
Ocean County Library

Slides, Video & Special Displays
Jersey Shore Artifacts & Memorabilia
Live Acoustic Folk Music

THURSDAY, JANUARY 21, 1999, 6-9 P.M.
834 Beaver Dam Road

Hosted by Robert Jahn
"Down Barnegat Bay: A Nor'easter Midnight Reader"
featuring Gary Struncius & Debbie Lawton
and participation by:
O.C. Cultural & Heritage Commission, O.C. Museum, Barnegat Bay Decoy & Bayman's Museum, Toms River Seaport Society, Office of Historic Sites: State Park Service, Island Beach State Park, Historical Societies of Bay Head, Brick Township, Point Pleasant and Squan Village!

Also featuring comments by Herman Bennett, Arthur Birdsall, Sean Fleming, Wayne Hartman, Harry O'Dell, Shaun O'Rourke, Wayne Scholl, Paul Taylor and George Williams!

on special display:
Captain Dorsett's 1880 Historical Cabinet
Made from Pieces of 26 Shipwrecks
and Arthur Johnson's Historic N.J. Map Collection!

also F. Alan Vogel's Underwater Video of Jersey Shore Shipwrecks!

Advance Registration Requested
Free - (732) 295-1555 - Open to All!

Improvement Association, O.C. Coastal Zone Environmental Coalition, and Swan Point Relay Clammers.

Save Barnegat Bay attempts to save land from overdevelopment by reviewing and, if necessary, objecting to permit applications, purchasing private land, and promoting Green Acres efforts by matching funds along with the William Penn Foundation. Its goal is to buy land for transfer to some branch of government, which will then manage it.

The group is best known for its work in conserving the Reedy Creek area, which harbors a diverse variety of plant and animal life, including migrating waterfowl. In 1996, SBB received $800,000 in Green Acres matching grants for preserving land around the creek, which runs one-and-a-half miles through twelve hundred acres of woods and wetlands on Metedeconk Neck, as well as neighboring bay sedge islands. The group has supported the purchase of two thousand acres in that area and in the vicinity of Herring Point. It has also waged a long campaign to successfully oppose a 367-unit development project on Bayville's Good Luck Point.

Save Barnegat Bay originally formed to protest the development of 135 condominiums at Pelican Cove near the Mantoloking Bridge, advocate powerboat noise and speed limits legislation, rein in jet skis, and promote a "No Discharge Zone" for the head of the bay. They also led the effort to include the last tracts of unspoiled open space along the west shore of the estuary north of the Seaside Bridge to be incorporated in the Forsythe National Wildlife Refuge. More than six thousand acres of the refuge are designated as National Wildlife areas, and the Barnegat Division extends from the Metedeconk River down to Little Egg Harbor.

The 275-acre area known as Kettle Creek Woods, which includes coastal forest and wetlands in Brick Township, was purchased for $3.5 million with assistance from SBB. It has also been active in promoting the preservation of Murray Grove in Lacey Township and recently established a friendly storefront staffed by volunteers in Lavallette, where in 1999 the group purchased Little Sedge Island, which it donated to the State of New Jersey. SBB frequently sponsors weekend trash cleanups along the mile-long Reedy Creek foot trail located at the intersection of Mantoloking and Adamston Roads in Brick Township.

"We're trying to keep land surrounding the bay intact and we've been at it for over fifteen years," says William de Camp Jr., the dedicated president of Save Barnegat Bay.

"The environment is currently undergoing changes of historic and, indeed, geologic proportions. Within the space of a few generations massive development will have transformed the face of our lands and water for all time. Pollution is epidemic. Open space and natural habitat are being lost permanently. Many species are becoming increasingly endangered, and the shellfishing industry is gravely threatened. The bay is overwhelmed by excessive boat traffic, visual access is being lost, and the natural beauty of our area is being greatly diminished. These ills all stem from the same source: unrestrained development," de Camp notes.

In 1997, voters approved a referendum to dedicate over $4 million annually with the Ocean County Natural Lands Trust Fund acquisition program, which was actively promoted by the group. You can visit Save Barnegat Bay's office at 906B, Grand Central Ave., Lavallette, NJ 08735 or contact them on the Internet at http://www.savebarnegatbay.org.

A Part of Nature

The mounting environmental challenges we are facing have brought many people together in concerted citizen action and also into a more conscious awareness of our relationship with nature. More people now realize and are taking responsibility for the fact that past human actions have inadvertently disturbed the balance of life to such an extent that our very survival is being threatened by the gradual poisoning of the air, drinking water, and food chain. Our hope for the future rests with the knowledge that we, too, are part of nature.

As Robert "Graywolf" Hamilton, president of the N.J. Native-American Association, commented during a recent "Down Barnegat Bay Symposium" at Ocean County Library: "The sacredness of every living thing, that which connects human beings to the place they inhabit — that quality is the single most liberating aspect of our environment. It is the fact that life is renewable, that all things which support life are renewable, and that they are renewed by a force greater than any living or individual thing. That holds the only hope for human survival on this planet."

Storm of the Century

Call it the "Storm of the Century" or a dire warning of things to come, the great Nor'easter of '92 struck with little warning, howling across the surging sea with wild one-hundred-mile-per-hour winds in the early morning hours of December 11th.

Blasting gales of freezing rain deluged the Jersey Shore from Sandy Hook to Cape May. Full moon flood tides breached the barrier islands and inundated the surrounding coastal area, while rivers and bays overflowed their banks.

Friday's high tide measured 9.3 feet at the Atlantic County National Weather Service station, exceeding the 1944 hurricane record.

Thousands of shore residents awoke to find their homes engulfed by rising tides, their cars dead in the water, and their power and heat gone with the wind. Ocean County authorities declared a state of emergency as shore communities from Seaside Park to Point Pleasant were marooned due to flooded highways and wind-blown bridges. Many stranded people tuned in local radio stations on battery-powered sets only to hear so-called "easy listening" music and minimal storm coverage, while the waters rose higher and higher.

Surging twenty-five-foot-high seas consumed the beaches, leaving twelve-foot cliffs where protecting sand dunes once stood, smashing boardwalks to kindling, and wreaking millions of dollars worth of devastation. Fences blew down, basements flooded, old trees uprooted, and telephone poles toppled, leaving high-voltage power lines writhing and sparking like electric eels.

Volunteer first aid and fire departments, as well as the local U.S. Coast Guard, went into action, undermanned and overworked to exhaustion, assisting local police in answering medical emergencies, fire calls, and evacuating hundreds of residents to shelters on the mainland.

Weathered by countless nor'easters and hurricanes, many lifelong clam diggers rode out the storm at home, helping neighbors, protecting their property, and gathering at night around candles, lanterns, and fireplaces, swapping tales of the great March Storm of '62 or the hurricane of '38 or, if very young, the memorable Halloween Storm of '91. New legends for future generations were in the making as their homes rattled in the windy darkness.

Nor'easters have their own mindless logic, and usually, after two or three days of pounding the coast, they disappear into the mists of local memory and folklore, leaving behind beautiful blue skies above devastated beaches as well as the flotsam and jetsam of broken dreams.

The hard truth is that the Great Nor'easter of '92 could have been much worse. We all feel relieved to hear experts refer to this one as the so-called "Storm of the Century." That means we're not supposed to worry about this sort of thing happening again until sometime around 2092 or so, long after most of us will be pushing up daisies. But weren't we told that the '62 storm was the "Storm of the Century," or was it the '44 hurricane?

A Nor'easter Classification System

In order to help understand this complex meteorological threat to the East Coast, Susan D. Halsey of the New Jersey Department of Environmental Protection – Division of Coastal Resources, has proposed a "Classification Scale for Major Northeast Storms Based on Extent of Damage," first published in the 1986 *Geological Society of America, Abstracts with Programs (Northeastern Section).*

"Northeast storms are capable of significant damage to the beach-dune system along our coasts, thus increasing the vulnerability of coastal development," Halsey says. "Confusion reigns for managers when comparisons are needed between storms, i.e., when tidal surges are equal ('20-year storm') for the 1962 and 1984 March storms but damage so disparate . . . no scale has been developed for northeast storms due to their diffuse meteorological characteristics. However, extent of storm damage can be correlated with occurrence on spring or perigean tides coupled with the number of high tides to which the coast is subjected," Halsey notes.

Ms. Halsey's classification scale is as follows:

Class 1: (up to 1 tide) Beach erosion and dunes sustain some scarping.

Class 2: (up to 2) Besides heavy beach erosion, dunes moderately to significantly scarped; overwash in weak areas, especially down street ends; sections of unprotected boardwalks popped or lifted off; flooding begins.

Class 3: (2-3) Serious beach erosion; dunes not only scarped but some areas flattened by overwash; flooding serious; widespread boardwalk damage.

Class 4: (3-4) Erosion reaching to marsh "basement" in some areas; most man-made dunes flattened; significant overwash, fans coalescing; deeper flooding widespread; breaching in natural dunes increasing.

Class 5: (4-5) Surge platforms and incipient inlets present; wash-over sands completely clog low-lying islands and roads; natural dunes heavily eroded.

"One element that can influence this scale is the 'set-up' factor: more extensive damage due to insufficient time between storms to repair systems," Halsey adds, noting that "tidal range, degree of development, and geomorphology of the coastal compartment may also influence this scale."

The real Storm of the Century may be just around the corner, brewing somewhere south of Bermuda or just beginning to churn somewhere out in the North Atlantic. And when it happens, we better be prepared. We were very lucky in '92. And we know we won't get much help from our local radio station or from our *Farmers Almanac*.

An Atlantis of the Future?

According to the latest weather research, the twentieth century was hotter than any era in the past millennium. Our climate may be changing because of the impact of modern civilization. Uncomfortably high temperatures occur more frequently, leading to failures in our power systems as people crank up air conditioners, many of which leak a gas that thins the protective ozone layer allowing more ultraviolet light into the atmosphere, leading to higher levels of skin cancer. Many people are afraid to go out in the sun these days.

By 2050, within the lifetime of many still living today, the Jersey Shore may have a tropical climate, along with more powerful and destructive storms. The resulting heat expansion of ocean water may result in the deluge of areas more than ten feet above sea level, as the barrier islands and Barnegat Bay move westward, leaving our present-day coastal cities and towns under water like an Atlantis of the future.

In the meantime, count your blessings and keep a "weather eye." Stock up on candles, matches, firewood, batteries, and canned goods. Consider real estate in the Poconos if you dislike being inconvenienced by Old Neptune's whims. And you might think about keeping a rowboat in your attic.

These Days

Where once the bay was a peaceful refuge for those seeking the salt-air tranquillity of surf fishing for striped bass or crabbing from a friendly public dock or taking to the water in rowboats, sneak-boxes, or catboats, today the air vibrates from the throbbing roar of offshore powerboats and the chainsaw whine of two-cycle jet skis. Overhead pass an endless succession of low-flying, droning, advertising-banner airplanes, hustling helicopters, commercial blimps, passenger jets, and circling C-141s.

A maze of luxury waterfront developments, with private docks and vinyl bulkheads on dredged lagoons, surrounds most of the 160-mile tidal shoreline not occupied by yacht clubs, marinas, public parks, and the Forsythe National Wildlife Refuge. Although over sixty miles of protected public waterfront remains, natural beaches, where a sea turtle can lay her eggs or a child can learn how to swim, are rapidly disappearing. Because of the danger of contracting Lyme disease from tiny ticks epidemic in the region, it has become hazardous to your health to wander in the woods or even work or play in your backyard.

While the bay has a capacity for over six thousand boats on weekends, more than 120,000 vessels cruise through during the summer season, according to Chief Naturalist Shaun O'Rourke. This unprecedented volume of traffic has created increased demand for public access to the water as well as more pollution from vessels leaking oil, gasoline, and sewage, along with high bacterial and microbial levels from non-point source contaminants flowing off the land with rainfall. Some of the aging bridges in the watershed are getting shaky, requiring constant repair and often seem to spend more time with their draws raised than in the down position.

Summer tourists, fondly known as "Bennies" by local year-round residents, begin their annual migration to the shore every June. By the Fourth of July, holiday bumper-to-bumper traffic often slows to a crawl, with sweltering drivers blowing car-horns and blasting rap music, in eager pursuit of season rentals and boardwalk fireworks, as automobile exhaust fills the sea air with a choking brown haze.

A few years back, local real-estate interests ran a contest to come up with a new name for the barrier strip from Bay Head to Barnegat inlet, whose varied municipalities often made coherent tourism promotions very complicated. The winning entry was "Barnegat Beach Island," selected in hopes that the catchy acronym "BBI" world become as popular as our southern cousin's nickname, "LBI," as it is called by those too busy to say Long Beach Island. Names come and go on this stretch, which in fact has been an island since the opening of the New Jersey Intracoastal Waterway Canal in 1926. Who remembers St. Elmo or Camp Osborn? Over the centuries, the area once known by Native Americans as part of Lenapehoking has been also referred to as Lord Sterling's Isle, Island Beach, Squan Beach, Squam, and even simply as Barnegat.

Welcome to the Jersey Shore!

Today, however, things are not as easy as they were during the time when whalers, wreckers, and rum runners had easy access to the shore. In some towns, armed beach police patrol the hot sands in all-terrain vehicles during the summer, checking to make sure all sunbathers, surfers, and swimmers have paid their dues for required beach badges, a controversial levy that originated in the 1930s as a way of discouraging "out of towners," and one that is nearly unknown anywhere else in the United States, where beaches are traditionally free to all. A protracted legal battle in the 1980s finally resulted in improved public access rights for the general public. But still, these days in some municipalities it is even illegal to walk on the beach after dark on full moon nights, a long-standing tradition at the heart of summer romance.

Welcome to the Jersey Shore! No wonder, then, that when tourists begin their migration north in bumper-to-bumper traffic at the end of Labor Day weekend, many year-round residents hold front-yard "Bye Bye Benny" parties to cheer them on their way.

We live in a time at the turn of the century when twelve-foot-tall plastic palm trees sprout in local soil around tourist motels; when the developer of a new condominium lagoon community advertises his project as "The Nantucket

Tuckerton, from *Harper's*, 1878

of the Jersey Shore"; when a real estate company hires annoying advertising-banner airplanes to remind us to "Catch the Spirit Down Barnegat Bay"; when even the dead are not safe from graverobbers and vandals who smash and topple the gray weathered tombstones of the region's founders; and when a classic seaside boardwalk amusement resort neglects its own colorful carousel past and chooses to use grant money to renovate its Main Street as an ersatz version of the Mississippi River city of New Orleans. Mark Twain would have something amusing to say about that!

With the bulldozing of the local landscape into "residents only" gated communities, strip malls and asphalt covered parking lots, and the overcommercialization of some beachfront towns that can't decide whether they are Key West, San Diego, or Honolulu, much of the authentic sense of place — which drew people here to this North Atlantic coast to begin with — is being lost forever.

A Natural Identity

Northeast winds are blowing in off a roaring sea, and the salty smell of a marauding hurricane whirling up from the Caribbean is in the air as this is being written. At times like this, with a red sun sinking over the bay, the elements energize the long, solitary work of completing a book — a process that, in the middle of the night, can feel like being stranded on a desert island, scribbling messages for unknown readers to be stuck in a bottle and cast out to sea.

This twentieth-anniversary voyage down Barnegat Bay is in memory of those lost friends and family members no longer with us. As we travel through time into the new millennium, perhaps Ocean County's Sesquicentennial celebration will help remind us of who we are and where we came from. We should remember that the Jersey Shore has a natural identity, a heritage that has made Barnegat Lighthouse a symbol of New Jersey, and a culture rich in history and resources that is worth promoting and preserving for future generations who will call this place home.

Robert Jahn
Mantoloking, N.J.
August 31, 1999

Down Barnegat Bay

(Part II)

So much for tales
of lost ships and sailors,
and things that once happened
under Barnegat's beam.

There's a red sky tonight,
sailor's delight,
watch the waves as they dance
across the blue sea.

Goodbye Captain John,
so long Uncle Jakey,
farewell Captain Bill
and wild Indian Will . . .

The voice of the dunes
whispers in moonlight,
on the bay the old ghosts
still raise up their sail . . .

Down Barnegat Bay
on the wings of a dream,
they wave to us
through the years —

We're here today
to watch over the bay
and to hear
the laughing gulls sing.

First Edition Crew

The crew for the first voyage included the following people:

Donald DuMont, publisher and research assistant; Wayne L. Hartman, literary advisor; Arthur Johnson, historical consultant; William C. Schoettle, historical consultant; Gail Reese, general consultant; David Rohde, production consultant; Ed Perella, halftone cameraman; Tom Boud, cover border; Frank J. Watson, maritime historian; Rick Gefkin, marine archeologist; Ken Birdsall, East coast promo; Robert Trout, West coast promo; Jake Jacobus, international promo; Winfield "Scotty" Scott, captain of the watch; Harry Kitchell, philosopher; and American Press, printing.

Grateful appreciation is extended to the following people and organizations who have helped make *Down Barnegat Bay* possible:

Inspiration: Louise Edgar Colie, Fred Colie, Donald DuMont Sr., Mr. and Mrs. Leroy DuMont, Polly DuMont, Bob Dylan, Florence Hulse, Curles Hulse, Pete Seeger, Fred Shaw, and Neil Young.

Special thanks to the following: the Mantoloking Yacht Club; the Bay Head Yacht Club; Ralph Autorino; Susanah and Alex Anderson; Tania and Daniel Hernandez Anderson; Eleanor Angott; Robert Bailey; Eleanor and Charles Ballou; Robert Joseph Bower; Betsy and Runyon Colie; Isabel and Norman Ginter; Sam Ginter; Norman Ginter Jr.; James Halleran; Richard Jahn; Richie Jahn Jr.; Roland Jahn; Laura Jahn; Veronika Jahn; Inger and C. T. Jenkinson; Lisa and Donovan Jenkinson; Pat and Robert Johnson; Leslie Matthews; Jimmy Matthews; Chris Matthews; Judy and Robert McGuane; Jamie, Jeffrey and Melinda McGuane; Sam Morris; Greg Morton; Bobby Reinert; Dana Richmond; Herbert Rogers; Howard Rogers Jr.; Diane and Linda Scheibe; Rev. and Mrs. James Smith; Annie Swanson; Mr. and Mrs. Hassle Totty; Greg Wayland; and Herb Whelan.

"Time is an ocean / but it ends at the shore . . ." — Bob Dylan

Sesquicentennial Edition Crew

Special thanks to historians Robert Bennett, Arthur J. Birdsall, Elizabeth Morgan, William C. Schoettle, Richard Strickler, Dick Updike, George Williams, and Jerry Woolley for generous advice, fact checking, and access to historical collections; to Robert Bower, Hotalings International, for proofreading and multimedia expertise; to Dover One Hour Photo, Toms River, for their high quality professional work and the extra effort they put into this edition; to Chuck Milliken, National Park Service, and to Janet Wolf, New Jersey Coastal Heritage Trail Route project manger, for special permission to reprint their new Barnegat Bay Region map; and to Tom Barry, Cliff Rollings, and Rich Wicker for adventures fishing and sailing on the bay and high seas.

I'm also very grateful to the fine people at Plexus Publishing, Inc., including John Bryans, editor in chief; Heide Dengler, production manager; Jacqueline Walter, graphic designer; Janet Spavlik, managing editor; Kimberly Mestrow and Pat Hadley-Miller, copy editors; Pat Palatucci, sales manager; and Thomas H. Hogan Sr., president and publisher. They enthusiastically gave me the time and freedom to integrate much more than fifty pages of new material. Their patience, hard work, and professional attention to detail helped steer this greatly expanded Sesquicentennial edition into port during a very turbulent time for me, marked by the passing of my brother Rich and my father, Harold E. Jahn.

My mother, Dorothy, also helped keep me on course while she was also dealing with a very difficult time. And, once again, Gail Reese has been involved with nearly every aspect of the endeavor, from double-checking galleys to hand-sewing a 10' by 4 1/2' Barnegat Bay Festival applique banner to enduring periodic breakfast slide shows of new material.

Finally, thank you to Peter P. Blanchard III, naturalist for the Trust for Public Land, New York, for taking the time to write a special preface to this twentieth anniversary edition of *Down Barnegat Bay: A Nor'easter Midnight Reader*. Anyone concerned with the future of the bay region should read his book, *The Century Plan: A Study of 100 Conservation Sites in the Barnegat Bay Watershed.*

Grateful appreciation is also extended to friends who have helped me navigate a long voyage by dead reckoning:

Peter Albano, Robert Anstett, Florence J. Asman, Chris Atwater, John Bandestra, R. J. Barklow, Vince Bologna, Chris Bongiorno, Coleman Brice, "Rib" Brice, Tammy and "Buddy" Brightly, Sandy Brower, Lois Brown, Frank Buono, Darby Busse, Cafe La Playa, Carolyn Campbell, Axel Carlson, Nancy Carlson, Carolyn and Jack Chapman, Deborah Coombe, Cynthia Coritz, Vince Creevy, Joe Crowell, Doris Daniels, Tony Daniels, Heidi D'Ascoli, William de Camp Jr., Bryan De Paul, Gene Donatiello, Inger and Larry Dooley, Gary Dubnik, Sean Farrell, Nancy and Sean Fleming, Theresa Fowler, Joe Franklin, Jerry Garcia, Pete Gilman, Betty Grant, H. H. Tenzin Gyatso, John Haas, Yvonne Hakze, Pat and Gene Hendricks, Sheryn Hendrickson, Stanley Hulse, Katie Jargowsky, Stacey Jeffers, Jersey Shore Postcard Club, Dale Kilian, Kelly Kincaid, Gail and Rich Kinney, Esther Kinsley, Larry Kirk, John Lennon, LeRoy Kutz, Dan Lieb, Corinne and Dick Lill, Dr. Scott Lloyd, Walter Lord, Pat and Jim Malone, and Mike Mangum.

Craig McLean, Meredith McLean-Francis and George Francis, Kathy and Jeff Heim, Mike McCarthy, Kim and Bert Mauro, Tony Monzo, Kirk Moore, Chris Myers, Lori Oliver, Andy Nuzer, Harry O'Dell, Terry O'Leary, Sean O'Rourke, David Oxenford, Allyn Paolicelli, Sam Peckinpaugh, Chris Peterson, Billy Preyer, Ruth and Dr. James Reese, John Rhody, Ricky Roland, the Sandpiper, Dave Satterfield, Marilyn Schlossbach, Wayne Scholl, Evalyn Shippee, Charley Sommo, Evan Spalt, Richard Spellman, Joel Stevenson, Dr. Paul Stumpf, Ned Swain, Paul Taylor, Dr. Hunter S. Thompson, John Tiedeman, Used to Be's, Dana Vanders, Robert Van Benthuysen, William Van Winkle, William C. Vibbert, F. Alan Vogel, Rich Weiner, and Janice Wheeler.

"Fare you well . . ." — the Grateful Dead